Uncharted Waters

Senator George Mitchell
Chairman of the Northern Ireland peace talks

S OMEONE STANDS FOR an election and loses, everybody in the country knows. And that takes real courage and that's where all these energies ought to be going. I find it inspiring that so many people have made that transition. Some of the most impressive members of the negotiations were men who had committed serious crimes in earlier years, had served long prison terms, had paid their debt to society, had become transformed in the meantime, and are now articulate advocates for peace.

A good example is David Ervine. Billy Hutchinson is another. Gusty Spence was a very active loyalist paramilitary. He did a long stretch in prison. He has now become a truly exemplary citizen and he was like a father figure to many of the delegates at the talks. One of the most powerful and emotional lessons of my experience in Northern Ireland is the possibility for personal redemption. For people who have made mistakes to learn from them, rise above their past and become valuable contributing members of their society.

There is not a more impressive politician in Northern Ireland than David Ervine. He did a long term in prison for committing a very brutal act. Now I think he is important to the assembly and he will be a leading figure for years to come.

The Times, 28 August 1998

David Ervine

Uncharted Waters

HENRY SINNERTON

First published in 2002 by
Brandon
an imprint of Mount Eagle Publications
Dingle, Co. Kerry, Ireland

10 9 8 7 6 5 4 3 2 1

ISBN 0 86322 301 X

Typesetting by Red Barn Publishing, Skeagh, Skibbereen
Printed by ßetaprint, Dublin

CONTENTS

Acknowledgements

I wish to acknowledge the following people for giving me of their time: David Ervine, Jeanette Ervine, Mark Ervine, Brian Ervine, Gusty Spence, Hugh Smyth, Billy Hutchinson, Eddie Kinner, Martin Snodden, Former OC UVF, Roy Magee, Chris McGimpsey, Briege Gadd, Edna Longley, Albert Reynolds, John Bruton, Fergus Finlay and Chris Hudson; and those who were kind enough to express their views in writing: Liz O'Donnell and Robin Eames; and Jennifer Mussen for kind permission to reproduce the school photograph of Orangefield Boys' School U14 soccer team 1967–68.

INTRODUCTION

IN THE WAKE of the loyalist ceasefire of October 1994, many were surprised, and some astonished, by the appearance as if from nowhere of a new personable breed of spokesmen, open-minded, down-to-earth and capable of expressing their unionism free of the banalities and grating clichés which merely encouraged audiences to turn away. One of these 'new' politicians was David Ervine.

Many have remarked that Ervine has brought to Northern Ireland politics a vitality and dynamism that has hitherto been in short supply. Passionate about unionism, articulate and coherent, he expresses his opinions reasonably, with an openness and tolerance that is unusual in a unionist politician.

His advocacy of unionism is remarkable for its refreshing and innovative tone. For the first time, many people outside, and some inside, the 'unionist family' are surprised to find themselves listening willingly and giving careful consideration to unionist arguments.

Ervine's journey started in east Belfast from a working-class terrace house. This book aims to describe Ervine's journey, the influences and experiences which formed him, and to gauge the impact he has made upon politics and politicians within and without Northern Ireland.

It does not take long in David Ervine's company to realise that this is no stereotypical working-class boy made good. When you watch his television appearances, listen to his soundbites, interviews and studio discussions, you appreciate his gift with words, his flow of ideas, his ability to capture the appropriate phrase and colourful image. This is someone who talks a unionism that is perceptibly different from that of the single 'constitutional' issue parties whose sloganising and sterility have long caused unionist politics to have little appeal, and which effectively propelled many reasonable citizens, of even the slightest unionist tendency, away from politics and into other fields and occupations. Ervine, a dyed-in-the-wool unionist, is a three-dimensional politician with policies on social, economic, industrial, health, educational and other mainstream matters which stem from his ambition for community and country. He is keen to engage with his political opponents – a rare quality in a unionist. Fortunately, he is not alone. Others from the same origins have shared the same brutal upheavals in their lives. Yet, despite their shared experiences of violence and imprisonment, they turned their predicament to advantage and, through mutual reliance, helped shape a new mould for a very different future. As Ervine himself puts it: 'I don't want just to solve a political problem. I want to change society.'

Ervine has attracted the attention of the thinking public. His electoral successes demonstrate that a surprising number of the middle class look upon him favourably, and his efforts to promote a confident unionism within his working-class community seem to be bearing fruit. Unusually, a wide span of Catholics regard him with approval. This unionism has its own distinctive edge: secular and civic, confident and positive, engaging and courteous, it tackles rather than evades issues, is of a left of centre tendency, and values and respects difference. The Rev Roy Magee, for example, who took the first crucial ground-breaking steps that set in motion the train of events which led to the loyalists' ceasefire in 1994, speaks of 'a man who has come up from the people to what seems to be a leader of the people. In a sense he's one of them, but it looks as though he has the ability to lead them from their own ranks – and when you think about that, there haven't been a great number of Northern Ireland [unionist] people in that mould.'

Professor Edna Longley considers the emergence of Ervine and his fellow loyalist politicians of importance from several perspectives. She was 'impressed by the loyalists' ceasefire terminology, the change of language, the flexible use of language which contrasted both with the hype of "unionist-politician-speak" and the "nationalist/Sinn-Féin-speak", the same jargon all the time. It was introducing a new kind of language on to the political stage.' She has also discerned a historical political tradition which had lain submerged beneath the waves of intercommunal strife: 'the vestiges of the old Labour tradition. Quite often the Shankill people who are involved in the loyalist peace-making seem to have connections back to that repressed left-wing ethos that used to be there years ago, back to "the thirties" and that period, through family connections.' Of particular significance, Longley points out, is the cultural diversity confirmed in the emergence of Ervine and the new loyalist political organisations, who, in marked contrast to their predecessors, are prepared to argue for an 'inclusive identity' for the North and are willing 'to take the cultural argument to Sinn Féin and its unchanging language'.

Professor Paul Arthur states that the perception of Ulster unionists by the outside world as bowler-hatted, be-sashed, inarticulate and dour is hardly appropriate as a description of Ervine. Indeed, these preconceptions of a humourless Ulster 'Prod', widespread in political circles in the Republic of Ireland, were soon dismantled once Southerners had met him, as was willingly stated by certain Dáil TDs on the RTÉ *Lifelines* programme of 14 May 1995. Arthur wryly sums up Ervine the politician: 'In terms of personality, he could almost be a nationalist politician.'

Ervine is one of the few unionists not to suffer from a siege mentality. With an abundance of courage, he was one of the first to set foot in places other mainstream unionists considered to be hostile. He was prepared to go to Dublin before the ceasefires to articulate honestly his political position and to return again and again to meet his opponents, seeking information with the express purpose of providing political analysis. He was positive and proactive on behalf of his community, for he is in the business of politics. Chris Hudson, a Dublin trade unionist and Peace Train activist, describes him as 'articulate, looks good, puts across a Protestant working-class point of view, is generous, is putting the hand of friendship out'.

How many mainstream unionist politicians would receive references in the same vein from such diverse and discriminating individuals?

Ervine's politics appeal. People believe he is a genuine advocate on behalf of a battered community which was hopelessly adrift in the doldrums because it was led abysmally by men of mediocre talent who were out of their depth. It is this contrast which underlies and gives force to Ervine's attractiveness as a political leader. Edna Longley aptly describes the frustration of disaffected Northern Protestants with their lilliputian politicians: 'When someone who is eloquent and presentable and intelligent gets up, you realise that the rest of Ireland ought to know about it.'

EARLY DAYS

ODAY, BEFORE YOU cross the river Lagan, a marvel of the 1990s
confronts you along the riverbanks. New, tall buildings,
unusual against the Belfast skyline, stand proud in a regenerated area which is a symbol of a different Belfast from that of the previous decades.

On the east bank, the mighty flyover that used to carry the traffic
from the humming shipyards of Harland & Wolff to the lone Queen's
Bridge is dwarfed beneath two yellow cranes, Samson and Goliath,
standing like sentries at the gates of east Belfast. A fan of roads – the
Albertbridge, Ravenhill, Mountpottinger, Woodstock, Cregagh,
Castlereagh, Newtownards – spreads eastwards and outwards from
where the River Lagan meets the tides of Belfast Lough. This area (the
notable exception being the Short Strand) covers inner-city, Protestant, working-class streets whose inhabitants are steeped in uncompromising loyalty to the British Crown. There is a tenacious allegiance
that endures, fed by folk, and often family, memories of the generations who fought in British military campaigns of two World Wars,
particularly at the Somme, where so many Ulster lives were sacrificed
for king and country. If not the traditional heart of loyalism in Northern Ireland, east Belfast is certainly a highly vocal lung.

It was into a socially tolerant and stable community that David
Ervine was born on 21 July 1953 in his parents' house, 11

Chamberlain Street, delivered, as was the custom then, by the local midwife. Chamberlain Street, a street of ordinary two-up, two-down rows of houses with outside lavatories, runs between the Newtownards and Albertbridge Roads.

David was the fifth and last child of the family. His mother, christened Elizabeth but called Dolly from childhood, was forty-two years old when he was born. Two years earlier she had had another son, Brian. There were two much older sisters and a brother, but the substantial age gap meant that they were, in effect, two families. David's father, Walter, was an iron-turner by trade. By the time the Second World War broke out, he had been working for twelve years as a crew member on oil tankers on the transatlantic route. He was asked to contribute to the war effort by accepting a 'shore' job in which he could make use of his skills as a tradesman, but he insisted that he did not want to stand idly by while the country was in crisis. Instead he joined the Royal Navy, where he was given a commission because of his experience in the merchant navy as an engineer. He served on the Russian convoys and returned home eventually with a form of shell-shock, an affliction that caused him to keel over on occasions.

Walter Ervine took up his trade again and found plentiful work in several places – the shipyard, Sirocco engineering, Hugh J. Scott's – moving around a lot since his skills were in demand.

His wife, Dolly, worked 'out' in Lines Brothers' pram factory on the Castlereagh Road and continued to do so during her two youngest sons' childhood. One of the older sisters who was still living at home looked after the two small boys, while her married sister who lived near by helped out, as was the custom in extended families in working-class areas of Belfast.

David nearly lost his life when he was about one year old. The family had a big tin bath which was used for boiling clothes. His two sisters lifted the tin bath, still boiling and full of clothes, off the gas cooker and placed it outside in the backyard where the two small boys were playing. In the hurry-scurry of a game, David accidentally tipped back over into the bath. Although Brian managed to pull him out, even today he can still visualise the horrific image of his infant brother standing there, his skin shrivelled into pink parchment, enveloped in clouds of rising steam. David lay on his stomach in a cot for twelve weeks in Haypark Hospital, so severely scalded that for some time his life hung in the balance.

Both boys attended Megain Memorial primary school at the end of their street on the Newtownards Road. David's reports said that, while he was intelligent, he did not care very much for school and refused to apply himself. Though nominally attached to Megain Memorial Presbyterian Church, the Ervines were not churchgoers. Each Sunday morning Mrs Ervine would put money in her church collection envelope, as Presbyterians do, but it was collected by a woman on her way to church, who would place it in the offering tray. At the end of the year each family's financial contribution was published in a church report. This disgusted Walter Ervine. There are Presbyterians who see this practice as democratic, open and transparent. Mr Ervine saw it as socially divisive and an intrusion. With both parents in work and the older children in jobs, the father's stance stemmed from social principle and a refusal to conform, not hardship.

Sunday mornings for the Ervines were spent at home. Mr Ervine always read *The Sunday Times*, and David would scan articles in the supplement. Social pressures and pretensions – the regular appearance in one's Sunday best, for example – were regarded as an empty charade by Walter Ervine and his family.

However, the boys could not avoid having to attend Sunday school. Every Sunday afternoon Mrs Ervine would comb their hair, any protest being met with a belt round the ear, and send them off to acquire their scriptural knowledge in 'a good Presbyterian Sunday school'. Like many other children from a Presbyterian home, the brothers can still intone: 'What is man's chief end? Man's chief end is to glorify God and enjoy him for ever.' David hated these Sunday afternoons. Sunday school meant nothing to him; it was merely rote learning. He would have preferred his father's more liberal regime of 'Look, make it their own choice.' As was the case in other Presbyterian homes, however, his mother's word was law, and so Sunday school it had to be.

David was persuaded to join the Life Boys of Megain Memorial Church for a time, but found he had no feeling of identification with the group, and his membership soon lapsed. For it was the street and not the church institutions with their arid ethos which lay at the centre of a boy's universe. The street was his civilisation, determining his

outlook and values. He lived by and conformed to the habits and cus-
toms of the society on his doorstep. And this was not a democracy.
Territory was marked out through your fists. The unwritten street law
dictated that you fought your corner or your life was made a misery.
It was the loudest voice, or the best at something, or the strongest arm
which influenced and held sway. It was also a strictly segregated
world: girls did not participate in boys' activities.

From his street the young David Ervine breathed in familiarity, the
oxygen to feed his organs of security and safety which were safeguarded by the muscle of collective action. The next street up the road
was enemy territory. Lurking round the corner lay uncertainty and
menace. And the street beyond that was everyone's enemy. The 'Indi-
ans' roamed other streets; only 'cowboys', his chums on palomino
steeds, rode in his territory.

David, inclined to be hot-headed, was always ready for a scrap. As
a young teenager he was sturdy and heavily built, though Brian was
'handier'. Having served his apprenticeship in the street, Brian
directed his pugnacious talents in his teens towards the boxing ring.
Aged seventeen he fought for his local boys' club, Ledley Hall, in the
cross-community Northern Ireland Federation of Boys' Clubs
championships. He weighed only ten stones two pounds, but under
competition rules he was classified as a heavyweight and found himself confronting opponents weighing anything up to fourteen stones.
In the semi-finals, held in a secondary school in a nationalist area, the
mere sight of his opponent's physique was enough to scare Brian, but
he won in the second round. At that, sectarian fights broke out
between rival supporters outside the ring. In the finals, held in a neutral city centre venue, against an opponent two stones heavier, again
the fight was stopped in the second round, and, under the Marquess
of Queensberry rules, Brian became Northern Ireland Boys' Clubs
heavyweight champion. David also had a go at boxing, but was too
restricted in his movements by the back injuries he had received in
infancy.

Any brotherly rivalry was confined to home, where they brought
the aggressive culture of the street inside. Outside, however, fraternal
solidarity was the order of the day. When 'big guys' would try to push
David around, then big brother Brian would sort them out. Northern
Ireland Boys' Clubs champion or not, Brian could still scrap. David

had no intention of being pushed around, but at times he found he had taken on more than he could handle.

On one occasion, when the boys were aged about fifteen or sixteen, Brian was alone in the house when an agitated young acquaintance called in. 'You'd better come,' he spluttered. 'David is in trouble. It's a mob. They've got him in Lord Street.' Brian rushed up to Lord Street, rounded the corner, and saw that a big member of the gang had grabbed hold of David. Brian sized up the situation in an instant, ran up to David's captor and socked him on the jaw. Just at that moment, a gang of about thirty youths appeared from around a distant corner and rushed towards them. 'Right, Dave,' Brian said quietly but insistently, 'on we go, home.'

However, there came the time when Brian retired as his brother's keeper. Young David was now big enough and tough enough to look after himself. And look after himself he did, having both courage and self-reliance. These qualities stood him in good stead when, late one Saturday afternoon, while returning with some friends after watching a football match at Windsor Park on the other side of the city, they were set upon by a group of hatchet-wielding supporters of the opposing team. David grabbed a pole with a banner on it from the marauders and fought a rearguard action while his mates were escaping. In the fracas, he received a hatchet blow in the back and was saved from more serious injury only because he was wearing Brian's thick donkey jacket. His assailants chased him as far as the Queen's Bridge across the Lagan, his escape route into east Belfast and home territory.

The Belfast street culture of the 1950s and 1960s was not the only influence shaping the personality of the young David Ervine. Other, more subtle forces were at work. Walter Ervine had the two boys out running down the street twice a week – to the library. He instructed them to pick three books, in any category, to bring home. He himself was a voracious reader, and perhaps it was his intention to expose his children to the riches to be discovered in books. At their age and in such a 'knuckle' culture, it signalled that there was nothing wrong with reading and that it was a perfectly sensible and reasonable thing to do, even though their main interests lay elsewhere. That was a powerful lesson and an enlightened example.

During David's teenage years he developed a strong, though temporary, interest in the youth organisations of the church which he had found so distasteful as a boy. He joined the Boys' Brigade and enjoyed it thoroughly. They were a rough-and-ready bunch of boys who 'tholed' the drill practice because their real interest in being there was games, physical education and the football team, a motivation shared by thousands of Protestant teenage boys. The great difference for David lay this time in the character and personality of the man who was the Boys' Brigade skipper, Geordie Magill. Geordie, who came from the same area and background as the boys he led, spoke their language and shared their interests; he was a keen footballer and served as physiotherapist to a football team.

Identification with his community was important to Ervine, even in his youth. So powerful was this motivation in him that he won promotion to wear the corporal's stripes, an attainment few reached in the Boys' Brigade. The company corporal was held in respect and had authority. Ervine, however, is more inclined to put his promotion down to the fact that he was now, at the age of sixteen, a really big lad, over five feet ten and built like a barge.

Many people today assume that Ervine, with his intellectual ability and great gifts as a communicator, was educated in a grammar school and university. This is incorrect. Ervine entered second-level education in 1965, at a time when a universal common curriculum and qualifications for all were unheard of. Instead, Northern Ireland retained the eleven-plus exam system of education, which was selective and elitist. Brian qualified for the local authority grammar school, Grosvenor High, while David attended Orangefield Boys' Secondary School, whose headmaster was John Malone.

In his book *Minority Verdict*, Maurice Hayes, a distinguished former civil servant in the Northern Ireland administration, writes about Orangefield and his fellow native of Downpatrick:

> John Malone was one of the really great educators. A member of an old Downpatrick family, he had become headmaster of Orangefield, a new intermediate school catering for the east of the city. John set about transforming this into a comprehensive school in all but name. In doing so he set new standards for secondary schools in Belfast, and more widely. He employed interesting people as teachers, and gave them their head, he was accessible to

pupils and engaged their interest and he was widely revered by teachers, especially those who were less than fully happy with the complacency of the system. He raised hackles in the educational establishment. He expounded unfashionable ideas about the dignity and worth of pupils who had been labelled as second-class by the selective system.

Some idea of the strength of opposition, and the originality of John Malone's philosophy, is gauged in an official survey, the MacBeath Report, 1955, which stated in its conclusions: 'The great majority of pupils at secondary-intermediate schools probably are not intellectually equipped to pass any worthwhile external examination.' Even in retrospect, the arrogance is breathtaking. In that era John Malone's task was daunting, matched only by his vision.

In 1965 some 20 per cent of pupils passed the eleven-plus and went on to one of the 81 grammar schools in Northern Ireland where all pupils took the compulsory GCE public examination in a range of subjects. In that same year the total entries for GCE in all subjects from the 137 secondary schools amounted to 587 candidates. No single statistic more tellingly illustrates the glaring inequality between the two types of school.

Ervine brought with him to Orangefield a combative nature and a disregard for authority. Naturally these traits soon got him into trouble. For a start he did not get along with his class teacher. Then there were the 'tough guys' among his fellow pupils, who constantly triggered his aggression. While his physical size withered any possible challenge from among his peers, it served only to arouse the interest of more senior rivals, and Ervine was always the type who would meet a challenge head-on, rather than waiting for differences to be sorted out by the school staff. Besides, he was having enough problems adjusting to the teachers' authority as it was. He saw the inside of the principal's office almost every day. His behaviour deteriorated so badly that the school requested his parents to come and discuss the situation.

Mrs Ervine took time off work to cross the Castlereagh Road from Lines Brothers'. It was she who told the teachers, 'Our David will be led, but he will not be driven.' They had the good sense to heed her words. David was made class monitor and things improved, and so did the behaviour of his class.

Picture a noisy physical education changing room: the games teacher is trying to quieten things down so that he can talk to the boys about what they are going to do during the lesson, but the boys are excited, chatting away noisily, throwing their bags on to the wooden benches with a bang. Somebody is whistling, a couple of latecomers charge in, feet drum on the floor. In exasperation the teacher shouts, 'If you don't be quiet, we'll spend the whole period here writing lines,' but only a few standing close to him can hear. One of them is Ervine. He is galvanised into action because he loves doing games. 'Listen,' he barks, 'if you don't be quiet . . .!' Instant silence descends.

Ervine was aware of what was going on. 'It was about controlling me as much as controlling them.' In fact, it seems that Ervine's reputation as a 'raker' has been exaggerated. Several of the teachers who were on the staff at Orangefield have no recollection of him as a particularly disruptive pupil; others, including some who were in positions of responsibility, do not remember him at all. This suggests that the tales of persistent misconduct on his part may well have gathered lustre with the passing of time.

Indeed, it appears that David Ervine contributed a lot to his school. During his first two years he played rugby for his year team as a number 8 forward. Then he switched to soccer and played as a stopper centre-half. One Saturday he played football for the school in the morning and in the afternoon ran for the cross-country team in Newtownards. He was a good swimmer and swam for the school team in galas. One in particular, at the Grove Baths on a winter Saturday evening, he recalls well. The boys had arrived very early, were refused entry and had to hang about outside, but when the teacher arrived he insisted that 'his' boys be allowed in off the street immediately into the warm building, and so they were. Clearly Ervine was responding through his involvement in school teams to the commitment of John Malone's hand-picked staff, many of whom he remembers with great affection.

In his fondness and respect for these teachers, we can discern a parallel to his experiences in the Boys' Brigade: 'You met a lot of young teachers at Orangefield. I identified very heavily with them. All young, good, no-nonsense people. Of course, they were serious people, too, but they had time for you. Certainly in my case they understood me.'

Orangefield also provided this schoolboy, whose culture was steeped in the industrial streets of Belfast, with opportunities to experience a totally different, almost alien, environment that he had never expected to enjoy. John Malone had bought Whinlands, a large house in its own grounds at Annalong, along the shore beyond Newcastle, County Down, and below the Mountains of Mourne. His intention was that it should be used as a school annex. Malone's was a pioneering venture for a school in Northern Ireland, an extension of the academic classroom, a field centre for studies and, importantly, a place to encourage and support social opportunities away from home for his pupils. It would serve as a forum where pupils and teachers could mix in a friendly atmosphere and get to know each other as individuals. It was the first opportunity many of the youngsters had ever had to spend time away from their parents and the streets. David Ervine was part of the 'Whinlands generation' in east Belfast, and John Malone's inspired experiment in the socialising of education undoubtedly added a vital new dimension to Ervine's life. He was at Whinlands in each of his terms at school, and still remembers, over thirty years later, the long walks in the mountains. It all contributed to a feeling of pride in the school.

Orangefield afforded Ervine opportunities to express himself through sport, gave him responsibility which he could use to good effect, provided occasions for him to socialise away from an atmosphere of aggression, and enabled him to develop a more rounded view of adults and those in authority – valuable lessons for a street scrapper.

Throughout his schooldays he was well aware that his sheer physical size could be used as part of a schoolboy's armoury against his teachers. Fortunately, their understanding attitude and professional teamwork ensured that he never seriously fell out with any of them. When anti-social behaviour did erupt, it was simply due to ordinary adolescent stupidity, which, in the nature of things, is never in short supply in a boys' school. One incident, which Ervine still regrets, occurred on the sports field. He was sent off once in a rugby match for retaliating violently when he went down on a ball and got kicked in the back, his scalded back.

Ervine left school at the end of June 1968, in his third year, as he was legally entitled to at the time, since his fifteenth birthday would be the next month. When he looks back at his schooldays, he remarks, almost apologetically, 'I think I proved in my early life at school that I was not a learner, or was not a practical learner.' But it was only in 1967 that the Northern Ireland government was persuaded that a Certificate of Secondary Education examination should be introduced into Northern Ireland for secondary-intermediate school pupils, following the scheme established in England and Wales in 1965. John Malone, in collaboration with Vincent MacGeown of St Augustine's and others, led a pressure group to extend parity of opportunity to secondary-intermediate pupils, and the CSE was eventually introduced for the first time in 1973. It would be only as a consequence of the coming 'Troubles', and in a very different institution, that Ervine was to find the motivation to apply himself and become a learner.

David Ervine's early life and schooldays reveal two fundamental aspects of his character that were to become dominant influences in his subsequent political career. First, it is clear how firmly his emotional roots reach down into the community of his native east Belfast. Second, his insights into people are perceptive and knowledgeable; he is able to see an individual's personality behind the functionary's facade.

MOVING INTO CONFLAGRATION

AFTER ERVINE LEFT school, society and his community were, to use his own phrase, 'moving into conflagration'. At home arguments about politics with his father changed from bread-and-butter issues to more serious and immediate developments, literally to matters of life and death. Morning, noon and night everybody seemed to have a radio tuned to the police wavelength. People became addicted to the latest news bulletin to find out what was going on in the city and elsewhere in the province. An anxious society in fear of itself was obsessed with listening to the news, watching the news and reading the news about itself.

Predictably, reactions depended on which side you were on. Like hordes of people of his age, Ervine resorted to 'little tribalism'. His father would try to put him right, but to no avail, for peer persuasion prevailed. A few hundred yards up the Albertbridge Road, a riot would be attracting youths like moths to a light. There was a level of excitement and a sense of belonging that were irresistible to the teenage Ervine.

Yet ordinary life continued. Brian Ervine emigrated to Australia soon after leaving school. David worked for a while as a carpet-fitter and then got a job in the Sirocco Engineering works, in east Belfast, where his father had once been employed. Sectarian attitudes were now overtly invading the shop floor. On his first morning the other apprentices had certain suspicions arising from Ervine's appearance.

They believed in some folk nonsense which says that Protestants and Catholics are differentiated by the distance between their eyes, and they thought he had the look of a Catholic. They confronted him to find out which 'foot he kicked with'. Outside the factory, situated in an almost totally Catholic area, attitudes polarised too. Taking the shortest route to work every morning, Ervine had to run the gauntlet of local vigilantes, but he could run fast. At that stage things were comparatively mild, and he only got his face punched once.

Irrepressible adolescent life continued, too, against a constricting backdrop of antagonism and suspicion. Now aged sixteen, Ervine had already met the girl, Jeanette, whose support, and ultimately love, were to be so crucial in his life. He recognised this at the outset of their relationship. He told her on their second date, 'I'm going to marry you.'

Jeanette's reply was brief: 'Like hell you are! You don't even know me. I'm off!' And she, as they say in Belfast, 'blew him out'. Ervine, typically, was not put off.

They met again soon afterwards at a mutual friend's birthday party in Holywood, a short distance away on the County Down coast of Belfast Lough. He left Jeanette back home into the city by taxi. She lived in Malcolm Lane, a narrow street at the foot of the Woodstock Road. As they were getting out of the taxi at the junction of the Albertbridge and Woodstock Roads, they suddenly found themselves in the middle of a gun battle between loyalist and republican factions shooting across the main thoroughfare, the Albertbridge Road. David led a frightened Jeanette home to be met by her worried parents waiting on the doorstep. Jeanette was impressed by his coolness and courage, and when he returned to see her a few days later, an enduring relationship began.

The job in the Sirocco works lasted only a matter of six months or so. He did not enjoy it. Restrictions, routine, close supervision, uniform compliance, machinery, all ran against his personal grain. Such a stifling atmosphere did not appeal to this young man.

At home events on the streets dominated discussions, and within the household divergent positions were openly taken up. The father was implacably opposed to Ian Paisley and saw him as a manipulator. Mr Ervine was a trade unionist and a member of the Northern Ireland Labour Party who never joined the Orange Order. His wife

did not obediently follow her husband's political opinions. Dolly
Ervine held her own views passionately and did not hesitate to express
them. When Bernadette Devlin, the brilliant and passionate critic of
the Northern state, would appear on television, Mrs Ervine stood
before the television set berating her furiously. Dolly was a strong
supporter of Ian Paisley.

In early 1969 David got a job as a storeman, again in a Catholic
area – Great Patrick Street. He worked for a family-owned wholesale
company which dealt with everything from fancy toys to marble
chippings. Here he was given his first exposure to dealing with the
public, which he found greatly to his taste. Variety, flexibility, dealing
with different people, with no two days the same: all combined to produce a sense of work satisfaction.

Outside work, however, sickening events seemed to be pushing a
province out of control into civil chaos. Social unrest among
Catholics, manifested in legitimate political protest, had degenerated
through civil disorder to social upheaval. People abandoned their
homes and fled for safety to nationalist areas which, in turn, became
spawning grounds for paramilitaries who emerged on a sectarian
bombing and shooting campaign.

East Belfast was not immune. That area, as well as other parts of
Belfast, Derry and indeed the whole province, was in a state of frenzy,
of suspicion leading to communal paranoia. Where would the IRA
bombers and murderers strike next? Rumour assumed the mantle of
fact. Fear fed on rumour. To hapless unionists, the reporting of mayhem in the media, all day every day, seemed to provide horrifying
proof to substantiate hearsay, relayed from street to street, of a
guerilla war whose aim was a republican takeover. Ordinary families
experienced feelings of confusion, insecurity and growing despair.
They sought, they craved, peace of mind.

Vigilantes offered protection from threat of attack, which, however
imaginary, nevertheless felt all too real among a community verging
on a collective nervous breakdown. The common will acquiesced to
self-appointed protectors recruited from among their own neighbours.
If anyone had misgivings, it is likely that they kept them private. Fear
of being the dissenting voice was enough to stifle opposition even
before it could be uttered. The beginning of the 1970s was a dread-
ful time.

Like all adolescent and adult males in the area, Ervine played his part in protecting a territorial strip, his street. They were given a rota, a shift to be on guard and keep the enemy at bay, and in the febrile atmosphere became ripe for exploitation by the paramilitaries who usurped effective control over the Protestant, working-class community in east Belfast. Ervine recalls:

> It seems ludicrous. At the time the Provos were not going to drive into Chamberlain Street and plant a bomb. There were bits of wood nailed together and pulled across the road at each end. You were given your rota that you had to do. I was about sixteen or seventeen. I can remember saying to myself, 'What am I doing standing here?' It showed the atmosphere that we were living in. There were places that were never going to be attacked by anybody, yet they had vigilantes! It was all about a communal hype and the circumstances we were going through. Therefore, one can see how it was relatively easy to go one step further, from the vigilante stuff to a structured paramilitarist circumstance.

Ervine dates his loss of naivety to these grim developments. No longer could he and his friends engage in the simple pursuits enjoyed by previous generations of the happy-go-lucky young: entertainment, dances and dates in all parts of the city; a game of football in the park of an evening; jumping on your bike and going for a spin to any old where just for the fun of it. Instead his world contracted and reduced itself in the cold name of security. If you lived in Belfast, you were careful where you went. Certain places you gave up going to because it would be simply too dangerous. You watched whoever was watching you. Into embattled local minds, a new city under seige, not marked on any map, materialised: East Belfast.

In local secondary-intermediate schools, teachers began to notice that some normally reliable senior pupils were not returning homework on time, or not doing it at all. Others appeared unusually lethargic in class. Individuals were sore and awkward of movement. Staff were unaware that many pupils were being drilled by the paramilitaries in the street during the night and being punished for misdemeanours of regimented discipline by being made to lean on their outstretched arms against a wall for prolonged periods.

Shifts in attitudes banished innocence from neighbourliness. Neighbours who were Catholics became Catholics who were neighbours. Catholics who were neighbours became Catholics who lived in your street. Catholic people in your street became people who should not be living in 'our' street, for were they not like the IRA? Relationships formed over years were shattered in the general upheaval. And all the time the vicious circle of intercommunal violence spiralled to crisis point. In 1971 alone, 174 people were killed and 2,592 injured in Northern Ireland.

Ervine tended to swim against the sectarian tide that was flooding his community by discriminating between Catholics and republicans. A neighbour, Mrs Neill, was a fine lady, and other Catholics in Chamberlain Street were as decent as anybody else. His problem lay with the threat of violence and its perpetrators, who mostly came from Catholic, working-class areas: the Falls, Ballymurphy, Turf Lodge, the New Lodge Road.

In personal relationships Ervine disregarded Northern Ireland's sectarian demarcation line, as his employment record clearly demonstrates. Had Ervine been sectarian, it is unlikely, in those bitter circumstances, that he would have taken another new job in 1971 in a wholesale paint company, this time in the city centre. Ervine still recalls his Catholic employer with undisguised warmth and respect: 'An absolute gentleman – treated me like a son.'

The benefit Ervine gained from the two jobs where his employers happened to be Catholic can be measured in human terms. Put simply, he enjoyed working both in the store and behind the counter because these jobs gave him what he valued most: 'exposure to people – Protestant, Catholic, whatever – all kinds of decent people'.

If the saga of bad news in 1971 was not bad enough, the new year had scarcely been born before its ghastly train of events began to roll. A bomb in Callendar Street, Belfast, on 3 January injured sixty people. 'Bloody Sunday' in Derry, where thirteen innocent people were shot dead, erupted on 30 January. A bomb demolished an army mess in Aldershot, England, on 22 February. Three days later the unionist politician John Taylor survived an assassination attempt on the streets of Armagh. A bomb in the Abercorn bar and restaurant in Central Belfast killed two women and injured 136 people, many badly mutilated, on 4 March. Sixteen days later six people were killed and nearly 150 injured when a bomb exploded in lower North Street, Belfast, where a hoax warning lured shoppers, who were being led by two off-duty policemen towards what they thought was a safe area, into a danger zone. The two policemen were killed in the explosion. Four days after that incident, it was announced that the provincial parliament at Stormont was to be prorogued on 30 March.

More happily, however, 1972 contained the most momentous day of David Ervine's life, for on 1 March of that year he was married to Jeanette Cunningham. Like David, Jeanette came from a working-class background devoid of privilege. Her family had to work for anything they got. Originally when Jeanette's parents married, they lived with the new wife's father in a large attic house on the Ravenhill Road. Later they moved to a small place of their own. To them it seemed like Buckingham Palace, but in fact it was a building that had already been condemned before they moved in and was falling apart.

Jeanette's father, Bobby, was a good handyman and was able to make improvements. He put in new windows and turned the stairs round so as to enlarge the living room of the small house. Sally, her mother, made all her three babies' clothes. She was a thrifty woman who also did the painting and decorating. Although times were not easy for them, there was warmth and neighbourliness on their street. People of different religious denominations lived together, got on well, and Jeanette had several Catholic friends, but there was also a good deal of political naivety. This became manifest during the Civil Rights campaign when the Cunninghams, along with most of their community, grew disillusioned with the direction of the campaign and its shift, as they interpreted it, towards the objective of Catholic power.

Jeanette's parents, who did not have business premises, held the same rights as their Catholic neighbours. She remains convinced that working-class Protestants were wrongly condemned at the time as exploiters of their Catholic neighbours. She, like most working-class Protestants, was confused over the 'one man, one vote' issue, exploited by the Civil Rights movement to highlight discrimination against all Catholics in Northern Ireland. She took it for granted that universal suffrage was already in place for all elections, part and parcel of her British heritage. So to join agitation for 'one man, one vote' would be supporting anti-unionist propaganda. Jeanette and her parents were ignorant of the cynical manipulation of the 'business vote'. They were simply unaware that those citizens, predominantly unionists, who owned business premises could exercise an extra vote per premises in local council elections.

Why were unionists like Jeanette and her family in the dark? Put briefly, it was because of the working-class culture of deference to the big political dynasties, the landed gentry, wealthy and influential businessmen, prominent members of churches, and all with the obligatory link to the Orange Order. Among the ordinary Protestant people, politics – apart from a determination to maintain the Union – was of little concern, something to be left to the established political leaders, no matter how remote and unrepresentative they might be. This unconcerned attitude was to cost them dear, for it kept in power an arrogant and incompetent oligarchy that was partly responsible for the desperate events now unfolding in the streets.

It was a very rough time to be in east Belfast. Even the primary schoolchildren were infected by the atmosphere of violence, sometimes marching along their school corridors in imitation of the illegal paramilitary UDA 'soldiers', whom they had seen in the streets.

The older, adolescent brothers of these youngsters formed themselves into 'tartan' gangs, based on their neighbourhood territory, such as the Newtown tartan, the Woodstock tartan, and so on. The term 'tartan', a word associated with Scotland, accentuated their repudiation of all things Irish and reinforced religious links with the sectarian division in Glasgow, a connection they revered. These tartan gangs were unruly and unpredictable, roaming the streets looking for trouble, specifically with anything or anybody Catholic.

In local secondary schools, even in those schools which normally would have permitted a certain latitude in dress, principals had to insist that strict school uniform be worn, because each tartan would try to incorporate its own slight variation to a school uniform. For example, the school tie would be worn in a particular knot, or shirt cuffs turned out in a certain fashion, or the jacket collar bent up, all to territorialise a form of dress that was intended to be common garb. School authorities were compelled to take preventative action to avoid gang warfare breaking out and to preserve the neutrality of the school environment.

If they were frustrated by the determined actions of schools to keep the Troubles out of the classroom or by the absence of sectarian targets, these young thugs could always vent their ire upon the soldiers of the British army now deployed on the streets of east Belfast in an effort to preserve some semblance of normality. Sometimes the local lads could plead provocation. It was frequently claimed that soldiers had shouted abuse at residents from their army vehicles; and once the resulting situation had got out of hand, it was quite likely that a full-scale riot would ensue. One of those subjected to army harassment was Brian Ervine, who came home from Australia for David's wedding and decided to stay when he was accepted on to a teacher training course at Stranmillis, in Belfast. One night, because of rioting in the area, he escorted members of his youth club safely home and on the way back picked up a used baton round as a souvenir:

> I was coming down Lord Street. There'd been rioting there, and an army snatch squad got hold of me and examined my hands and realised I wasn't throwing anything. But they gave me a going-over. There was shooting at the army at that time on the Albertbridge Road, and they laid me spreadeagled out while they were being shot at. It was incongruous. There was this English officer with a hoity-toity accent who was effing and blinding. I couldn't keep my face straight. Then they took me in the pig to Chamberlain Street because there was rioting in our own street. It was like Zululand. A few of the soldiers got injured and they began to take it out on me. They took me back to the barrack, and they were going to charge me with possession of a live round of ammunition. They were rough. I saw guys with blood pouring out of their heads.
>
> In the end the police realised it was a dud cartridge. The officer – not the one who scooped me – apologised. They humiliated me. You know the sort of thing: 'You Irish, you're only good for digging roads.' Of course, I said, 'If it hadn't been for us, you wouldn't have won the war' [a typical, if inaccurate, riposte of unionists frustrated when Ulster's Britishness is impugned]. They replied, 'You're only good for navvying.'
>
> When we'd gone into the barrack, the police had asked me, 'What O-levels have you got?' Me with eight O-levels,

two A-levels, studying for a degree in education, and they were calling me everything – Paddy, road-builder. It was horrible. It's insecure being brought up in a working-class area.

In east Belfast people's nerves were raw. A sense of lawlessness was stalking the district, and yet Her Majesty's forces, sent to protect the law-abiding citizens, were behaving like gangsters. Shoppers going into town were being blown up: killed, their limbs torn off, scarred for life. The IRA campaign had restored the Protestant and unionist working class to the postures of their folk history as painted on Orange banners and Lambeg drums. Now the ancient siege mentality was revitalised and thriving in east Belfast.

Like everyone else in the east of the city, David Ervine knew the loyalist paramilitaries were active:

I remember before I joined the UVF, they took the army on in east Belfast. I heard on the news that there was a gun battle in that area and, absolutely demented, I drove through the gun battle to get to my mother's because the UVF men were lying at the corner of my mother's street with rifles, firing at the army at Templemore Avenue. At the bottom of Chamberlain Street, I saw them openly carrying their weapons. I dived down and got into the house with my mother and father.

Ervine had rejected invitations to join the paramilitaries despite the mayhem around him. His whole upbringing told him that religious bigotry, with its suckling violence, was repugnant. 'I don't believe with the rearing I had and exposure to my father's political opinions that there was any great degree of sectarianism within me.'

And yet in 1972, at the age of nineteen, he did march in the opposite direction: 'That was the year I made a conscious decision to become a paramilitary.'

Why did he take a decision that so obviously denied all that he thought he stood for? Two things drove him. First, in the summer of that year he and Jeanette were awaiting the birth of their first child, and then on 21 July, Belfast suffered a horrific day of slaughter. Ervine describes vividly the effect on him of that day:

I was sitting in what was called Clancy's Tavern, at the corner of Albertbridge Road and Castlereagh Street. There was a ground-floor bar, a middle lounge and a top lounge. I was in the top lounge, and I could see the puffs of smoke go off in Belfast. I think that was the beginning of the end. It was so brutal, so raw. The best means of defence is attack. Maybe that sounds simplistic but that's how I felt.

The merciless savagery on that agonising Bloody Friday, when twenty-two bombs killed nine people and injured 130, sickened a city that had stomached vicious brutality until it thought it could take no more – and it caused David Ervine to walk straight into the arms of the loyalist paramilitaries. Like many young men on the other side of the religious divide, he had reached the point when he felt he had to do something to protect his own:

It was a sense of belonging to a community. That community was massively tense. Where's the next attack coming from? The sense of being under siege, the sense that this is against us. This is not against the government, this is against us. It's not against the rule of law, it's about people. They're killing our people.

On that day Ervine's inner dilemma reduced itself to a simple matter of kin – 'to whom I belong and to whom I do not belong'.

The second thing that drove Ervine towards the paramilitaries was more personal. At a time of high emotion, a bizarre, heart-breaking coincidence brought home to Ervine with disturbing impact the randomness of death and survival on the streets of Belfast. On that Friday of infamy, an Ervine was among the fatalities. Of the same age as David, the unfortunate victim only lived four streets away from Chamberlain Street, and agitation spread among parents and neighbours as to the exact identity of the local boy who had perished. Eventually there was relief for the Ervines of Chamberlain Street but great sympathy for the bereaved home.

Now Ervine decided to take up a 'long-standing invitation' to join the 'armed and disciplined' loyalist paramilitary Ulster Volunteer Force (UVF), whom he had already witnessed in action during the gun battle along the Newtownards Road.

There are three points that are worth bearing in mind when considering Ervine's decision to join the UVF. First, he had not meekly followed the flock. Characteristically, personal conviction was necessary before he would act. A tide of reaction was flowing through east Belfast, but only he, and nobody else, would decide if he was going to swim with it. Secondly, he was invited to join the UVF. Ervine says that he never discovered the reason why. This may be modesty or disingenuousness. After all, he was a big man, well built, had a reputation for being able to look after himself. He was a 'battler', and a courageous one at that, a decided asset to any paramilitary force. Thirdly, he joined a group which, in his estimation, appeared to be well organised and capable of undertaking its business with precision.

A document which appeared in November 1974, entitled *UVF Policy*, and referenced Policy Document 1/74, printed and published by the Ulster Volunteer Force, indicates the nature of the organisation Ervine joined. Inside there are sixteen paragraphs, and without reprinting the entire text we read:

UVF Military Policy

1. The ULSTER VOLUNTEER FORCE is a military organisation composed of loyal Ulster patriots who are pledged to support the maintenance of the Union of Great Britain and Northern Ireland; the preservation of our Protestant Faith and Liberties and the restoration of peace, contentment and stability to the people of Ulster.

2. The prime objective of the ULSTER VOLUNTEER FORCE is to train, equip and discipline a dedicated force of loyalist volunteers capable of supporting the Civil and Military Authorities in protecting the people of Northern Ireland in the face of armed aggression from foes foreign and domestic . . .

3. The ULSTER VOLUNTEER FORCE maintains that there is no essential difference between official Government action and unofficial loyalist action in the struggle against terrorism subversion, so long as that action is morally justified . . .

5. The ULSTER VOLUNTEER FORCE further maintains the right to resist, by force of arms if necessary, any attempt

by any Government to impose an unjust and undemocratic system of Government upon an unwilling majority. We acknowledge the fact that rebellion against lawful Government is a grievous sin against God...

6. In formulating its military policies and strategies the ULSTER VOLUNTEER FORCE has applied to it criteria similar to that governing a just war... Torture in all forms, the holding of innocent hostages and the indiscriminate killing of innocent non-combatants – which destroy the soul of the perpetrator as surely as the life and health of the victim – form no part of UVF policy.

8.... we must employ the same tactics as our enemies, but we must be more ruthless and determined.

9. In order to destroy the forces of terrorism and subversion the ULSTER VOLUNTEER FORCE is pledged to:

   (a) Track down and eliminate the Command Structure of the enemy

   (b) Seek out and destroy enemy active service personnel

   (c) Uncover and disrupt enemy supplies and sources of finance

   (d) Harrass and intimidate those who give shelter and support to the enemy.

10. The ULSTER VOLUNTEER FORCE recognises the Provisional IRA and Provisional Sinn Féin as the number one short-term enemy of Ulster...

11. The most dangerous and deadly enemy in the long-term will prove to be the Official IRA and its Marxist-Leninist associates. In the struggle against these Republican Socialists the ULSTER VOLUNTEER FORCE recognises the need for both political and military action. To this end the UVF shall seek to expose the errors of doctrinaire socialism and to expose the myth of the supposed class struggle...

16. In order to build up its financial and material resources the ULSTER VOLUNTEER FORCE DECLARES that all individuals, associations and business concerns which support the enemy are legitimate targets for procurement operations.

Ervine was attracted into the ranks of the balaclava-wearing gunmen as a comparative latecomer, a reluctant novice. For others, entry
into paramilitarism went with the territory. It was part of the street culture. You did not play marbles along the pavements; you threw petrol
bombs through the air enthusiastically. You did not go to the local park
to play football and get rid of your aggression by kicking the living
daylights out of the opposition or by making them look silly with mazy
dribbles. No, you and your comrades tried to invade an alien enclave,
do as much damage as possible and get out, leaving your mark behind
to teach your enemies a lesson. You did not give too much thought to
what this was all about. What you definitely did know was the excitement and the feeling of togetherness with your marauding mates. It
was a heady mix. You started young. Maybe you were heading for
Long Kesh jail, but you did not give that a thought. Who would, when
the adventures in the street out-performed what you saw on television,
except when you were watching yourself on the news?

With thoughts like these shaping the mind-set of countless young
Protestants in the back streets of Belfast, it is easy to understand why
David Ervine was not alone in his journey into the world of paramilitarism, though some started earlier than he did. His future prison
acquaintance, Eddie Kinner, for example.

Eddie Kinner was born and reared in the heart of the Shankill
Road, in Dover Street. His family is steeped in loyalty to the British
Crown. His great-grandfather fought in the Boer War. His grandfather, too young to join up during the Great War, forged his age and
enlisted in the original UVF regiment, fought at the Somme and was
wounded twice. Kinner's father volunteered for the RAF and served
for five years in the late 1950s.

At the age of eleven, Eddie was spending his evenings after school
making petrol bombs for the 'big fellas' to throw. School itself was an
irrelevance; his real stimulation and commitment were with the
Shankill tartans. He enjoyed going to football matches, especially when
Linfield was playing. Not that he cared much about the technical intri-
cacies of soccer: 'I didn't go to watch football. I went for the riot on
the way back home past Unity Flats. That's what I was going for.'
Unity Flats, a Catholic enclave, stood at the foot of the Shankill Road.
After 5 o'clock on a Saturday evening, a raucous mass of expectant
supporters parading homewards up the Shankill would wave their red,

white and blue scarves and Ulster flags in provocation; they shouted
and sang and swore their enmity to the embattled residents. Then,
shepherded by slow-moving Land-Rovers of the RUC, they marched
on home, their weekly show of hostility and defiance achieved. The
transfer of this street-hardened apprentice into the ranks of the hard
men in balaclavas was an easy, almost predictable process.

Another of David Ervine's contemporaries to make the same
smooth transition from random street violence to paramilitary
involvement was Martin Snodden. His motivation was fear – 'fear of
what was likely to happen to my family, my friends and my neighbours'. Snodden had lived in the Donegall Pass area, a short walk
away from the city centre, until he was seven years old, and had then
moved to the Suffolk estate on the southern edge of Belfast, at that
time a predominantly Protestant area. However, in the disturbed
climate of the early 1970s, Suffolk, in common with other districts in
Belfast, suffered migration of people from 'mixed areas' to 'safe
areas', where their neighbours would be solely of their own religious
persuasion. This population movement may have affected as many as
700 Protestant families on the Suffolk estate.

Snodden could not remain untouched by what was going on in his
neighbourhood:

> My first encounter would have been in my last year at
> school whenever a couple of fellows from the top of
> Lenadoon had come to me, a couple of friends from my
> class, and said they were being intimidated by this guy
> from Andersonstown who was coming along the top and
> abusing them. Would I come up and give them a hand? So
> I'd gone up and had a fair dig with them – that was the first
> sectarian thing I had done, not even realising it as such at
> the time.

Encouragement to get involved in more serious violence came from
a respected but unexpected source. To be just, it was the kind of
remark that could have been misinterpreted by youths like Snodden,
who felt they were under threat.

> I remember the church in Suffolk being attacked and going
> up to defend it. We had been walking up towards the

church and had come under attack from a crowd of Catholics. They'd come charging at us from behind with hurley bats. I got hit on the shoulder. We all spontaneously bolted. One of us got left behind, and they were blattering him in a garden. So we turned and went back and got him. They ran away and fired a couple of shots at us, but we pulled in at the church. The minister was there. I can't remember the exact words that he used, but it was a case of if he got hold of them, he knew what he would do with them. This was influential to us at the time. If a minister can say that sort of thing, then we can do it.

For impressionable teenagers with adrenalin still pumping after a deadly chase, such intemperate language provided the crucial impulse that would tip the delicate balance between restraint and retaliation. This incident, where a pillar of the community felt so impotent and isolated by the state's law and order agencies, indicates how far society in Northern Ireland had moved down the road of lawlessness. Further, it explains how paramilitaries gained acceptance in a host neighbourhood which endorsed the state, and whose civic leaders, while disapproving of the paramilitaries in public, gave an impression of private, if reluctant, support.

From east, west and south Belfast, the three young men – Ervine, Kinner and Snodden – who did not know each other and had never met, each separately accepted an invitation to join the UVF. Yet already they shared common bonds: they were working class, from stable families, had attended secondary-intermediate schools which they had left without any sense of achievement and did not have criminal records. All three made a conscious decision to get involved with the UVF because the British security forces seemed incapable of protecting their community.

If Northern Ireland had not been in a state of virtual civil war, these young men would not have been destined to spend an extended period of their adult lives in prison.

SENTENCED

MARTIN SNODDEN WAS caught on a bombing mission that had gone wrong. One of his comrades, who had been standing only a matter of inches away from Snodden, was killed when the bomb they were placing exploded prematurely. His immediate reaction was a feeling that he was lucky to be alive, combined with a sense of guilt. But strongest of all was a sense of grim determination that, no matter what the future held for him, he would never give in to the police and prison authorities.

He needed that determination. He was caught first of all by local Catholics and was then beaten up by the military police when they took charge. Snodden was handed over to the RUC, who in turn beat him to the ground on the way to hospital. Finally, when he was transferred from hospital to Crumlin Road Prison, he was subjected to physical intimidation.

In Snodden's case, this kind of treatment only strengthened his resolve to resist. He refused to admit to his crime or even to give the police a statement: 'The police weren't going to get a word out of me. The prison officers weren't going to break me. I was convinced of that.'

This may seem heroic, but paramilitaries on both sides included training for such an eventuality and instructed recruits in which procedures to adopt. Capture would have to be faced at some stage, interrogation was inevitable, and anyone caught would be on the receiving end of brutality and beatings.

Martin Snodden was nineteen years old when he received a life sentence. Eddie Kinner, too, jailed for the same abortive bombing mission, was also given a long sentence. At the time of his crime he was underage, so he received a sentence of undetermined duration, an 'SoSP prisoner', to be detained in jail during the secretary of state's pleasure.

At the time Ervine did not have any influence in the UVF. His main function then was to be merely one of their number and do what he was told. Perhaps he was being tested, vetted for suitability, for he wasn't used as often as he had expected. The training he experienced was in stripping weapons, cleaning them and putting them together again. He was taught how to take up defensive firing positions, attack firing positions, and lay ambushes. This training took place mostly in Belfast, with never more than a handful of people. To Ervine it all seemed very exciting. The people he met during those sessions were almost exclusively working class. They were not that efficient, but their potential killing power was phenomenal.

In 1974 a debate took place within the UVF about sectarianism versus militarism: i.e., should war be waged against the Catholic population as a whole or focused on republican militarists? Sectarianism won the argument. Consequently, a bombing campaign was launched, during which a hundred bombs were planted in a fortnight, resulting in a lot of damage and lives lost.

The purpose of the UVF was to kill. Their analysis was based on the argument that since the Catholic community was harbouring the Provos, the way to damage the Provos was to hurt the Catholic community until the Provos would be expelled or renounced. This policy depended on killing ordinary Catholics, any Catholic, rather than the specific targeting of Provo volunteers and commanders.

The brigade staff of the UVF decided policy. Ervine had no knowledge of who these people were. However, it was possible to guess by watching who deferred to whom in a pub, at a meeting, in private homes.

Ervine continued to be active in the UVF for two years until he was arrested. 'I was arrested for possession of explosives with intent to endanger life. I was arrested on the Holywood Road on 2 November

1974, driving a vehicle which was stolen, with what turned out to be five pounds of explosives, of commercial explosives, detonator and fuse wire.'

He is quick still to deny that he was responsible for the bomb when asked directly. His response – 'No. I always have denied that I put it there. I was operating under duress.' – is layered with meanings. Is he stating a straightforward legal cover? Or is he saying he was following orders, or disagreed with the orders, or that he disagreed with the policy of the UVF but as a committed activist was obeying orders? The undisputed facts are that when Ervine was apprehended by the RUC, they secured him to the vehicle and told him he would stay there until he rendered the bomb harmless. The fact that he did so is irrefutable evidence that Ervine knew about bomb-making and informs us on reasonable grounds of his complicity.

Given all the circumstances, one would have to be a sychophantic sympathiser – or a complete mug – to contradict the court's verdict. The court found Ervine guilty as charged and handed down a sentence of eleven years.

Jeanette Ervine was horrified when she discovered her husband's clandestine actions. She found it almost impossible to come to terms with what had happened because she was convinced he had done wrong. While understanding why young men thought they had to do something for their country because that was the way they had been brought up and because the circumstances at the time were frightening, nevertheless, she disagreed with the use of violence. From her point of view, all that had been achieved was another unhappy home. She struggled to come to terms with the recurring image in her mind's eye of her husband carrying 'a tag around his neck, like "murderer"'. Her only consolation was the enormous sense of relief arising from the fact that no one had been killed as a result of his actions.

Jeanette also had to cope with the impression her husband's arrest for a terrorist offence would make upon her neighbours, who had previously thought so well of him. Would shame be brought down on her head? It has to be remembered that the unionist population identified with the forces of law and order, and had borne the brunt of terrorist violence in its community, civic centres and often within families. She worried that this distaste would result in antagonism towards herself and their son. 'I suppose it is highly different living in

a unionist or loyalist area, or growing up i
for you're worried about what your neighb
ilar circumstances in other areas in the city
cans would have felt proud that they had th
haven't got that type of unity. And a lot of p
totally against . . . I really worried about how   ople.'

Jeanette Ervine's devastation at the thought   husband going
to prison was totally debilitating. Attending the proceedings in court
was traumatic, and there were times when she felt she simply could
not cope. On the day David was sentenced, she was allowed to visit
him in prison: 'There was no way I could hold on. Dignity went out
the window. It was just tears.' It seemed that an aching eternity of
separation stretched ahead of her.

That day David told Jeanette that since he had done the deed, only
he should pay. He did not expect her to share the punishment as well
and offered her freedom from their marriage. She refused with a
candour reminiscent of their first disagreement: 'I didn't feel I wanted
my freedom. I was his wife and I wanted to be with him. If it was
going to be hard, well, that was it.' Even today, rarely can Jeanette sit
and talk about that difficult time without breaking down, so raw are
the feelings the memory still revives. Ervine, who had already spent
seven months on remand in the Crumlin Road Prison in Belfast, was
transferred to HMP Maze, or Long Kesh, outside Lisburn and eight
miles south-west of Belfast.

LIFE IN LONG KESH

ONG KESH WAS the wasteland to which society consigned its
criminals, a desert region beyond all civilisation. Stern, for-
bidding grey walls reared up into the heavy clouds. A visitor
could not discern north from south, east from west; nowhere was
there a tree or a patch of green. It was a soulless place.

Ervine's first reaction was: 'This is new, this is different, and it ain't
very pleasant. What am I going to do? What has happened to me?
What am I going to do with this? How am I going to cope with this?'
The camaraderie of a common experience helped, but it was no com-
pensation for his predicament. At night, alone in bed and with the
lights switched out, his thoughts were his only company. They were
depressing companions. A sense of gloom pervaded his cubicle: 'What
does this hold? Is this the way this is? Is this my life? Here I am, I
make no apologies for who I am or what I am, but: phew! I don't
fancy this. I'm not sure I was ready for this.'

No one could have been prepared for the life in Long Kesh. The
conditions were intimidating, the living quarters spartan and such
facilities as existed rudimentary. Not only did the prison bring to mind
cinematic images of Nazi prisoner-of-war camps, the terminology
used to describe where the prisoners lived reinforced that impression.
They were housed in Nissen huts, thirty-three men to each hut, inside
compounds fenced off by wire; there were two or three huts in each

compound. The Nissen huts were freezing in winter, with icicles on the inside and dripping with condensation in the mornings; in summer they were roasting hot. Prisoners were allocated to compounds on the basis of their membership of an organisation. Compounds were built within a 'phase'. Each phase was surrounded by high and massive walls. Access was through a huge hydraulic gate, reinforced, operated by guards twenty-four hours a day. A phase in some cases kept prisoners of only one organisation. Others contained several organisations, but even here the rigid segregation by compound was accepted by all: Provos in one, UDA in another, Official IRA in another and the UVF in yet another.

On arrival, prisoners were transported through the phases in a minibus with blacked-out windows, with the obvious intention of keeping them ignorant of the prison layout. When a minibus approached a gate, it stopped. All the doors would be opened by the driver, the guard would inspect the interior, and then, if he was satisfied all was well, he would operate the hydraulic gate and the minibus would be permitted to pass through. For a disoriented newcomer like Ervine, it must have seemed as if he was being taken blindfolded into an impenetrable maze.

Ervine's great strength, right from the start, lay in the unbreakable support of his wife. Her own 'sentence' on the outside had its own severe problems and challenges, but fortified by their mutual assurance he, too, determined to make the best of his predicament in Long Kesh, Compound 18.

The camaraderie helped. More importantly, so did the military regime organised by Gusty Spence, who had served in the British army. Such a regime was Spence's statement to the prison authorities, and especially to UVF volunteers, that since a war was being fought, their capture and imprisonment rendered them prisoners of that war, and they must expect to be treated as such. They were not to be considered, or consider themselves, as criminals. There was to be no disintegration of morale or discipline, and since Spence was the UVF camp commanding officer, discipline would emanate from him.

Lying in bed during the day was forbidden, for wallowing in self-pity did not benefit an individual and, worse, could be contagious. Spence knew that a military *esprit de corps* was essential for all their sakes, and the militaristic structure he devised promoted survival with dignity. Movement towards a less militaristic regime could be permitted gradually and in a controlled manner.

Spence's method was to foster an atmosphere that kept men alert by encouraging them to think about themselves, about why they were in prison, about ideas to improve their conditions, and then to go ahead and try to have them introduced. The message was to exercise control where possible over their own lives within the restrictions and responsibilities of communal living. Eventually, from this foundation, men with talent and ability might emerge who were capable of exercising enlightened leadership to encourage others to make something of themselves, something positive out of their deprivation.

At the beginning there was a lot of military training. Its purpose was simply control. Here were these young paramilitaries consigned to conditions that they did not find in the least agreeable. They would look around and think, 'I'm not putting up with this,' and refuse to accept the authority imposed from above by the prison. This was because Spence provided a framework which prevented men from becoming individualised, the means by which prison authorities maintain their power over prisoners. He also knew from his own experience of deprivation in jail the importance of retaining dignity and self-esteem.

Spence's problem lay in the uniqueness of the loyalists' situation. No precedent existed. While republicans did have a history of penology, the loyalists, who traditionally supported the institution of prison as a place for those who rebelled against the state, were now being punished by that same institution. Other difficulties exacerbated his problem. For example, as the prison expanded, new staff were recruited, some of whom were former school classmates of the men they were now guarding. What Spence, along with several other ex-servicemen, had to do was to write the loyalists' handbook on incarceration, and he based it on military lines.

Spence knew that he had to be very careful in the implementation of his policy. A primary concern was that discipline should not deteriorate to the level of abuse. It ought not to mean brainwashing, nor 'French Foreign Legion type discipline, buried up to your neck in sand'. Spence's experience of issuing commands and interpreting orders while serving in the British army, where part of his life had been spent in Nissen huts, reinforced his belief in the importance of a liberal, interpretative discipline.

He started with their living conditions. An outsider would have been astonished at the standards of cleanliness and hygiene in the compounds. Discipline dictated that they be kept in pristine condition.

Every morning the huts were rigorously cleaned. Each person had responsibility for his own area. It was inspected every morning by the 'officer' of the hut. If he found a speck of dust with his finger on window frames, on the window, on skirting boards, or in a locker, a punishment, such as an hour's fatigues cleaning the toilets, was meted out. In addition, every Sunday morning there was a 'bung-out': everything except the beds was put out of the hut, and the whole place was thoroughly washed out and cleaned until it was spotless.

This type of strict organisation continued throughout the day. As well as maintaining standards of cleanliness, it gave the men a sense of work and obligation and group cohesion. Every prisoner had his own particular responsibility within the compound, something which it was his duty to carry out at a particular time of the day.

Compounds were litter-free zones. Cigarette ends were not to be thrown down, for example. The thrust of the compound command's outlook was that this place was to be treated as the men's home, not a barracks, and domestic standards had to be maintained. The rules were obeyed by consensus. People knew what was expected of them.

In Spence's original policy, education and physical education were compulsory elements. A typical day started at 8.30 a.m. with a run of at least two or three miles around the inside of the compound perimeter, then breakfast, a wash, followed by muster parade at 10 a.m. After that the day was taken up with military activities, such as arms training or going over fabricated assault courses. Spence was conscious that 'I had to deflect those men's minds in positive directions, because if I didn't, if they were left to vegetate, I would have had a bunch of psychiatric cases on my hands.'

A daily structure which excluded military training evolved very quickly out of Spence's rudimentary plan, because his officers had the sense to interpret orders creatively. Physical education could take the form of exercises in a gym or playing football, or even simply running. Education took on a wider remit and was allowed to develop according to the scholastic, academic and political needs of the men.

By the time Ervine arrived in Long Kesh, a typical day in the compounds had evolved to a jog before 9 o'clock, followed by a shower and then breakfast. Then, after cleaning up their living area, the men attended classes in a communal hut that served as a classroom, often conducted by teachers brought in from outside, or passed the time reading or doing handicrafts. They would then return to the compound and perhaps spend an hour at various forms of exercise in the gym. After lunch they studied until 4 o'clock and then went for another jog until it was time for tea. This was followed by a free period, which might be spent relaxing, walking round the compound or playing a game of football. Evening classes were also held. At 9 p.m. the prison officers came in and closed the doors. The men watched television or otherwise occupied themselves until it was time to go to bed.

The prisoners' day was thus completely structured. The men themselves were quick to realise its immense positive potential. Billy Hutchinson, lean and reflective, from the Shankill Road in west Belfast, was among those who saw the benefits:

> Gusty prepared a situation in Long Kesh where people didn't have idle hands. You used your time constructively. He wanted you to exercise your brain and your body. 'You don't think about it. You get out there and train and also do something mentally.' Not everybody did all those things. Maybe some did one thing, maybe some didn't do any of it at all, but some of us took part in it all. The opportunity was there. And there were discussions. It was healthy to have discussions.

In those compounds he controlled, Spence demonstrated that a positive regime did work in prison. He had stated to the men from the outset: 'If you say that you are a political prisoner, if you say that you are a prisoner of war, do you understand what that means? Do you understand the responsibility that that carries? Because, as one who wants to change a society, you have to be virtually without fault. Now you have to act accordingly, by your demeanour, by your approach, by your fairness, by almost everything if you say that's what you are.'

Most of the men, of course, fell short of these high standards, but there were some, such as David Ervine and Billy Hutchinson, who fully accepted those responsibilities and worked hard to build upon them. These were the men whom Spence had hoped would emerge as leaders in the compounds.

When these new leaders, i.e. compound officers, appeared, Spence stressed a further responsibility, which will seem bizarre to those, including many unionists, who were convinced that these people were criminals who deserved to be locked up behind bars, where their behaviour would descend naturally to a base of their own worst devices. 'You only obey lawful commands,' asserted Spence. 'If you find yourself in conflict with a command, then you must question it.' An order involving the placing of a bomb in a public bar is an obvious example of an 'unlawful command', but circumstances could also arise within the jail where a command could be interpreted as unlawful. Spence's officers had power, but it was not an unfettered power. There must be no 'little Hitlers'. In fact, in day-to-day living orders were rarely questioned, because officers were conscious of the burden of responsibility placed upon them. Some commands may not have been liked, but, as Spence says, 'You weren't there to run a popularity contest or a democratic seminar.'

The men Spence appointed, such as Ervine and Hutchinson, followed his precepts and practised a kind of benign control based upon the rule of law. Ervine perceived the philosophical outlook:

> In communal living the rule of law is all, not for the sake of the rule of law but for the sake of those who have to live together. There was no toleration of total individualism, even though that is a Protestant trait. The determination to have primacy in the rule of law within the compound system was not to stultify the notion of individualism but to make sure that each individual had the same rights as every other individual.

By this basic principle enlightened leaders, informed by consensus, regulated activity and balanced rival interests.

Increasing control over their conditions and helping to create a society where decency and dignity could flourish entailed a grinding attrition against the prison authorities on all issues. Nothing was freely given. Each single item had to be wrung from the governors, but, once given, was taken eagerly and absorbed into the pattern of daily compound life.

It was to be a long and tortuous process to have a negotiating procedure put in place. When the prison first opened, in August 1971, the authorities were impervious to any idea of change. Agitation by the prisoners was followed by retaliation from the authorities. For example, the prisoners would withdraw their cooperation, and as a consequence routine inspections of the compounds would be shifted to the middle of the night.

The priority of the authorities was to maintain their power to run the prison, and they did not welcome suggestions from inmates. Refusal followed refusal, met by another refusal, not for days or weeks but for months on end. The possibility that a request might improve conditions, be a psychological support or improve a person did not figure in the authorities' considerations. If a change in conditions were acceded to, it might bring about a reduction in the degree of punishment – an outcome foreign to their thinking.

It was ironic, yet fully in keeping with the confusions of the situation unfolding in the early 1970s, that the prison governor, Mr Truesdale, had served in the same regiment of the British army as Spence. He was considered to be a hard man. He and Spence understood each other and would speak to one another in forthright terms so that there was no misunderstanding. The polarity of their relationship and the disparity of their functions was summed up in a retort from Spence: 'You do your worst and I'll do my best.' Spence was well aware of the three criteria that barred concessions to prisoners: inconvenience, security and the all-important propaganda aspect. Spence knew, just as the authorities knew, that if the loyalist or republican prisoners were treated any differently from ordinary prisoners, it would confirm that there were political prisoners in Northern Ireland, which, as Spence put it, 'all the world and the crows knew there were'.

To reinforce the reality that no preferential treatment would be meted out to loyalists, English and Scottish officers, who had been seconded to the Northern Ireland prison service to enable the authorities to cope with the rapidly increasing prison population, were put in charge of the UDA and UVF compounds.

The uncaring actions of the external authorities, which the inmates usually regarded as callous, boosted collective prisoner morale inside the compounds and justified Spence's leadership strategy. He knew also that a long-drawn-out campaign, as this inevitably would be, demanded stamina and inspiration. The source of his inspiration lay in defiance. If someone suggested that something could not be done, he determined to prove otherwise.

The generally accepted wisdom in Long Kesh maintained that it was impossible to run a marathon in the compounds – so Spence ran one. A more important issue was the appalling quality of prison food. The staple prison fare consisted of greasy fried food conveyed from a centralised kitchen in big Dixie cans: wafer-thin slices of Spam with dollops of mashed potato, tureens of soup and an interminable supply of sliced pan loaves with every meal. Spence organised direct action, endorsed by the camp council which comprised the leaders from each paramilitary faction, to reject the unsatisfactory food. The result was that eventually the Northern Ireland Office had to involve itself in the matter, and a negotiating procedure was set up that enabled Spence to put forward what he insists were always 'reasonable requests'.

Spence was still not satisfied. As part of his strategy of self-reliance, he thought that his men should cook for themselves, but cooking facilities were not permitted in the compounds. He had the heaters taken down from the walls and, through some minor technical adaptation, transformed into hot plates. The solution of this problem caused another for the prison authorities: lack of heating in Nissen huts. Spence used this situation to have heating restored by arguing for the installation of proper cooking facilities at little cost. He negotiated to obtain small gas rings, frying pans, spatulas, raw eggs and bacon, baps and various types of local bread, such as soda and farls, so at last the men were able to prepare their own meals.

On the recreation field, negotiations took place on the issue of poor-quality plastic football boots, which were not allocated individually but were shared out on a communal basis. After a prolonged period of complaint and negotiation, real football boots or trainers could be supplied to prisoners by their relatives, despite the clear security implications.

Spence wanted to paint the huts, but initially the authorities would not provide him with paint. This caused another row. He negotiated that if paint were brought in, at no expense to the jail, the men could paint the place themselves, and that is what happened.

Such initiatives on Spence's part were seen on the authorities' side as a challenge to their regime – as, indeed, they were. The prisoners felt that they had put one over on their captors, and morale was boosted. Spence was demonstrating at the same time to these men, who were where they were because they believed in the force of arms, a radically different approach about effecting change and getting things done. His long-term strategy of principled resistance combined with negotiation had a tremendous impact on the men under his command.

Billy Hutchinson was listening and learning when Spence advised:

> You want to negotiate with the prison authorities, then you want to make sure you're going to get things. So you don't embarrass them. If you decide to embarrass them, it's because you need to embarrass them to get to the next base. But you always use reasonable arguments, and you see how far you can get. If they refuse to do that, then you have to look again at how you are going to do it. But you always refrain from using violence.

Spence's agitation created a benign backdrop of improved living conditions against which prisoners could reflect on why they were in prison in the first place. Thinking about this was the essential first stage in the process that Spence devised. One of the first questions he would put to prisoners when they came into Long Kesh was, 'Why are you here?' For most of them the first reaction would be, 'Because I was caught.' Spence would then say, 'Why did you do what you did?' And then, perhaps for the first time, men would begin to try to articulate why they were in their present position.

It was a revelatory process for them, and it was Spence's purpose that it would eventually lead to the emergence of capable and intelligent individuals to take on the enlightened leadership envisaged in his original plans. Hence his tactics of 'trout fishing' – constantly provoking, constantly challenging, seeing who would rise to the bait.

Discussions about politics played a part in the daily social intercourse of the compounds and took several forms. Men who had formerly been accustomed to unthinking acceptance of everything they were told now found themselves asking questions. It was a radical and positive development. Occasionally these discussions could shake the foundations of their political beliefs. For example, during a debate on the issue of special category status, it was revealed that negotiations had taken place between Spence, Billy McKee of the Provisional IRA and the secretary of state for Northern Ireland, William Whitelaw, by telephone from Crumlin Road Prison. For committed, rock-solid foot-soldiers to find out that their leader had been in direct, one-to-one communication with the enemy would be disconcerting to say the least, for they had been brought up to believe that talking to 'the other side' was treachery. This concept had nothing to do with the message you delivered. It was more fundamental than that. The mere act of opening your mouth to contact your opponent was an act of betrayal, a treasonable offence. However, their own leader had done it and had survived and was not less of a loyalist despite the 'contamination'. Most certainly it would have been an awakening, albeit in a crude and rudimentary form, to one way politicians go about their business.

Spence continued to challenge the loyalists' preconceived notions of themselves. One has to be reminded the loyalists were loth to be critical. Inherent in that very term 'loyalist' lay a contradiction which inhibited open discussion: to whom or to what did they owe allegiance? Eddie Kinner explains their dilemma:

> At that stage, a lot of us, because of our circumstances, were fighting to remain British, and all of a sudden we were now being punished by the British. We were being forced to question our own loyalty. There was a fear to do that openly, and it was Gusty who brought that out in Long Kesh. He encouraged you to ask those questions. You weren't treacherous when you questioned the British government and your own people, and that then allowed the debates to take place within the cubicles.

One question on which Spence encouraged discussion was the issue of capital punishment, an issue of some direct relevance to the prisoners. He then widened the debate to include the authority of constitutional unionist politicians, a taboo issue. Ervine describes how typically the matter was raised:

> Spence would have said, 'The attitude of these people is they want you hanged. We've been manipulated. These people can wind you up one day and condemn you the next.' All these things were provoking to us because we were on the line. We were in many ways unaware. We weren't at the top

of the ladder of the organisation, knowing who was doing any kind of manipulating. But Spence was aware of it, and Spence was provoking us all the time in terms of not so much saying, 'Hate these people' or whatever, but, 'Think about these people. You're taking too much at face value here, son. There's more to this than meets the eye.'

A reassessment of affiliation and loyalties might be a natural reaction for these footsoldiers who had always considered themselves close to the bosom of unionism, cherished by that community. How much deeper, then, the sense of rejection when a hero, a man who had inspired many among them to take up 'Ulster's cause', a politician who embodied in the eyes of the world the unionist fight against republicanism, seemed to endorse the consensus against them. Spence invited Ian Paisley to address the loyalist prisoners on the question of capital punishment. Paisley's attitude was one of 'Hang them all, hang all terrorists.' And when he was asked if that included loyalists as well, he replied that yes, of course, it included *all* terrorists. 'Well,' the loyalist prisoners told him, 'you're not welcome here. Go away.'

Spence's policy of provocation was also clearly apparent in his invitation to another distinguished visitor. What must the reaction of loyalist prisoners have been when, in March 1980, they saw Archbishop Tomás Ó Fiaich enter their compound and Spence introduce him? Ervine admits:

> We were all provoked. The debate was certainly stimulated. It was back into the question 'Is Gusty right or is he wrong?' And you were back into considering: 'Well, Ó Fiaich did say this and he did say that.'

The prisoners were able to draw their own conclusions as to the difference between the Roman Catholic cardinal and the Free Presbyterian moderator:

> Ó Fiaich was very supportive on prison issues, and very supportive no matter who the prisoner was. He wasn't selective whether you were a Protestant prisoner or a Catholic prisoner. His concerns were about conditions and attitudes. So that was a provoking circumstance, a Catholic cardinal coming into our compound.

Loyalists came to appreciate Spence's nerve: 'That's a bit risky! – and then you became respectful about how it was done and how he carried it out.'

Respect for Spence allowed time for reflection to arrive at an understanding of why he had done what he had done:

> He had done it for us, because we had to confront these things: 'Who is this ogre? Who is this ogre, the cardinal? What does he stand for that is so awful that we can't come to terms with it? And, what's even more important, are we not living in a cocoon?' How dare we think we know everything about everything! We are the people? No, we are a people.

Spence, by affording his men opportunities to consider different perspectives, was leading them to question their inherited political beliefs, was allowing those who had ability to reassess what they thought they stood for and to reconstruct a personal political view. The process was, as Martin Snodden recalls, not an easy one:

> Through the discussion and dialogue we had around the tables and walking round the wire, we examined all our previously held values, beliefs and attitudes and really broke them down, and had to put in place new ones. And it was tough. It was very tough when you consider that we had gone into prison, taken up arms in defence of the state and in defence of our people.

It was an inverted version of classic adolescent psychology where the truculent teenager discards his disapproving parents' moral code in order to be free to find his own values. Here, however, Spence was playing the role of the rebellious parent who caused affront by challenging his conformist charges to kick over their political, not moral, traces.

In this situation, fraught with the tension created by sharp division between men in jail for some of the most serious and violent crimes imaginable, the potential for violence was high. In one loyalist compound in the early 1970s, a prisoner had his throat slit one Christmas morning, and vicious brawling among prisoners was an unsurprising outcome of disputes, but it did not happen in the UVF compounds. This was due to Spence's 'no violence' regime, by which the tensions were brought under control. Agreement and consensus were the watchwords, as Billy Hutchinson recalls: 'There was agreement among all of us that the bully did not dictate, that cliques should not manipulate.' And Spence taught them about how to deal with difference: 'There were those discussions, it was healthy to have discussions, and you didn't lift your hands. You used dialogue to debate things. Gusty also taught us that negotiation was the most important thing. You always refrain from using violence.'

Confirmation of the success of Spence's policy comes from the observations of a professional working in Long Kesh: 'They learned in the Maze [Long Kesh] to manage conflict positively and peacefully to a large extent.' However, this was not the United Nations General Assembly. When disagreement raised tensions that threatened to boil over and damage the pattern of non-violent coexistence, Spence would take action to restore equilibrium. Eddie Kinner describes a typical scenario:

> Gusty would have been watching, and he wouldn't have allowed it. The way Gusty used to deal with it would have been, 'Right, out for a drill.' And he had everybody out drilling. Everybody used to dread going out to drill. When Gusty had you out drilling, he would have picked on a few people that deserved a bit of stick and given them stick. The whole place would have been in stitches. If he catches you laughing at them, then he turns on you. Some of the stuff was brilliant. I used to love going out to drill just for the crack.
>
> We took turns at drill sergeant, trying to get the timing right, get everybody in precision. You could hear most of the people hated it because they'd be marching round the place and doing all sorts of different manoeuvres and panicking, 'We're going to be out here all night till we get this bloody manoeuvre right!' But then Gusty would have thrown in a bit of levity. The crack was brilliant, everything that he did and the way he did it.

When they went back in, they were totally exhausted. They were that tired there was no getting up to any mischief or into anything negative.

This benevolent and fair regime, as far as was possible, engendered solidarity and more sharing attitudes among inmates. The callousness of the authorities would not be reciprocated among themselves; rather, an atmosphere of mutual support reflected the civilised respect they believed they deserved as political prisoners. That motivated their reactions when a particular issue was bothering them, or when one of them was having a hard time.

Nobody was allowed to feel sorry for himself, because depression is infectious. Ervine is adamant that 'People weren't allowed to wallow in their own self-pity. There was no sympathy for them. "Pull yourself together" was the theory, which was right, because had you given sympathy we all would have ended up lying on our beds feeling sorry for ourselves.'

As an officer, Ervine took seriously this kind of responsibility for his men. On a wider scale, he supported wholeheartedly Spence's strategy and his policy of striving constantly to improve compound conditions. He seemed always to be in discussions not only about the internal workings of the system but also about what was going on outside.

A continuing source of irritation was the cumbersome and lengthy means of finding a resolution to their grievances. The procedure was that 'board papers', forms for filing complaints, and petitions had to be submitted to the Northern Ireland Office, which could take up to six months to respond. So unresponsive and unyielding were the authorities that, under Spence's tuition, Ervine and the other compound leaders served an arduous apprenticeship and eventually qualified as master craftsmen in the trade of challenging the status quo. It was a relentless, uphill struggle, but they saw themselves as constantly working to 'get one up on the system'.

When you have been negotiating against some of the cleverest and wiliest brains in the Civil Service, who are clam-like in receipt of your communications and who have the power to refuse you everything you propose without explanation, and you have the resilience not to be put off, as well as the persistence to fight your case consistently with the stamina of a zealot and win just once, the exhilaration is a narcotic. You seek quicker and more effective ways of ensuring a second win, and then a third, and a fourth. How should you put your case? Which language best expresses your argument? Which words will persuade your reader? How do you set out your case on paper?

How can you make sense of the reply? How can it mean the opposite of the sense you take from it?

Out of this felt need to express themselves better grew an appetite to learn. Now confident, enterprising and self-reliant through their experiences in Long Kesh, they were bitten by curiosity and ambition for self-fulfilment. Their informal education was the key that had led to better compound conditions, but this was not enough. This dynamic for self-improvement owed its origins to the energy generated by the twin motors of Spence's maturing policy, personal responsibility and choice, which encouraged positive behaviour. The UVF initiated an education process to allow people opportunities and choices. It was not compulsory, though there were inducements, and it was available to all.

Those few whose education had been interrupted as a consequence of paramilitary involvement renewed their studies, while others like Ervine, Hutchinson, Snodden and Kinner took it up eagerly. Men who had regarded themselves as hopeless academic rejects now belatedly sat their O levels, and passed them.

Ervine's enthusiasm for education paralleled his attitude to life in jail: 'You've got to make something of your life. It is a life after all. You're not in there doing time. You're in there living your life, and life is what you make it. It's up to you to do something about it.' He became a wholehearted participant in the various educational courses available in the prison. In this, he was greatly sustained by the support and encouragement of his wife, who never missed her weekly visit and who constantly urged him not to waste his time when he could be doing something worthwhile.

Ervine's first step in the educational process in Long Kesh might astonish those who know him as the polished, discriminating and fluent performer in the media. He enrolled for remedial English classes. He felt that he needed a thorough grounding in grammar, punctuation and all the essentials of good English necessary to enable him to express himself on paper. The overwhelming urge to write stemmed from his need to evaluate how his thoughts were developing.

The ferment of ideas brewing among the men under Spence's benign regime had intoxicated him. They needed to distil their thoughts, and Ervine felt that 'the only way I was going to get anything was to get it down on paper and let people read it and debate it. I wasn't the only one. There were lots of us, guys who were bouncing things off each other and jotting things down, and saying, "What do you think of that?"'

He went on to take O levels in English, English literature, German, maths, geography and sociology. He also learned Irish, though he had no intention of taking an exam in it. Building upon his O level successes, his self-confidence led him to embark on an Open University foundation course in arts/humanities and social sciences, which he saw as comprising a 'third of a degree'.

The prison authorities had not facilitated these opportunities easily. Spence, along with the other three commanding officers, of the Official IRA, the Provisional IRA and the UDA, set up a joint council to fight what he called 'the big battle' for provision of OU courses. They agitated through political pressure, common sense and speaking to Northern Ireland Office civil servants to have a representative of the Open University brought over from Britain to discuss the introduction of OU courses for prisoners in Long Kesh. Their approach was rebuffed on the pretext that no precedent existed for such an initiative. Spence, accordingly, referred them to the case of a prisoner in Crumlin Road Prison who had been granted leave to pursue an Open University course. Thus precedent was established, and the provision of OU courses followed soon afterwards.

After spending a year or so getting some O levels, Ervine continued his studies by taking an OU course. What had brought about this radical transformation of the former self-confessed tearaway at Orangefield? He was, of course, now an adult with the support of a loving wife; he was living under a regime which offered few distractions, but which positively encouraged personal pursuits; and he enjoyed the mutual support of his fellow inmates. Yet, deeper motivations inspired fundamental change in his attitudes. Ervine's perception of the benefits he received from education is revealing on two levels.

Firstly, he derived immense enjoyment and a strong sense of satisfaction from his studies. He felt that he had 'confirmation of the wisdom of education. Confirmation that this is the right road to go down. There's a warmth in this. There's something for me in this. Just for me; didn't have to be for anybody else; didn't have to tell anybody about it, but there was a comfort in it. This was the right thing to do.'

Secondly, it gave Ervine the mental equipment necessary for thinking about his society and its problems, and about the use of power in

solving those problems: 'Power is about my society. Power is at the
very core of our existence. Evaluating not only what I think power is,
but the manipulation of power, the circumstances of political power,
the historical attitudes in relation to power, all those things were
important in understanding my society.'

The various facets of his daily circle of interests – debating, arguing and discussing in the compound, negotiating with authority,
exercising his leadership responsibility, academic study and exams –
had focused Ervine's reflections back into one central and personal
conclusion, another equally significant shift, of utter dissatisfaction
with the nature of the Northern Ireland political system in which he
had grown up.

Other forces besides education were at work in changing his character and outlook. These multiple environmental influences provided
what he termed 'the real education in life itself. But also, I think, the
safari through books, through ideas, was very valuable. It was a journey – for me it was anyway.'

Nobody pointed the way, though Ervine's learning experiences in
jail revive the image of two young brothers running through the
streets of east Belfast every week to borrow books for their father
from the local library. The muscular adolescent's energy and excite-
ments were now channelled into satisfactions of a different kind. The
young married father, eager for his family and sucked into paramilitarism on a tide of revulsion, had evolved in the compounds into a
man independent of thought, reflective, decisive, his self-confidence
boosted by his experience of formal education, keen to spar verbally,
with a bit more 'savvy' about the nature of politics and the function
of politicians, and with his commitment to his community intact but
radically transformed.

THE SPENCE REGIME

BRIEGE GADD, FORMERLY chief probation officer for Northern Ireland, has no doubt that the provision of education in Long Kesh 'made a huge difference. It was the one thing the prison services got right.' She formed the impression that many of the prisoners, particularly among the loyalists, were very intelligent but had, for a number of reasons, been unable to realise their full academic potential while at school. Indeed, the limitations of education and lifestyle imposed upon these individuals may have had quite a lot to do with their eventual involvement with terrorism.

The overwhelming majority of these prisoners had attended secondary-intermediate schools which were intended for the majority of pupils who were rejected as unsuitable for an academic education by the selective exam at eleven years of age. A contributing factor was the entrenched socio-economic outlook which pervaded the educational system in Northern Ireland. Access to grammar schools was difficult for clever children from working-class backgrounds, and, for those who succeeded, integration across the social divide into a grammar, which tended to be the preserve of the middle classes, was not easy. They almost invariably ended up at a state-run secondary-intermediate school, where academic objectives were comparatively limited.

Such considerations as these determined Eddie Kinner's initial reaction to suggestions that he should enrol for an Open University course. 'You need to be born to it,' he thought. He was absolutely convinced that he was not capable of anything higher than the couple of O levels he had passed in jail. He rejected the initial approach, but his friends persisted, and eventually Martin Snodden tackled him again. 'Well, Eddie,' he said, 'what about doing this OU course? Do you fancy having a crack at it?'

'I'm not able,' replied Kinner; 'don't have the wherewithal.'

'What have you got to lose?' asked Snodden.

After thinking about it, Kinner agreed: 'You're right, I don't have anything to lose and, anyway, it's going to cost the authorities more.'

So Eddie Kinner joined his mates, and from that time on they integrated study into their daily routine, disciplining themselves to use their time constructively. An important factor, too, was the way the OU courses were structured. A system of continuous assessment was employed, and soon the students were scoring high marks in all their assignments.

That he had not even sat the eleven-plus, owing to a bout of pneumonia, had left Billy Hutchinson with a sense of failure. However, while in Long Kesh he sat both O and A levels, including A level politics. Politics was also part of his OU social sciences degree. Hutchinson also gained a diploma in town planning.

The extraordinary success of the education services provided in Long Kesh was attributable to a number of factors. First, the courses were offered on a free choice basis. There was no compulsion and no attempt at any government manipulation. Courses were organised on a strictly utilitarian basis and were conducted by dedicated teachers, who were clear about what they were doing. Briege Gadd says:

> I think education was delivered by those teachers in such a way that they [the prisoners] were enabled to learn what learning is all about – the model of excellence . . . I get the sense that life-sentence prisoners were much more into education than fixed-term guys; particularly the OU route was one more taken by lifers than fixed-term men, which is very interesting, because I actually think lifers have made more use of their time in prison for their own positive benefit and for their own change than the fixed-term men. And more so, I reckon, over the last ten years where I think the

prisoners, by their education, realised that there was no
future in a continued war in Northern Ireland. So they
began to train themselves to be community resources for
peace on the outside.

As well as achieving high levels in their formal education studies,
the prisoners excelled, too, in 'informal' subjects. It is here that full
credit is owed to the prison authorities who permitted top-class
experts, acknowledged in their fields, to lead courses. Across an
impressively wide range of enthusiasms, from boxing to women's
rights, athletics to budgerigar-fancying, weightlifting to art, prisoners
were allowed full scope to acquire knowledge. In this way education
played a crucial role in enabling many of the prisoners to reassess and
develop their lives in directions contrary to the diminished aspirations
expected of them after a normal school experience.

The spirit of inquiry fostered by the educational regime in Long
Kesh is illustrated by Ervine's curiosity about the Irish language. Why
should a loyalist want to learn Irish?

I've thought about this a few times, and I've been asked
about it several times, and I think it was because it was so
alien and so unheard of, and I wanted to know what it was.
I think also I felt for a very long time that much of my
culture had been hi-jacked. The greatest Irish speakers in
Ireland had been Presbyterians, are still, and some of them
are ministers of religion. Two hundred years ago our
people spoke Irish. Was there anything I was losing? I don't
think there was, truthfully, but I did go through a process
of attempting to learn Irish. Why not?

That process led him further to study Irish history; and here he
learned, perhaps, the most important lesson for people who live on
the island: 'In attempting to understand Irish history, I suddenly
realised that it depends on whose history, who wrote it.'

The depressing hardships that stalked the dreary world of the compounds could so easily have broken the spirit of individual prisoners,
but a buoyant communal philosophy enabled the men to survive and
triumph over their blighted surroundings. One manifestation of this
positive outlook was a growing awareness of health issues which

caused many prisoners to change their diet and adapt their daily
behaviour. Given the emphasis on environmental cleanliness, physical
exercise and education, such a development was an obvious progres-
sion. The prisoners were determined to show that they would not suc-
cumb to a designation of criminals. They rejected outright the label
of animals attached to them by public opinion, determined to hold
fast to their nature as human beings, and so demonstrated a model of
good practice on health issues that would have gained the stamp of
approval of any health board.

It is also very likely that, in order to reach that level of performance, the prisoners would have gone through a period of soul-
searching, would have hit a low point at some stage, and realised that
they had to redeem themselves. Spence's regime allowed each prisoner
space and a framework to make up his own mind and arrive at a personal decision about lifestyle.

Humour and fun were characteristics of that UVF compound life,
despite the deprivation. Prisoners employed their wit and imagination
to keep themselves amused and bright. The football pitch, in particular, afforded humorous rivalry between loyalists and republicans. As
the republicans in the compounds alongside the pitch cheerfully
jeered, the loyalist players got their own back by their deliberate mis-
chievous use of the Irish language they had learned. Billy Hutchinson,
who fancied himself as a referee, was conscious that the entertainment
they provided for their IRA neighbours had little to do with their
playing skills: 'But, by the same token, when we were on the football
pitch and they were doing drill, those of us who could speak Irish
could mess up their drill. Especially one guy who was brilliant at it.
He would shout in Irish and they would do about-turns. We gave it
a birl in Irish.'

On some occasions proceedings descended into sheer farce. Taking
their cue from the prisoners of war in the Second World War, both
sides attempted to excavate escape tunnels. According to Spence:

> Colditz was a tea-party compared with Long Kesh. They
> had a big *schloss*, a big castle. They could have drawn from
> timbers and done this and done that. The compounds were
> a rabbit-warren of tunnels. I remember, humorously, a
> fellow who shall be nameless, at two o'clock in the

morning came up and shook me awake, saying urgently:
'Sir, there's funny noises down this tunnel.' I said: 'It's probably water seepage.' Long Kesh gets its name from the bog
(it's all a floating bog, you know). So anyhow he says: 'No
sir, it's not.' So I put on the swimming trunks – that's the
way they dug – went and looked down into this place, and
funnily enough there were strange noises. So when we got
almost up to the tunnel face, there were voices. And I said,
'Get the hell away out a that!' It was the Provos! They
were digging from another compound, and they'd come in
the wrong direction. This wee voice says, 'What's that?'
and I hissed: 'Hey, Kevin, you're digging into our tunnel.
You're in the wrong direction.' I didn't want it to be a joint
tunnel. I was always conscious of retrograde publicity and,
God knows, people went out of their way to do it to us.

Christmas and the Twelfth of July were special times when efforts
were made to lift morale. Poteen played a potent part. At Christmas,
however, it dulled the ache of separation from family for some, while
for others it helped them pass the festive period in oblivion as a way
of getting through the celebrations as painlessly as possible. The
Twelfth was celebrated with bunting, regalia, white gloves and as much
pomp and clamour that could be managed in a 'parade' inside a hut.

The authorities knew that the prisoners were likely to distil poteen.
At first it was not difficult to find out which huts were being used for
this illegal business. All prison officers had to do on a cold winter's
morning was to observe which roof was not covered in hoar frost, for
the pipes of the still were led up around the roof. They would then
search the hut and confiscate the hooch. In summer they simply went
in and searched the compounds.

As the prisoners became more skilled at concealing their secretive
business, a cat-and-mouse game ensued with the authorities. On one
Eleventh Night, the loyalist prisoners had hidden their poteen by
injecting it into Coca-Cola cans stored in the foodstore which they
were allowed to keep. Unfortunately, one of the prison officers taking part in a search of Compound 21 decided to help himself to a can
of Coke. That was the end of their stock of poteen intended for the
Twelfth.

But it was not the end of all the poteen in that phase of the jail; with a little bit of improvisation and cooperation from the Official IRA prisoners (the Stickies) in an adjacent compound, plus certain prison officers turning a blind eye to what was going on, the celebration was saved. As Eddie Kinner tells it:

> We shouted down to Compound 19 to throw us up other tins for us to celebrate. They threw it over into Compound 20, who caught it in blankets and then threw it over to us. You should have seen it that day: four sets of blankets – one sailing it up over the wire, a second catching and a third throwing it through the air from their compound over to our blankets. The screws were standing watching; they knew what was going on. We let the Stickies keep some of the poteen, and they celebrated the Twelfth that year with us.

The incident did not end there. At that time the Twelfth was broadcast live on television, and the prisoners were allowed to watch the parade. As one of the lodges passed by, they noticed that among its members was the very same screw who had been in charge of the search team which had confiscated their poteen. Immediately everyone in the hut sprang to their feet as one man, calling him 'all the Orange sods of the day'.

Stickies enjoying the Twelfth with the UVF that year and the UVF hurling abuse at the Orangeman triggered a level of mirth which was lost on no one. Through the laughter, the loyalists realised the distance they had travelled in their political thinking.

Questions have surrounded the relationships between republicans and loyalists in prison. Did they meet? How did they get on? What did they discuss? Were friendships formed? Did they collude? Did they discuss a solution to the Northern Ireland political situation? Was any agreement reached?

Of course they met, but they were in prison. In specific instances, though still with security the top priority, it was inevitable that meetings would occur. A *modus vivendi* was worked out between the camp leaders of the various factions. Ervine explains:

> There was precious little contact between loyalist prisoners and the Provos. We effectively lived in different

phases. You did meet going to and from visits and if you were in the prison hospital, but, in the main, there was no cohabiting as such. There weren't great opportunities; there was segregation. And I think in the main it was wise. Where there was contact, there was a realisation that 'today there are ten of us and two of you, so we are top dogs', but the next day there would have been ten of them and two of us. So there was a 'no conflict' policy in relation to the prisoners, not because we were being nice to each other, but because of the practical way we had to live our lives. I can remember one instance where one of our guys was attacked on a visit, and the Provos refused to admit their two men back into their compound – removed their political status.

Opportunities to meet did arise through education, says Ervine:

We would have met in education with the Official IRA guys because they were in the same phase as us. There were communal study huts outside the compound, beside the football pitches, where we and they would have gone to see tutors from the Open University. But we had to get away from the compound when we were approaching exam time. So we negotiated to be able to use study huts that were remote from the compounds, in which you had peace and quiet and space. That's where we would have met the Stickies. Frankly, I have to say there was more political debate took place than there was education.

Billy Hutchinson elucidates:

We learned quite a lot from republicans, no question about that. We learned politics. The whole time I was studying in Long Kesh, whether it was O levels or A levels or OU, I always had republicans in my class, particularly the Official IRA, because the Provos were in a different phase. We watched them, we listened to them, we analysed what they did. And we said: 'That's how we need to be if we are going to survive. We need to make our arguments.' Very talented people, and to get thrown into an argument with them about the Westminster model, or about the British monarchy, or about the coal-miners' strike in 1984 or whatever, it's unbelievable. And you learned from them, the arguments, how to perform. Then you started to talk about political structures.

What was it like when these bitter enemies, the personification of all the hatred and brutality of their warring communities, met face to face? When a loyalist met a republican for the first time, suspicion and distrust soured the air initially, but he discovered eventually they had things in common, as Martin Snodden described:

> When I started going to the study huts, I had by chance chosen a room, and an Official IRA man had chosen the same room. So we're in the same room, and we got talking. I can remember him making me tea and me thinking, 'I wonder is he putting anything into that tea?' And I'm sure he was thinking the same when it was my turn. Whenever we had tea breaks, we would have been chatting, and we were saying where we came from and why we had ended up there, with the realisation that we had a lot in common and had almost been hoodwinked into being involved in the conflict, and the irresponsibility of the so-called leadership in the country. Not just politicians, but so-called prominent people in the community.

Ervine has expressed regret that similar opportunities did not arise to meet and debate with the Provisional IRA:

> In some ways it is a pity that we didn't have to face the Provos in the same way, because their attitude to ourselves is one of second-class citizenship. Provos rather look upon people like me as some kind of deluded Irishman. Their attitude was that 'One day he'll waken up and realise we had the right philosophy all along.' Which is absolute rubbish. They would have been quickly disabused of the notion that we were fools and didn't have the ability to think for ourselves. They operated on the basis that only when an SAS man was driving the car could loyalists carry out a military operation effectively. In other words, you

were in cahoots with the British, the Brits tell you what to do. All this is crass nonsense. From that point of view, it would have done them a world of good. Of course, it might have stimulated a bit of debate, and, I've stated it publicly, we're not afraid of debate. Far from it.

Ervine concludes:

I think that one of the things that was interesting, for all of us, was that neither, really, was going to change the other's mind. That became evident very early. Nobody was going to win a political victory in a discussion. I remember, after being exposed to them just for a short time, going back to our compound and saying, 'You know, I must have sounded like an absolute pillock in that debate,' because I was trying to win that debate. In those circumstances there is no win. There is the exposure to other ideas. The debate doesn't just sharpen your own ideas. Why would you want to throw the baby out with the bath water? Why would I be so keen on victory if his idea is a better one than mine? Why don't I listen? They were all learning processes for me in terms of listening carefully to what people were saying, and adapting what they were saying to the world and thinking: 'Now how does that fit? Is it real? Is he saying something to me that I can live with that's accurate? If he is, then I have to take it on board. I must pay attention carefully to what he's saying.'

Comments of this type clearly indicate that Ervine had reached a further stage in his intellectual development. The ferment in the loyalist compounds, under Gusty Spence's encouragement, had allowed him to form his ideas about unionism. However, everyone with whom he was arguing shared a basic premise: the validity of unionism. So debate would be informed largely by familiar ideas and concepts, sympathetic to the British position. Now through engaging with the Official IRA, who were very talented men but more focused politically, experienced in coherently arguing their stance, and who presented arguments from a perspective totally foreign to Ervine, he was learning to value an idea for its own worth, disconnected from the

influences which dictated the flavour of an argument. He had the wit
and awareness to know that he was a student of the art and, into the
bargain, one who was keen to graduate. He was conscious, too, that
'there was something healthy being exposed to somebody with a different opinion'.

This is not as simplistic in Northern Ireland terms as it first
appears. A maturing had occurred, and it had taken place in an academic environment normally associated with universities. A loyalist
accepted that a republican had a case. He saw value in that case, even
though he disputed it fundamentally and no agreement had been
reached. The first steps had been taken along the road of political dialogue. On an interpersonal level Ervine had gained, too, although the
political fence remained intact.

> We had a relationship that was cordial and respectful. I
> think there may have been a couple of friendships that
> grew out of it. But we were us and they were them. Maybe
> we proved something: that 'them and us' can actually
> cohabit, that 'them and us' can get on, that 'them and us',
> without losing one ounce of principle, can function
> together. That was important. Another lesson learned. And
> remember, these guys came from Catholic backgrounds.
> They came from Catholic, working-class areas. They came
> from sectarianism, as did we in many ways, and yet we
> learned the capacity to cope with each other, and they only
> had one head, two arms and two legs, just like me.

The contrast between the lesson Ervine learned through meeting
with republicans and the message relayed to his community by its
established political leaders was stark. His conclusion, born out of the
limited social and political interaction with republicans in Long Kesh
and Spence's tutelage, was positive and confident: his community had
nothing to fear from engagement with its political adversaries.

The robust young street fighter who had never walked away from
a physical challenge, who had revelled in looking after himself in the
tough east end of Belfast, now, through force of circumstance, had
had his energies channelled into a different enthusiasm. He had
argued intellectually with his fellow inmates over the new political
ideas Spence had placed before them, had demolished the old ideas to

his satisfaction and articulated his reworked convictions against top-notch republican opponents. Ervine learned to punch his weight in debate, in a style reminiscent of his father.

However, even though they learned and took a great deal from their meetings with men in the Official IRA, Ervine, Hutchinson, Snodden and Kinner were in a small minority among loyalists who met those republicans regularly, and only because they were following Open University courses. In the 1970s there were three UVF compounds in Long Kesh, a total of nearly 300 men, and few loyalists were in contact with the Stickies.

That minority expressing opinions at odds with the fervent and aggressive 'unionism against the rest of the world' mentality so prevalent in the Protestant community in the 1970s caused argument and resentment among loyalists. It was bad enough that they dared to step out of their station in order to acquire an education and criticise unionism from a left-wing perspective; worse, they then broke ranks by talking to republicans. Finally, and worst of all, some friendships were established.

Contacts with another group, prison officers, coloured the daily life of prisoners. Resentment, distrust and suspicion, at least initially, were emotions that affected prisoners' attitudes towards their guardians. Beneath the surface, this hostility had the potential to erupt into clashes. However, the day-to-day relationship which the UVF command managed to establish with the prison staff was, in Ervine's words:

> Pretty good. They made sure we didn't escape. There was the same number every morning and every night, and we got on with our lives. The important issues as far as we were concerned were establishing respect, a mutual respect between prison officer and prisoner. You never would have called a prison officer 'sir', ever. You called him 'Mister'. If you knew his name, you might well use his name, but you called him 'Mister'. By the same token, when they entered our huts we expected them to take their hat off. Not because it was about standing on ceremony; it's about, 'You are entering my home.' Those people came in and took their cap off and in that little symbolistic way offered

a degree of respect, which was returned. It was OK, in the main. They used to come in and walk around the compound and nobody bothered them. In fact, you would have got the odd time when you would have said: 'What about you? Keeping all right?' There was no antagonism. We wanted life without antagonism.

Individuals harboured other sentiments, but these were kept in check by the command discipline. Nevertheless, all was not constantly smooth. Strip-searches provoked confrontation. Prison officers inflicted recurring acts of humiliation upon individuals, who were forced to submit, and yet the prisoners learned from each other to turn humiliation to their advantage. One of those was Eddie Kinner:

> When I went in I lacked a lot of confidence in myself. Strip-searches were designed to humiliate you. Initially it worked, when you weren't sure. Within the compounds one of the confidences Gusty and all the rest of the lads said was: 'Don't allow them to do it. Reverse the whole thing on them.' And the way I adopted it, as soon as I was identified for a strip-search, I just pulled all my clothes off and threw them at them, to show them, 'I'm not the one who's perverted here. You are.' And they quickly said, 'Wow, wow! Hold on!' It reached the stage where, on a lot of occasions, they weren't interested in searching. Once they saw you were prepared to remove your clothes, and it wasn't having any effect on you, they weren't interested. At seventeen, I would have been terrified, in a corner, terrified of what was coming. But because of the confidence that instilled in me, I wasn't afraid. I could see what they were aiming to do, and I wasn't going to allow them to do it.

The prisoners believed their custodians' suppressed antagonism manifested itself in petty acts of retribution. A constant grievance concerned the food parcels which were regularly sent in to the prisoners: these frequently arrived with their contents damaged and uneatable, having clearly been deliberately tampered with in transit. Occurrences of this type gave rise to a general perception that 'we weren't being treated as human beings' and embittered relations between staff and inmates, provoking some of the latter to erect barriers that were to their own detriment, as was the case eventually with Kinner:

> It was about the release procedures. There was none for lifers. The governors came in with this proposal that all lifers had now to go out for an interview with a governor, with a view to release. The likes of myself refused to take part in the interviews for years. The effect of it, I now certainly feel, was that I served three years longer than I needed. Another prisoner, in very similar circumstances, who took part got out after ten and a half years, and I served fifteen and a half years because I refused to go out and be interviewed by a governor. Their perception of me would have been probably somebody who was hostile towards the whole system and would have been disruptive. They hadn't come in and had a conversation with me. They formed an opinion of you because you didn't conform. Beyond that, they didn't see any development of us as individuals in the compounds.

Kinner's case points up a negative aspect of the *de facto* dual regime whereby the authorities ran the prison and the prisoners made their own lives within the compounds. Although for many of them this informal arrangement helped to make their years in Long Kesh the most significant period of their lives, Kinner is critical of the lack of vision displayed by the prison authorities:

> I think it was only towards the end they realised how productive Compound 21 was. Generally any time they met us, all they met were the representatives, the OCs, and it was always debates, always conflict. 'We want better conditions' – that was our image. It wasn't a question of 'These fellows are doing something positive.' They hadn't a clue. A whole community had developed there, and it was streets ahead of any other community. The authorities did not realise the personal growth that was taking place.

Consideration of the fluctuating relations between captive and captor (between 1976 and 1979 seventeen prison staff were murdered outside the jail) leads one to draw contradictory conclusions; both parties were locked into an unorthodox pairing where there was always a negative to nullify a positive. If it were to be described as a relationship, then it was like a dysfunctional family, simmering with mutual antagonisms. If one tries to describe it as a partnership, which implies positive collaboration, then it was never that.

The underlying character and complexities of the Northern Ireland penal system have been analysed and described by Chief Probation Officer Briege Gadd:

> I don't think when history is written, the Northern Ireland Office will be assessed as having done a good job as regards prison. Teachers were escorted in by prison officers, who themselves lacked basic skills, to teach Spanish or whatever to people who had murdered. And if I had been a prison officer, I don't know how I would not have been resentful.
>
> I am not denying education for the prisoners, but I think the NIO should have said: 'We're going to have the best trained, educated prison service in the world.' And what they did was they neglected proper education and training of the prison officers. Instead, they offered financial incentives. They threw money at them. If they had given them half the money and put the rest into education, you would have had guys who didn't become demoralised. The prison officers should have been as educated and skilled as the prisoners.
>
> As for the prisoners, in a sense that feeling that the prison was totally against them, the prison officers were against them, the prison service, the NIO, the security services – that was the big external threat. And when there's a big external threat against you, your internal morale is high. That's good psychology. I don't actually think the government sat down and thought: 'How are we going to get the republicans and loyalists to have high morale?' I think it was accidental rather, but it worked.

It suited the government's purpose to implement a policy of containment appropriate to a passive criminal mentality. The loyalist prisoners' sense of resentment at this treatment was a big factor in motivating them to do something positive with their time, even to the extent of persistently trying to revise the prison rulebook to further their ends.

The prisoners did not consider themselves to be criminals, and their behaviour tended to prove their contention. Such an attitude is directly counter to the thinking of society that if you are put in prison, then you must be a criminal. Once again, the professional observations of the chief probation officer reveal that this simple-minded notion is at odds with the real situation:

> The typical prisoner in the paramilitary sense is different between republican and loyalist, but they in turn are more similar to each other than to the ordinary criminal.
>
> The bread-and-butter work that any other probation service would have anywhere with ordinary prisoners is about burglars, thieves, people who have been criminals all their lives, and for many their fathers and grandfathers before them. They are very different from the sort of people who ended up in the Maze [Long Kesh], in terms of background, in terms of prognosis on release, in capacity to learn and change, and basically almost from a separate tribe altogether.
>
> Now, particularly on the loyalist side, there were some young men who had got involved in paramilitarism who probably would have been gangsters anyway. But even they are quite different in a sense from your ordinary prisoner. The ones we are talking about, both loyalist and republican, as a rule would have had stronger family support. They would probably have a higher IQ. Before getting into terrorism, they would have had quite a good lifestyle. Whereas the ordinary criminal, you will find, is from a dysfunctional family and was a low achiever at school. Most of the paramilitaries would not have had the lifestyle of criminals. Many of them on the loyalist side, when you analyse their job patterns, were skilled tradesmen; and, most importantly, a lot of them would have had jobs before they were arrested.
>
> On the republican side, actually, you didn't have the skilled craftsman so much. Now, that's about the

employment patterns developed in Northern Ireland. But you would have had guys who probably would have done fairly well academically. You had a sprinkling of teachers, social and community workers. So they tended to have more academic education. But that was due to the patterns of education in west Belfast.

I would say that that the type of social behavioural development which occurred in the compounds was the biggest example of the difference between the paramilitaries and the ordinary criminals. Ordinary criminals never form groups to fight for better conditions. They form a subculture which is a criminal subculture, in prison. And they become very tolerant of prison conditions because a lot of them have grown up in institutions. It's not all that different to them.

Although the prisoners in the compounds were clearly very different from the 'ordinary' criminals, nevertheless these men were in prison, and with just cause. No matter what mitigating community circumstances are raised in their defence, it is not the purpose here to argue against offenders' removal from society, or to excuse their deeds. Yet society has forgotten, or does not care, how severe and devastating that removal is. It is in the harsh and degrading conditions of imprisonment, and how a crushing regime was surmounted, that interest lies.

The juxtaposition of the prisoners' notion that society was not at all free of guilt for their predicament and the prison officers' notion of their punitive function dictated an awkward coexistence. The prisoners had to provide their own salvation; hence the rigorous self-discipline and the quasimilitary organisational system by which it was imposed and maintained. Initially these military structures had indeed been set up as a means for the prisoners to start the journey back, but the structures evolved later into what was, to all intents and purposes, self-management within the compounds.

Gusty Spence's tough regime and persuasive philosophy of self-help:
• allowed the human spirit to flourish and gave men a chance to regain their dignity;

- permitted men to take a long, hard look at themselves;
- afforded through education, political and formal, a measure of control and influence over the future direction of their lives;
- gave them the confidence to be able to see opportunities when released back into their communities;
- promoted a sense of initiative which enabled men to capitalise on opportunity.

A prevailing autonomy, with the benign though grudging and always reluctant approbation of the authorities, driven essentially by the prisoners themselves, created a climate in which many remarkable developments would occur.

SPENCE UNIVERSITY

ANY CONSIDERATION OF David Ervine's journey is incomplete without reference to Gusty Spence. He was the key figure in Ervine's political awakening. Indeed Roy Magee, a Presbyterian minister who encouraged loyalist moves towards ceasefire, refers to Ervine having attended 'Spence University'.

Spence was the crucially influential figure for a small group of loyalists who, after release, made an impact out of all proportion to their numbers in Protestant working-class areas through community work, and is the *eminence grise* behind the Progressive Unionist Party, which played an important part in the peace negotiations. He is the inspiration for many young Protestant people, and others of different ages and backgrounds, to become actively involved in party politics for the first time. However, the image in the public mind is different altogether.

Spence's role in terrorism is common knowledge. It is documented in the grim roll-call of shameful deeds perpetrated in the name of one ism or another in the province. In the mid-sixties he was convicted, with others, for the murder of Peter Ward, a young, innocent Catholic who worked as a barman in the former International Hotel which stood behind the City Hall in the centre of Belfast. By contrast, little if anything is in the public domain about his role as would-be reformer of unionist politics and an acerbic critic of unionism's stewardship of the Northern Ireland community.

Spence's background, like that of Ervine and Hutchinson, is of the very stuff of working-class unionism. He was born and reared 'in deprivation and squalor', as he himself says, at 66 Joseph Street, now gone, at the bottom of the Shankill Road in west Belfast, in a row of two-up, two-down houses. 'We had a scullery,' he says, 'and if you had swung a half-decent cat you would have bashed its brains out against the walls. And the outside toilet, of course. In the winter nights, if there was one available and only if there was one available, you took a candle out with you to the toilet.' There were nine of the Spences living in that house; he had four brothers and two sisters.

> We slept in this onion box of a house. My father and my elder brother slept in the 'box room' and we slept in the big room. It took two double beds squeezed in, and four of the younger brothers slept two-up and two-down, or top 'n' tail as they say today, and my mother and the two sisters slept in the other bed. The four feet of the beds sat in Cherry Blossom [boot polish] tins, into which had been poured some lamp oil or paraffin oil, in order to stop bugs and cockroaches getting up to the children.

Spence's father, William Edward, 'Ned', was an old-time soldier who could recall the cruelty and slaughter in the trenches of the Great War and never forgot where to place the blame: on General Haig, the great 'donkey'. 'You weren't allowed to mention Haig's name in our house. And you weren't allowed to buy a poppy. And that struck me as very strange, but my da said, "I don't know anyone who has ever benefited from the Haig fund." He hated Haig, the butcher.'

After primary school and having gained his leaving certificate, grammar school was out of the question. 'It cost fifty-two bob to buy a rudimentary uniform – a coat, a wee skull cap and a couple of books. They might as well have asked my parents for fifty-two million pound. So I went where I was destined to go to right from scratch, for sixteen shillings and eightpence a week: the dark, satanic mills, placed strategically on what is now the so-called peace line.' On his first day it was made clear that sectarianism would play no part in the workplace. 'All the boss said was, "Get your shoes off, keep your head down, do your work. I don't care whether you're a Prod or a Taig." And that was it.'

Youngsters baptised in closeted backgrounds could emerge and become acquainted with those who prayed in a different pew on a Sunday, 'people who spoke a little bit stranger than we did. They acted a bit stranger than we did, funnily enough. And on Saint Patrick's Day you would have seen the girls coming in in their green aprons with green ribbons in their hair.' On the Protestant Shankill it was celebrated in a quieter way, but no less seriously. 'It was the norm in working-class Protestant districts, I suppose all loyalist districts, to wear shamrock on Saint Patrick's Day. I came from a family that was heavily involved in the [British] forces. We were all in the forces. All the shops on the Shankill Road sold shamrock in boxes, and my mother sent it to Singapore, Hong Kong, wherever my brothers happened to be soldiering or sailing.' This custom has disappeared now, as Spence observes: 'It's sad today whenever you see a kind of an anti-Irishness. I suppose maybe it's understandable because of the Provisionals' campaign. Whatever little bit of Irishness people felt or some people felt – I feel greatly Irish – it was kind of way driven out of them by these people who purported to be absolute Irish, and dogmatic Irish, by bombing and shooting them.'

People could move about from one mill to another, either to earn a few pence more or having been given the sack, and Spence moved among other Belfast mills: Ewarts, Edenderry, Rosebank, Brookvale, Grieves' and New Northern mills.

Spence got married when he was twenty-one, moved out of the Shankill and suffered culture shock. Yet his new home, in the same city, was just two roads away.

> I moved into a whole different planet from the Shankill to the Grosvenor Road, because my wife was born and reared there. For the first year I hated it. Every moment I could spend on the Shankill Road I spent there. My new neighbours were different people. I was relatively naive. But after the first year I came to love the Grosvenor Road. Catholics and Protestants virtually lived side by side, which was extremely strange, for there were no Catholics living on the Shankill Road.

It is here that Spence gives an insight into the tribal nature of Northern Ireland society: 'On the Shankill, politics of a rudimentary sort, or even religion of a rudimentary sort, would have been the topic of the day. On the Grosvenor Road it was something different. I wouldn't want to give the impression that it was religion and politics that drove the Shankill Road; indeed it wasn't, but the politics and religion were of the same, and one didn't want to become different from the rest of the houses.'

Because of economic circumstances, Spence followed his father and brothers into the Crown forces in 1957. He enlisted in the Royal Ulster Rifles and, among other places, served in Cyprus as a military policeman. He returned home in 1961. As an ex-serviceman, he had a choice between three jobs. He opted to become a postal sorter with the GPO because it paid more than the RUC, and he never fancied being a prison officer in the first place.

His military experience led to an invitation in the mid-sixties to involve himself in politics – not in orthodox activities within the mainstream unionist party, which has always, he claims, been wracked by division, but from some individuals who had illegal activities in mind for him.

> I myself joined the Ulster Volunteer Force because there were certain unionists who reconstituted the UVF in 1965. I was approached by a unionist politician, unelected, and another person to join the UVF . . . I was assured that all types of things were going to happen in Northern Ireland. Republicans were going to do this and do that and do the other. Little did I know that I was only a pawn. And there was a series of incidents designed to overthrow O'Neill. [Captain Terence O'Neill, then Unionist prime minister of Northern Ireland, who was attempting to reach across the sectarian divide to Catholics and nationalists.]

Spence's time of illegal activity was brief. In 1966 he received a sentence of life imprisonment for his involvement in the murder of Peter Ward, with a recommendation that he serve at least twenty years. He spent the first six and a half years in Crumlin Road Prison, a place he detested. He was in a primitive jail, allowed to see his family for only half an hour a month, but it was there that he acquired the mentality that enabled him to cope with adversity. His strength lay in his own resilience:

I suppose what inspired me initially was defiance. I remember the first time I said to the governor, 'No.' He said to me, 'What did you say there?' I says, 'No.' He said, 'No one has ever said that to me before.' I said, 'Well, I'm saying that now. No. Do what you will. No. That's it.' That was when I wouldn't work for him. Said I, 'I'm a trade unionist. Give me trade union wages and I'll work for you, but not for half an ounce of tobacco a week.' That's what you worked for, half an ounce of tobacco a week.

Because of his insubordination, Spence spent the next seven months in solitary confinement, but, with the help of friends outside and the support of some individuals in the legal profession, an opinion was delivered: 'The deprivation of one's liberty is his punishment. It's no part of our purpose to make prison disagreeable.' And so Spence's solitary was ended. His defiance achieved one reform within the penal system. He had won the first of a series of victories and adopted a positive attitude towards prison life, which saw opportunity where others saw only submission, and which later invigorated the likes of Ervine and Hutchinson.

In addition, in prison Spence also realised the necessity for education. 'People use big words in order to create disadvantage. You use bigger words to put them at a disadvantage . . . But there is only one way to get to know big words and use big words, and that is through education.'

He used his time in Crumlin Road Prison to take seven or eight correspondence courses, the only provision at that period. A sympathetic peripatetic tutor who worked in Borstals passed material on to Spence, who worked through them, though without any accreditation at the end. The tutor marked his work and informally assessed it. Later when Spence moved to Long Kesh, on 4 November 1972, he worked to formalise that educational provision. With his critical faculties awakened, Spence's assessment of his own predicament then followed. He asked himself the question he was to put later to the young men who entered the compounds of Long Kesh: 'Why are you here?'

Spence would not have been behind bars if he had not joined the UVF, an invitation he could have refused. Now he had time to consider why he had not refused it: it had not occurred to him to turn it down. As a Protestant working-class man, he believed what his 'betters' in the Ulster Unionist Party told him. There was one common aim and one great amorphous group. Most certainly he did not have his own opinions. He belonged to the great mass whose truth lay in Britishness and the right to maintain that citizenship. There was no question of asking questions.

At Long Kesh Spence had all the time in the world to contemplate his predicament. He asked himself why was the Unionist politician who had got him involved not suffering? Spence's thoughts turned to the hierarchy of the party to which he had given unthinking allegiance. His faith shrivelled before the evidence in front of him: 'Stormont as such was only a building. It's those people who manned it – the government – who were abusive. It was power and they allowed a certain amount of power to seep from between their fingers in the shape of patronage.' Spence had heard reliable stories about eminent people in positions of influence who used their political contacts to line their own pockets from deals made from inside information about government contracts.

Local government was not excluded from this corruption:

> The difference between City Hall and Stormont? One was petty larceny and the other was grand larceny. A businessman is a very busy man, and if he is running his business properly, he has very little time. But yet these people were taking time off to become councillors.

The hand of corruption stretched down into the local unionist community and electoral wards. 'You are talking about contracts and jobs and houses. It was patronage.'

Where were these prominent unionist politicians now? They certainly did not share Spence's cell, or take up the concerns of the prisoners in the Crumlin Road Prison, one of the worst jails in western Europe. The sole exception was Peter Robinson MP, of the Democratic Unionist Party, to whom even today Spence is grateful for the continued efforts he made to gain the latter's release.

The feeling among loyalists that they were rejected by the wider unionist community was reinforced during the agitation for special category status in 1972. Dearth of support from the unionist public revealed the repugnance felt by the man in the street for 'Ulster's' freedom fighters. Clearly loyalists were going to have to be self-reliant and find their own salvation. And they did, seeking support from whatever source. 'The SDLP played a leading role with us. None of the Unionist Party wanted to know anything about it. We worked with the IRA. We worked with anyone.' The strategy was successful, and special category status was introduced on 20 June 1972.

Disillusion translated into Spence's re-evaluating his unionism and himself. He found it to be a difficult personal experience: 'If you are truthful, self-questioning is the most hurtful aspect of human nature – to admit responsibility.'

Given his position of authority in Long Kesh, Spence determined to provide conditions where the new influx of loyalist prisoners in the early 1970s could lead productive lives instead of the dismal, demoralising existence of his first years in the Crumlin Road Prison.

Some others who had transferred with him shared his outlook. 'There were some of us who were thinking along political lines, positively: "This is no use. Violence is no use. There has to be an alternative to violence." Any human person must think in those terms, including the IRA. There has to be an alternative.'

Among Spence's embryonic ideas for a different society was power-sharing in government between unionists and nationalists, and integrated schools in education. At that time, controversy raged about the acceptance of the Catholic Mater Hospital in Belfast, with its religious ethos, into the National Health Service. The loyalists had no doubts. The answer was yes. To take such a stance was a radical departure from the policy of mainstream unionism, which opposed providing financial support for the hospital. The loyalists reached their conclusion based upon the right of any man to be paid for his labour. This represented a significant shift for those unionists who were moving towards rational politics and away from prejudice.

To stimulate new political thinking among loyalists, Spence invited personalities from diverse backgrounds into the compound as part of an integrated strategy to promote a reformed unionism. His aim was to break through the orthodoxy which had stunted the political growth of the Protestant community, fostering internal strife, strangling initiative and ensuring that its naive followers were now shunted down a road to disaster. A couple of unionist Westminster politicians did not receive invitations because they favoured capital punishment.

The purpose of these occasions was to expose loyalists to diverse views and to engage in political debate with visitors. Participation was not compulsory, but for those who were interested, the opportunity was there. In addition, conditions in the compounds were conducive to inmates' continuing arguments among themselves. On top of his daily pursuit of improving living conditions in the compounds under his command, Spence was attempting to create a climate that would breed a reformed unionist, who, when 'planted out', would flourish and prevail in a hostile atmosphere. David Ervine was one of those who enthusiastically embraced Spence's project. His energy and enthusiasm, combined with Spence's initiative, spelled opportunity.

The three UVF compounds in Long Kesh – 18, 19 and 21 – were all situated in the same phase. Ervine was in C18, Spence in C21. Ervine impressed Spence because he displayed the attitudes that Spence was looking for in enlightened leadership. As Eddie Kinner confirms: 'Initially you'd have seen Davey as a hut sergeant, who would have ensured you obeyed all the rules within that particular hut, but all of it would have been fair. Most of the things would have taken place within people's cubicles. There was always debate and discussions taking place.'

Eventually Ervine was promoted to compound commander. His style of leadership was based more on consultation and persuasion than on a dogmatic, regimented approach. One former regimental soldier who, to quote Spence, 'went a wee bit overboard on discipline', was removed from office. It was 'a question of interpretation. David interpreted those rules and regulations, those orders, in a very liberal way.' There was a standing obligation on all men to engage in physical education, for example, but if a man was disabled or had a medical complaint, Ervine excused him.

Martin Snodden said that Ervine was 'a man of the old UVF school of thought. Very traditional in that sense, a people's person. He had come up through the ranks, was a highly principled person, and wouldn't have been open to any form of gangsterism or some of the exploits that were going on during the time of his incarceration. Principled without a shadow of a doubt, and motivated politically. He had become involved in the conflict in defence of his people.'

Now with maturity and, crucially, with time, Ervine could reflect upon the views he had heard when his father talked politics in their house in Chamberlain Street. Kinner recalls a vivid impression of Ervine's passion for discussion: 'No matter where Davey was, there was always a debate going on. You couldn't have walked past Davey's cubicle without seeing a group of people there in discussion; and most of them key people. They were sitting debating with Davey, not just about inside but outside as well.'

Ervine's reputation as an unorthodox thinker grew among fellow loyalists. Opposition to such non-conformity was inevitable. Though he was not alone, Ervine had dared to step across the line and had broken ranks by criticising the mainstream unionist leaders. He was always promoting an alternative unionism. Among the ranks of in-step loyalists, this created resentment and antagonism.

Generally within the loyalist compounds, opposition existed on three fronts. Number one was the 'we are soldiers' mentality which rejected involvement in politics. Number two was a small faction who were in tune with Ian Paisley's political ethos of Protestant majority rule. A third grouping saw themselves as soldiers fighting for their country who would follow mainstream unionist politicians.

Such opposition failed to deter those who were convinced that there had to be a better way, and the opposition was not as articulate or as analytical. In the mid-1970s, there was a gaping chasm between 'thinkers' in the UVF inside and the supporters of embattled tradi-tional unionism outside. This internal opposition showed itself on the sports field. Ervine, from his schooldays, was a big defender, whose devotion to football outdistanced his finesse and subtle touch. Matu-rity had not changed his playing style. On the pitch, when his politi-cal opponents attempted to retaliate for the lost debates, he responded in kind to the physical and verbal challenges.

Antagonism against Ervine was orchestrated by a man who had gathered a group around him to wage a campaign against Ervine as an individual, his leadership and his views. A serious feud against him was developing within the compound. He never backed down, but, as on the football pitch, met every challenge, intellectual and physi-cal, head on.

Suddenly Ervine resigned as commanding officer of Compound 18. Ervine was at a turning point in his life, weighing up his future direc-tion. To this day he is reticent about discussing this period in any detail, but when pressed about the matter, his recollections are revealing:

That actually was one of the most painful periods of my adult life . . . I suppose as commanders go, I was very liberal, wanted to be very liberal, because we'd always run pretty tight ships. It was evident to me there was no influx of prisoners any more coming into the compounds because they were being redirected to the H-blocks . . . And I felt, at that time, that maybe we should liberalise a little. It was my feeling that that was what I was going to do.

He became aware of the opposition against him. 'It would seem that there were a few who were not happy with the idea of my leadership, and they, if you like, flouted my leadership.' Perhaps from a sense of loyalty, Ervine does not go into detail. 'I couldn't say they directly challenged my leadership, but I felt that if they were not ready for liberalisation, they shouldn't have liberalisation. I just think they couldn't do their time, were struggling to do their time. They were all people relatively "close to the gate" in terms of the time they had served. I had no problem with life prisoners or guys who had a long time to do.'

He denies that discord stemmed from differences over practical politics, allegiances or political philosophy, but Ervine can be an abrasive critic. The personal resentment he caused among some loyalists is comprehensible. His willingness to speak out against the traditional unionist parties and their leadership was bound to cross the supporters of those parties. For Ervine, there was nothing controversial – indeed quite the opposite – in airing criticism of the established unionist parties since he had heard it often before from his father, but to many of his unthinking fellow inmates, who voted on automatic pilot, merely voicing such thoughts would have bordered on sedition.

Ervine kept his integrity intact by refusing to be provoked into the desired physical response and chose to continue to fight on his own grounds: politics and persuasion. Typically, he threw his opponents by doing the unexpected. It was not the first time he had done the unheard-of. In his youth he had switched his support from Linfield football club to Glentoran, his local east Belfast team, a change that would shock any Belfast soccer fan.

By relinquishing command in Compound 18, he says he could concentrate on getting on with what he wanted to do for himself:

education, reading, handicrafts. But he had crossed a Rubicon. Disillusion clearly played a part in his resignation, but a retreat back into the crowd was not on his agenda. He was changing direction and was moving on to a new phase in his life, motivated by personal needs, emotional, educational and political, and not concern for the 'group'. Ervine opted to move to Spence's compound, 21.

The significance of Ervine's move is profound: he was now opting for politics and rejecting militarism; he was choosing peaceful methods and rejecting war. By associating himself with Spence, he was reaffirming those honourable values which unionists attached to the original UVF, who had returned from the trenches of the Great War expecting a better society – the defence of democracy, rights and freedoms – which had lost vigour, enfeebled in the torpor of politics in the North.

Spence's intent was to apply philosophic surgery to the diseased unionist body politic. This combination of abstracts, Spence's 'fundamental' plus Ervine's 'radical', was to create a real challenge within unionism. In retrospect, it is possible to say that Ervine, in jail, made the right move at the right time. He, like many others, thrived in Compound 21, shorn of all military responsibilities. Right away he made an impression. Comrades recall that he was always reading and studying. Snodden recalls that 'he got that hunger for knowledge and he pursued it'.

Although now without military rank, Ervine continued to be an influential figure and continued to lead the way in debate and argument. Now, however, he was in a more sympathetic atmosphere.

Chief among the issues debated in the compound were those which touched prisoners' lives and were relevant to their predicament: why they were in prison; what was going on outside; what or who was influencing events.

Kinner remembers:

> We would have debated all the actions that were being carried out by the organisation that we were affiliated to. Every time they carried out something, we would have come back and said, 'What did they do that for?' We were looking for the political direction of it, why they were taking it along a particular line. Why did they let Lenny

Murphy [leader of the notorious Shankill butchers] get away with all that stuff he got away with? As far as we were concerned, we were politicising ourselves.

Politicisation of the prisoners by the prisoners was accelerated by the conditions in which they lived, as Ervine himself remembers: 'You are living cheek-by-jowl. You might see the same fellow twenty times in the one day.' Sometimes an unguarded comment would highlight sharply differing viewpoints. For example, when the three Maguire children were tragically killed by a car driven by IRA men who had been fired at in the street by the British army, which went out of control and mounted the pavement, on 10 August 1976, Ervine and some others watched the television news in silence. Suddenly someone remarked, 'Ah, sure they're only Fenian bastards anyway.' The speaker was verbally attacked and had to be protected by the command structure. Ervine and others were coming to realise that 'This is not us. We are not like that.'

With so much happening in the outside world, the debate might have changed ten times a day. In a hut there might be five or six fellows sitting in a cubicle on one side talking about football, while on the other side there would be a debate about politics. And somewhere else they would be discussing how they all used to go to the disco. Kinner describes what he overheard many times:

'Ah, no, I don't think that's right.' 'Well I'm telling you it is.' And then somebody would say, 'Well, I'm going to see how many people here think that.' And the next thing he's away, for it's the easiest thing to do an opinion poll in the compound. He'd have gone along and said to half a dozen fellows, 'What do you think of that there?' and he'd have got half a dozen answers and come back and said, 'Well I'm telling you the vast majority of people in this compound totally disagree with what you're saying.'

Since physical force was against camp policy, Ervine and everyone else learned to use persuasion to get their views across and influence others: 'You learn to trust. You learn not to be antagonistic. You learn to discuss and to debate, and find ways of influencing.' Basic training in the skill or art of debate, practised in these informal and spontaneous talking-shops, dovetailed with Ervine's growing concern with politics. Spence noted qualities in Ervine that showed promise in the political field: 'He had a feel for language; his vocabulary was reasonably wide. He had a good basic grasp of socialist politics, caring politics.'

The impromptu and unorganised arguments, responding initially to the natural combustion of enthusiasm and camaraderie, helping to burn up the long hours of a slow day, began to be conducted in a more formal manner from about 1975 onwards. Due to a combination of government prison policy (all new prisoners were kept in the H-blocks) and prisoners' releases, prisoner numbers in the compounds had dwindled to the extent that only Compound 21 remained for the UVF prisoners. Those who remained were, in Spence's opinion, the *crème de la crème*.

The concentration of these UVF thinkers living together in one compound, close to Spence, gave them unparalleled opportunities to focus upon fashioning their own brand of unionist politics. Spence provided a channel to harness the enthusiasm of their wide-ranging ideas: 'There had to be a better way. The underlying theme among our embryonic ways, in Long Kesh and outside, was "There has to be a better way," not only in a non-physical sense but also in a political sense, also in a social sense – everything that goes to make up a population.'

Spence established a system of seminars where matters could be debated in a formal manner, in addition to the ad hoc discussions which continued to be part and parcel of daily conversation:

> What happened was we used to have a place called the study hut, so I said, 'Right, there's going to be a seminar for anyone who wants to attend, free, open to anybody.' There were some genuine people who had no interest in politics; they just went their own way. There were people who were interested in politics who came initially, but through force of argument they found themselves on the back foot all the time. They couldn't articulate and they couldn't put their case in a structured way.

Obviously, the prisoners dealt with matters that directly affected them. They discussed the plan to build the H-blocks, incorporating a conventional jail regime, to replace the compounds, and the message that Spence relayed to the authorities resonates still today: 'You must be joking! These men, even when they were in Crumlin Road Jail before the advent of political status, would not observe what you call "prison rules and regulations". Now what are you going to do with the man who says, "No"?'

During the hunger strike, the UVF men concluded that the British government was stupidly giving the IRA and Sinn Féin a big weapon. Allowing the hunger strike to continue, they believed, defied all logic. It wasn't a question of surrender, as they saw it, but of acknowledging reality. Prisoners housed in the H-blocks wanted to wear their own clothes. The men in the UVF compounds wore their own clothes every day of the week, and there was only a wall dividing one part of the camp from the other. It was illogical. Like the republicans, they, too, expected Margaret Thatcher to bring the hunger strike to a halt.

For the men who had no formal knowledge or history of involvement, Spence set up remedial classes using any expertise that existed within their own numbers. Two men who had been members of the old Northern Ireland Labour Party spoke first and foremost about socialism and capitalism, without getting too deeply into the dialectic, for example.

Spence used his input to expose the deficiences of Ulster Unionism, which had opposed every piece of enlightened legislation, like the National Health Service and family allowances, because they believed that Catholics might outbreed Protestants so as to receive extra payments. He attacked that classic pillar of Northern Protestant power: 'I think the Stormont regime was one of the abuses of inclusive/exclusive. As Carson said, any democracy must take great cognizance of the minority, but the Unionists did very, very little. For instance, in the field of jobs there wasn't all that much done for the minority. In the field of housing, too, there wasn't all that much.'

For those UVF militants who believed they had been reared on a diet of British parliamentary democracy, Spence gutted the local variety to reveal its rotten core:

> In the last few years of Stormont, Eddie McAteer brought the old Nationalist Party in as Her Majesty's loyal opposition, even took on the title leader of Her Majesty's loyal opposition, and yet from 1922 until 1972 the only thing

nationalists were able to get through was an amendment
to the Wild Birds Act. That was in 1931, and was the only
bill in 51 years by a non-unionist member that was passed.
What sort of democracy is that? That's not democracy.

Spence's vision for unionism was predicated upon inclusivity. He
used discussions with republicans about ways to reduce hostility
between all factions within Long Kesh, to broach how their efforts
could be transferred into the community outside. He was disappointed. The Provisional IRA mooted things about working-class solidarity and eventually passed him a paper setting out their views, but
Spence saw nothing in it for Protestants. The Official IRA talked
about a place for Protestant and Catholic and Dissenter living
together in a new United Ireland, but to Spence this was merely a variation of the old nationalist theme, that unionists were self-deluded
Irishmen who would see sense one day.

Although decidedly left-wing and unorthodox, Spence pitched his
policy securely within the unionist fold. He laid out his principle for
unionism without compromise or ambiguity: anyone who is for the
Union could be a unionist. He stated that a unionism that is genuine
and reasonable should be honestly and openly argued. Anyone at the
seminars he organised had to keep that in mind. Spence's radical
stance, and republican lack of imagination, provided impetus for
political students like Hutchinson, Ervine, Snodden and Kinner to
consider a new unionism as an essential element in any potential solution to Northern Ireland's crisis.

A speech delivered in 'Cage Twentyone, Long Kesh Prison. 12th
July 1977' demonstrates Spence's radicalism and the challenge he
encouraged his men to take up. It included:

> We never tire of celebrating the advent in history when
> William of Orange achieved for us in 1690 Civil and Reli-
> gious freedom. We, the Protestants of Ireland, were the per-
> secuted in those days and now things are somewhat reversed.
> But is persecution necessary for the establishment of the
> inherent freedoms of mankind? Has persecution ever
> changed a person's views? Do we really want freedom and
> the pursuit of happiness at the expense of some other unfor-
> tunate soul? . . . I submit that it is fear which makes one

people oppress another . . . We are living in the most socially and legalistically oppressive society in the Western Hemisphere . . . Polarisation complete with one section of the community cut off from the other except for some middle-class contacts which appear to be more concerned about their class than community . . . We are a police state with the accompanying allegations of torture and degrading treatment to suspects undergoing interrogation . . . Even yet we still have men nonsensically counselling that victory is just around the corner. Victory over whom – the IRA? Or do they mean victory over the Roman Catholic community? . . . The fears of Roman Catholics will not go away because bigoted Unionist politicians say so.

We in Northern Ireland are plagued with super-loyalists . . . If one does not agree with their bigoted and fascist views then one is a 'taig-lover', or a 'communist' . . . Unfortunately, we have had too many of these people in our own ranks. No fascist or bigot can expect sympathy or understanding in the UVF compounds . . . The sooner we realise that our trust has been abused, and the so-called political leadership we followed was simply a figment the sooner we will attempt to fend for ourselves politically and to commence articulation in that direction . . . ours was a sick society long before the fighting men came on the scene. Life in Ulster before the troubles was artificial . . . We want employment and decent homes like all human beings, and Loyalists will no longer suffer their deprivation stoically lest their outcries be interpreted as disloyalty . . . The politicians seemingly cannot or will not give us the peace we so earnestly desire, so I therefore call upon all the paramilitaries to call a universal ceasefire. To open up dialogue with each other in order to pursue ways and means of making such a ceasefire permanent. Eventually Loyalist and Republican must sit down together for the good of our country. Dialogue will have to come about sometime, so why not now? There is no victory in Ulster, not for the IRA, or the UVF, the police or the army. There is only victory for humanity and common sense.

After chewing over these myriad ideas, a shared conviction formed between the UVF participants. When the plethora of impromptu daily discussions and focused weekly seminars are combined with the necessary discipline of formal Open University studies, we begin to understand why Roy Magee has labelled Ervine, and the others, graduates of 'Spence University'.

Like other wise university students, Ervine determined to live as rounded a life as possible behind his prison walls, and in Compound 21 he used the time and space to exercise his awakened intellectual curiosity. He refused to look upon his sentence as a halt in his life where one day of numbing routine would be followed by another. His declaration 'Live your life! Live your life!' sums up not only Ervine's intent but that of the others, too. They breathed in camaraderie and fed on mutual encouragement. They weren't so much 'doing time' as remaking their lives: new ideas, achievements, courage and hope that would signpost their way forward. They enjoyed fashioning out of their dehumanising conditions ways of reconstructing themselves, invisible from the public's gaze, especially the sober unionist burghers in leafy suburban avenues, who had they known what was happening would have demanded that Siberian deprivation be reimposed immediately.

Paradoxically the Belfast east end boy's life expanded within the narrow confines of that intimidating jail: 'I was twenty-one, and before I didn't think it was possible, really, to laugh until your sides were bursting without a beer in your hand.' But he did at Christmas Day parties and sports days, and many other days when the human spirit refused to break on the rocks of hardship and sadness.

PARALLEL SENTENCES

L IFE WAS NO joke for relatives outside the prison. Each man was some mother's dear son, some demented father's worry, or left behind some saddened brother or sister, disappointed some admiring girlfriend or caused confusion and anger in a child when his 'Da' was never there. When a man was put inside Long Kesh, the web of family relations trembled. Whether it shrivelled and blew away usually depended upon the character and tenacity of the wife. While our paramilitary 'hero', whether soldier of destiny or fighter for God and Ulster, was in jail, his wife was expected to pick up the family pieces and carry on as usual, despite the aching gap at her side.

To this day Jeanette Ervine finds it hard to talk about going to prison to see her husband. She had no idea how she would cope. To survive, Jeanette had to abandon her plans of training for a good job. She was doing a grant-aided course at Rupert Stanley College, an east Belfast further education centre, which she had to give up. She lived off supplementary benefit, but at least was there for their child, Mark, who was already missing a parent. He wouldn't let her out of his sight. Mark had just turned two, and every night he would run to the window looking for 'Daddy'. At Christmas time he fretted for David, and Jeanette had to comfort him. That was heartbreaking. However, David's employer did not forget her but kept in touch regularly. In fact, they kept up a correspondance until he died, while David was still in prison.

Letters, too, were important between herself and her husband. There was only one half-hour visit a week in Long Kesh, when there was pressure to include everything, to tell him about both important matters and trivial details, too. Often something or other was left out, and letters filled that gap. Letters also allowed time for contemplation of one another. A little timid at first, hesitant because of the censor's intrusive eyes, their inhibition soon decreased. Still, Jeanette was always conscious of what she put in letters because she knew someone else would read them, whereas David said, 'To hell with them.' Away from the hurry of the half-hour visit, they could spend time exchanging their innermost thoughts: 'I remember he wrote in a letter that it was like a wheel, and he was a cog. He could see things clearly, where he had gone wrong. He was able to sit with nothing happening around him and reflect. He knew things were going to be different, that violence wasn't a path he was going to go down.'

Keeping their marriage secure was a joint victory over daunting circumstance. Coping with the harshness of daily life was a private battle Jeanette waged constantly. The initial shock and suffering of her 'parallel sentence' meant that she, like her husband, had to choose: go under or survive. She was determined, not for a cause, not for a philosophy, not just for herself, but to survive and regain the life that had been snatched away from her. Life revolved around their child and building a home for David when he got out. Many wives and mothers devoted, or perhaps sacrificed, themselves to the same end for five to ten to fifteen to twenty years at a time during Northern Ireland's Troubles.

The first part of the challenge was to establish a routine that enabled her to fill the empty days, so she got a part-time job in a nearby shop. Jeanette's parents were a huge support and looked after Mark. When they saw how stress was affecting their daughter's appetite, her mother took action. Soon it was arranged that Jeanette would go to her parents' house and stay for dinner there before going home with Mark, and she spent every weekend with her parents.

Being able to shelter in the bosom of your family brings comfort in times of heart-breaking distress, but support is one thing; over-reliance and lack of self-confidence are different altogether. In order to restore Jeanette to some kind of domestic normality, Mrs Cunningham shrewdly decided to move the 'wee housewives night' to Jeanette's house. On a Monday night about half a dozen ladies who lived locally would get together at the Cunninghams' where they just sat and chatted, or maybe knitted something. That meant that Jeanette had to go home from work on Mondays to prepare supper. Soon she was collecting Mark from her parents' house every evening after work and going back to her own home.

She was once more in possession of her characteristic patience and calmness, capable of concentrating anew on some plans which helped soothe her pain. When David was arrested, the couple had been planning built-in furniture in their bedroom. The wood was still there, so her uncle and cousin built it for her. The return of her postponed happiness obsessed her. The whole time David was away, she kept herself busy planning for his homecoming. She sat up at night sketching and drawing, planning for their 'wee house': this for the working kitchen, that for the bedroom.

Jeanette encountered the common misconception that families of prisoners were well looked after financially. Neighbours would remark that she had no worries because she was having her household bills paid for her. This was not the case. She had to pay all the bills herself and economise as much as possible. A UVF welfare officer had approached her with an offer of financial assistance, but Jeanette's negative reaction was typical of the distaste in the unionist community for the loyalist paramilitary organisations. She regarded it as 'blood money'. Eventually, she relented, persuaded by her husband to use such funds for his benefit, if not for her own. She was approached again, and this time accepted so as to be able to send Ervine the weekly parcel that each prisoner was allowed to receive from home.

Like so many other wives, Jeanette's week hinged on the Thursday visit to her husband in Long Kesh. She and Mark went every week, while either her mother or mother-in-law went with her, on alternate weeks. Jeanette detested being processed into the jail. Naturally shy and quiet, she never adapted to being herded as one of the crowd. Over the years it became a routine that, decades later, she could follow blindfolded:

> You went into the car park, and from the car park you had to go over and get your visiting card from a small office into the left, and to the right was a big waiting room. That

was the first stage. I went in, left my card in for the visit and took the child over to the Quakers' playgroup. I sat with him until our name was called and then went through the turnstile and into another waiting room where you would wait until you went through a search. Then you boarded a bus, which took you to another waiting room.

The public expects jails to be impersonal, unfeeling buildings where compassion and sensitivity are minimal, but Jeanette's experience one December makes one wonder if the authorities were, on occasions, deliberately crass. During that visit the music played was: 'It's lonely this Christmas without you' and 'We'll have a blue Christmas'.

Jeanette, like many mothers, was protective towards her small son. She had told him that Daddy was a painter, away working every week. Mark would ask, 'Daddy, how long now?'

However, during one visit, Jeanette was in the waiting room listening for her name to be called. It was packed to suffocation, standing room only. Everybody, from all factions of the sectarian divide, was together. Different visitors were heckling each other, like on the raucous terraces at a soccer match. It was summer, and Mark was playing outside with another child. Suddenly, as Jeanette was called for the visit, he came in crying. When she asked what was wrong, Mark told her that the other child had told him that his Daddy was in prison. Up to then she had not even mentioned Long Kesh, or anything about prison, in front of him. Tears flowed from the traumatised child, and his mother was plunged into feelings of guilt. Had she been right to protect him?

The incident confirmed to Mark his suspicions about the real reason behind his father's absence. Playing with other kids in the street, he, now six years old, had been harangued about his father, for the whole neighbourhood knew who was in jail, and why. One evening a drunk staggering out of a pub told Mark where his father was. But all queries were fobbed off at home, where sectarian sentiments were never uttered. Although always delighted to go to see his father, Mark was uneasy, because he knew there would be people where his father 'worked' who did not like each other. On one visit, Mark commented to his mother that his father would be away for a long time if he still had to paint all the walls of the place.

Although Jeanette found all visits difficult, she managed. Towards the end of her husband's time, however, an incident soured the atmosphere, and succeeding visits became even more of a strain:

> They were pleasant with me and I was pleasant with them. I took only the basics in my handbag. There was no point in bringing a lot in it. One week there was just a pen and some tissues on the floor of my bag. I went through the visit, left my property in, got a body search, they searched the child, and went through to get on to the bus. That particular time, when I went back to collect my belongings, the pen was missing. It was a present from my daddy, so a special thing. I was always civil because there's no point in not being. They were carrying out a job. I didn't want to cause offence or anything. But, on this occasion, I said to the woman officer that my pen wasn't there, that I had had a pen in my bag. She said, 'We have had things taken on ourselves, our own property. I feel you should report it.' I didn't want to report it. She said, 'Report it because we have an idea it's one of the other prison officers.' So I reported it, to my cost. The following week they were very churlish towards me. When I came back from the visit, everyone in front of me was handed their property, and people behind me, too. I was kept waiting until the last, and I asked the prison officer who was giving back the property if he was looking for my bag. The next thing, a woman prison officer arrived. She said that she had my handbag and gave me a lot of abuse. I was dumbfounded. She was like an SS woman, that's the only way I can describe her. My pen never turned up.

From then until David's release, Jeanette dreaded facing this woman.

Why did Jeanette let the matter rest and not complain to the prison authorities? Prisons are intimidating. They are not department stores where complaints may be taken to Customer Services. The semi-military procedures and surroundings may cower the ordinary visitor, who becomes grateful for a visit being granted at all and no longer perceives it as a right.

Jeanette did speak up forcibly, however, when her husband mentioned that he was considering the possibility of refusing temporary parole in 1979. David could have taken his parole earlier, but had postponed it until Christmas, and now he was thinking of not taking it at all because of agitation among the prisoners. She told him he was thinking selfishly, and that he must take his parole because he was entitled to it and because he should spend time with his family. The agitators must include in their thinking the people who were outside, who had gone through the sentences with the prisoners, and not deny them parole. David took his parole for Christmas.

One would expect the period of parole to be a time of unalloyed joy, for the prisoner returned home to a world of freedom, of high expectations come true at last. Instead, for most it turned out to be a time of harsh disappointment and fear, when unforeseen horrors arose from everyday behaviour. The Ervines were no exception.

They wanted to do everything. They went into town, but going on the bus was very upsetting for David. The centre of town was crowded, and he just could not cope with people milling around him. Jeanette had not even considered that. She thought he would come home and things would be much the same:

> The worst thing I could have done was to take him into town after him living in an enclosed space. I thought it would be magical. We went into Anderson and MacAuley's and took Mark to see Santa. In the coffee shop, David couldn't go up and order a cup of coffee. He wasn't used to money. That was such a big thing. Then I started to realise what I had put him through. And colour, he talked about colour, colour TV, which he hadn't seen, and colours of socks, and colours people were wearing. It was a totally different world. It was like beginning all over again, except you were an adult and you had to be trained to it.

David was not the only paroled adult to find himself disorientated and confused when first released back into the intimacy of family and familiar surroundings, only to be disturbed by a childlike inability to cope. It manifested itself in many of the ordinary things 'normal' citizens do without thinking, like coping with stairs. After living for years on ground level, they had lost the habit of negotiating a series of steps. Money was not used inside jail, so making simple transactions became difficult outside. Embarrassed, they would opt out of purchasing or travelling on public transport on their own, thus putting restrictions on their temporary freedom. One prisoner spent the happiest and most contented part of his Christmas parole sitting alone on the roof of a shed in his backyard, in the middle of the night, looking up at the stars and listening to the silence, in sheer relief.

Jeanette got through those years thanks to the crucial role her family played. They responded positively, and if she needed anything, they gave it to her. Not all wives were so fortunate, or appreciated. Briege Gadd recounts the tribulations of another young mother, also from east Belfast, left outside to manage as best she could while her activist husband did his time:

> This loyalist wife got up on Saturday morning at half-past six. She had four young kids (they kept having kids, even though he had been sentenced). So she dressed them all up, got them into their white knee socks, to visit Daddy. That took about four or five hours. Hot day, lift down in a tiny car, young kids, kids are quarrelsome, knee socks get dirty, and there she is with the Nike trainers for him, for his fitness, and a nice piece of steak. And she's trying to keep those kids, you know the way it would be, under control. There was nothing for them to do. That was at the time when you had to wait for hours, and there was no tea, no coffee, no television while you waited.
>
> Eventually, they go in on the visit. Meanwhile, husband was all geared up to see them, but his instant reaction was, 'Could you not put clean clothes on the kids?' So, she felt, 'God love him.' She did not say, 'You bastard.' She was nice to him and she felt sorry for him. He had another twenty years to do, so, 'Here's your steak, love, and here's your trainers.'
>
> That Saturday evening, she made it back home just in time to go into the local butchers who sold her mince because by Monday it would be off, or the chicken pie that was past its sell-by date, for the tea for the kids that night.

And that was replicated all over the place. The 'heroes' were in prison. The families made sacrifices. The signal sacrifices that wives of prisoners made to keep families and community together cannot be exaggerated.

With remission, David's (and Jeanette's) sentence was reduced to five and a half years of an eleven-year term. They were given their release date.

The glorious, longed-for day, 2 May 1980, was upon her. Her brother drove Mark and her, the two mums and Brian Ervine to the prison, while at home:

> My sisters and everyone were waiting at my house, with full instructions: 'Make sure you have a great big fire. Keep the fire going, and as soon as he arrives put on the record, "Welcome Home".' Mark didn't know his daddy was coming because I was afraid of telling him and something going wrong. So, I thought it best to wait outside the prison and then we would know, for certain, that David was coming. Mark was in the playroom. I couldn't stay in the playroom. I was in the waiting room with my brother standing outside, and I was watching, looking for his hand signal that David was coming. And then eventually, it seemed like for ever, it happened.
>
> I went for Mark and said, 'Mark, come on, there's someone to see you.' And, as Mark entered the waiting room, David came through the door. It was like an electric bolt. The child just stopped dead. He couldn't believe it. And then he ran into David's arms. Mark said, 'Daddy, this is better than Christmas. This is better than Santa.' Of course when I saw all that I wept, tears of happiness.

After five and a half years, the convicted paramilitary, who had gone into Long Kesh fearing he was not going to be able to cope, had done more than merely survive. His characteristic ebullience had ignited a confidence that drove his talents to invigorate themselves anew, to discover different satisfactions, and find himself. Violence had been rejected and replaced by politics as a conscious means of exerting influence in society.

Education emancipated Ervine. He was smitten by the control it gave him when arguing his own point of view, deriving pleasure from articulating ideas effectively. Equally, he was hooked when he found education to be a mine layered in rich seams of knowledge he could explore. Satisfaction lay now in the battle of wits.

Billy Hutchinson characterises how Ervine changed: 'He doesn't worry about being Number One. He's a team player. The most important thing is the team. Now, in the team he is the captain, and what he'll do is to talk people through the game. He'll make sure everybody knows where to be. At the same time captains will lead. But he doesn't have to be Number One. That's not what he's about.'

Ervine had gained insight into effective leadership, the type that is caring, creative, prepared to take a considered risk in order to move the group interest forward. Such a risk was Spence's invitation to Cardinal Ó Fiaich: imaginative yet within reach of its constituency. Effective leadership is not a self-satisfied, indolent one which positions itself in the middle of its group, is inward-looking and whose chief quality is inertia. Instead, Ervine believes it should lead from the front, address real issues, put its case with integrity while recognising dignity in its listeners, respect for opponents, and above all be genuine, because if it tries to dupe people, it will be found wanting.

Ervine learned other lessons in Long Kesh that are relevant to a civil society:

> Not only should you not have to go into jail to learn, to have an education, you shouldn't have to go into jail to learn how to live communally. When I was a kid, every door in the street was open. That isn't the way the world works any more. The communal responsibility that we learned in Long Kesh is not something that's very evident here. We all require each other. We all impinge upon each other and we all should have common sense and decency towards each other.

Ervine had also come to accept that no one section of Northern Ireland society retains a monopoly on suffering: 'We all suffer. Only by recognising that each one of us has a responsibility to do something about it will we make a change. And if Long Kesh had anything to offer, it was about accepting responsibility.' Prisoners had to learn a hard personal lesson about their predicament, with an application for

the wider community: 'Northern Ireland suffers from a benefit mentality. I don't mean just the dole queue, but that it's always somebody
else's fault for our predicament. There's no acceptance of responsibility, and yet taking responsibility in society is fundamental. And
everybody having a portion of that responsibility.'

Paradoxically, prisoners who were locked up for years together in
the compounds benefitted greatly personally. Ervine recognises how
much he learned about people. He got to know the real person, not
the label created by place of origin or associates: 'I think that that was
valuable. And it teaches the lesson that we are all too simple about
friendships, about who is a friend and who is not a friend, and why.'
This is how Ervine's friendship with Billy Hutchinson began. By their
local allegiances. Hutchinson, coming from the Shankill Road in west
Belfast and a Linfield supporter to boot, was a friendly rival in the
loyalist scheme of things. However, in the enclosed environment of
prison, they got to know each other as people and became firm
friends.

That attitude colours personal relationships for Ervine now. From
party sympathisers to political opponents, to the public, through
officers of statutory bodies to ministers of state, and up to heads of
governments, Ervine will draw his own conclusions. 'Nobody tells
me who's a good guy and who's a bad guy. Or they can tell me, but
it will make no difference. I judge people on what they are capable of
in human terms, the person they are.'

Reliance on personal antennae to evaluate others stems from
Ervine's sense of let down when, as a fresh inmate, he had looked to
effective leadership in the loyalist and unionist communities to make
political gains and retrieve the unionist position, and thus lend justification to his sacrifice: 'You had to trust the guys who were in charge.
You'd no choice. You had to trust the "parent body" on the outside.
You had to trust your politicians. In fact, very little of that worked
for me.'

Trust developed internally and matured into discriminating
relationships which created camaraderie. Camaraderie made things
happen, as Spence knew: 'Comradeship is 90 per cent of your existence in any state of deprivation. For anyone who is suffering any
form of adversity, comradeship strengthens because there's a feeling
of oneness, "We're in it together." You are a little bit challenged, too:

"Is he as good a man as I think he is? Is he as bad?" There were trials and tests that men met.'

Ervine surmounted those tribulations. No one waved a magic wand. There was no secret formula. It was the hard graft of looking at his experiences and finding both courage and stamina by facing up to himself and asking hard questions:

> Who am I? What am I? What am I doing? What are my responsibilities? What have I done? How did I abdicate my responsibilities? That process I went through in jail, and it is painful. I haven't experienced childbirth, but self-analysis is a massively painful process. The first and foremost issue is, 'Confront yourself.' I can remember an incident in jail that was an interaction between me and me. It was almost like the oxygen level in my lungs was more voluminous. I felt light and powerful, within myself. Not my power over others, but within me. Power to do good. To do what I know is right, to advocate changes that are about human kind, rather than the narrowness of the life we have lived. To value people as human beings as opposed to being told what human beings are about, or not about. To think for myself, free to assess and analyse for myself, that freedom.
>
> That does not mean that anybody who argues from a different perspective is likely to have me lambasting them, because it does not fit with my notions. I found a sense of quiet calm. It was not a road to Damascus conversion. The process started when Gusty asked me, 'Why are you here?' Maybe it was working away prior to that. It is hard to tell, but he certainly kick-started it. I discovered me.

A moral courage defined itself after Ervine examined what he considered self-evident political and cultural attitudes and rebuilt a set of beliefs to which he could commit himself with an honest heart.

People in the street might feel justified in demanding blunt answers about a former paramilitary's actions and his responsibility for them. Ervine argues that circumstances created the atmosphere which caused upheaval. Further, those circumstances derived from a corrupt society. Thus, guilt cannot be apportioned in an absolute sense to individuals. The host society needs to recognise its shared culpability.

Ervine points out that, since the starting-point of his mature acceptance of personal civic obligation towards society originated in self-questioning, then similarly, the onus is on society to ponder its collective responsibility, with courage and honesty, painful though the outcome may be.

That said, given the intellectual integrity that Ervine and others demonstrated, it is unlikely that in their private moments these UVF prisoners would have evaded moral issues. Why else do the words 'painful' and 'difficult' occur time and time again, when each one talks about the process of self-questioning? What is being described is a personal coming to terms with the deeds that put them in jail. On that, a ravaged Northern Ireland society would remain sceptical without a public display of private penitence, but one incident, in the H-blocks, offers insight into the personal turmoil of some prisoners. One hot June evening at the end of evening classes, as the iron doors clanged shut behind him, one of the teachers who was leaving met a lifer coming the other way. The lifer was relaxed. Slightly suntanned, dressed in a white T-shirt, summer shorts and flip-flops, and carrying a sheaf of study books under one arm, he was ambling nonchalantly towards the wing the teacher had just left. They recognised each other. 'Jeeze,' said the teacher, 'people would think you were coming in from a balmy beach on the Riviera.' The prisoner passed by, his flip-flops slapping the floor. 'Yeah,' he said without looking back, 'no doubt.' The teacher stood waiting for his escort. 'Hey!' the teacher suddenly heard, and turned round in the direction of the prisoner, who was waiting to re-enter his wing, books still under one arm and leaning against the locked door. 'Hey, boy! Not if they saw me at 2 o'clock in the morning they wouldn't.'

Some prisoners did confront themselves and emerge from that questioning process positively. What more have the public the right to demand of 'the class of '76', as the Provos christened them? Perhaps the question should be reversed: why should the public not learn from the experience of prisoners like Hutchinson, Kinner, Snodden and Ervine, convicted felons who left jail to make a telling impact upon their community and wider society? Prison changed Ervine's life. Kinner developed and widened his interests, emerging a much more confident and understanding human being. In Compound 21, Snodden learned about himself and the foibles of others, with a strong appreciation of the values of life and liberty; moreover, he developed a healthy, independent attitude towards politics and, especially, towards traditional politicians. Self-scrutiny transformed lives. People themselves changed themselves.

Their success was recognised at an unofficial level. A prominent unionist politician, visiting the loyalist compound, commented that they were just a bunch of psychopaths. Before Spence could respond, the prison official who was escorting the politician intervened. 'Sir, is this the first time you have been in this compound? I deal with these men every day of the week, and let me tell you, there is no bunch of men that I know who are more stable, who are more constructive and more positive.'

Spence is all too aware of establishment prejudice within the unionist community, intent on dispossessing the prisoners of mitigation advanced on their behalf. He argues that each man knew he could end up in prison for a long time, or dead or maimed, when he joined the paramilitaries. There was no sense of personal gain, yet he chose that path. Normal society should not recognise those motives, but Northern Ireland, a society in turmoil, was not normal. Spence accepts that an organism as unsophisticated and untrained as loyalism was will commit excesses. And he recognises that its fundamentalist unionist host will desire extreme retribution. He rejects the notion that the death penalty would have been a panacea for violence in the turbulent streets and has no doubts that its effect would have been counterproductive. The hanging of any form of paramilitaries in Northern Ireland would have been disastrous. Better by far, is his explicit conclusion, a productive prison regime of the kind he was instrumental in establishing in Long Kesh. To those hurt by such sentiments, perhaps Ervine's comment on the matter may encourage them to pause and reflect further:

> For us it was a place of learning, plus a place of debate. It was the first time we had ever had an articulate conversation in our lives upon issues that were beyond football, horse racing or the weather. It was new for us, vibrant. It was also a learning process that said, 'Our society has to change, has to be different. Who would you see about that?' If you believe that society has to change, and others

don't – well, you have to create the dynamic for change.
So, I see it as taking on the responsibility that we vested in
ourselves when we first entered the debate.

Spence's 'students' ask no more of the rest of the unionist
community than they demanded of themselves. In a fundamental
reassessment of their unionism, loyalists debated core beliefs and subjected them to analysis. Spence points out: 'It was a slogan that we
were "superior". Similarly, that these people [Catholics] are lazy and
they won't work, and they have all these children and they want pur-
posely to be a drag on the state. These things were questioned.' Spence
sums up their root and branch reformation: 'We are in a position to
say, Yes, we were in Long Kesh. Yes, we bombed. Yes, we shot. Yes,
we killed. No secret about it. That was then and this is now. We
climbed up out of that pit.'

As Ervine sat in the car carrying him away from Long Kesh, he
could have drawn up a CV of his personal development: management
experience employing an inclusive approach; strength of character
demonstrated when resigning his command on a point of principle;
proof of academic ablility; skill in political analysis and commitment
to anti-sectarian policies based upon civility and diplomacy; appreciation of the fun side of life with enthusiasm for the cut and thrust of
debate; confidence. His working-class reluctance to criticise one's
social superiors, a reticence to stand out from the crowd, inability to
take on opponents in political debate – all had been swept away. He
was his own man, independent and sure of himself.

Spence had drummed into Ervine and the others their obligation to
cultivate future generations: 'After you go out, what do you do? Do
you just fade back into anonymity, or do you try and do something
about it? If you go out there knowing what you know, having done
what you did, having served what you served, and don't do anything
about it, then you are cowards.'

Which is nothing to do with curling a finger round a trigger, but
everything to do with stretching out your hand to grasp opportunity.

But this was to come. On 2 May 1980, as he sat in the car beside
his wife, Ervine's overriding feeling was delight at being reunited with
his family. Jeanette's sentence was over, too.

MOVING TARGET

SIXTY-SIX TURBULENT MONTHS after his arrest on 2 November 1974, Ervine came home. He had two interrelated priorities: to rekindle his family life and to find an ordinary means of supporting his wife and child. Future events would be subservient to the needs and welfare of his loved ones.

Their initial steps towards a normal life were tentative, as he and Jeanette had anticipated. First of all, like any family, she and David spent a lot of time together, away from the outside world, helped by the unswerving support of their relatives. 'At that stage I was pregnant. David had got his parole at Easter, and then he came home on 2 May. We got the loan of a caravan, the three of us, and we spent a fortnight beside the sea. It was good. It gave us space together as a family.'

Jeanette knew that adjustment of relationships was bound to happen and realised how delicately those changes would have to be treated in the shift from her role as Mark's sole parent to accommodate the return of his father. Balance would have to be struck with care. Like other women afflicted by the Troubles who had had, through necessity, to redefine their role within the family in the absence of the 'man of the house', she had become more self-reliant and had taken upon herself control of decision-making. Many women such as she refused to return to traditional, demarcated roles once the husband had returned from jail. Sharing had to be renegotiated from both sides.

It was a difficult period for all. Jeanette recalls:

> For both of us it was a time of adjustment, and for Mark
> as well, because this man is on the scene, taking over a
> house, and leaving his personal belongings round the place.
> You had to be careful. If Mark needed scolding, I was the
> one who had dealt with it, whereas David had to be care-
> ful of making Mark feel that he had stepped in and was
> 'the Master', someone taking over. The child wasn't used
> to his dad being there. So it was one big adjustment for the
> three of us. We managed it. We worked together.

It was prolonged hard work. Mark's initial jubilation turned sour.
The loving and humorous father he had visited in prison for as long
as he could remember, for just half an hour a week, now became a
stranger laying down the law. Ervine knew the temptations in street
activities that could lead one up the ladder of paramilitary involvement. He was absolutely determined that his son would not end up
inside. Perhaps he overreacted towards the ten-year-old, but Mark
resented being given orders: what television programmes he could
watch, what time to be home, what time to go to bed, not to go here,
to stay away from there. He would not be disciplined, and he rebelled.
He used to resort to his maternal grandparents and confide in them.
He lost trust in his mother, because he knew she would share everything with the father he was growing to fear, but to whom he would
not bend. Mark felt betrayed; formerly the principal object of his
mother's affection, he now felt supplanted.

Innuendo from his pals in the street angered Mark. Snide comments about his mother walking down the road with a strange man
made his blood boil. He replied with his fists, and that meant more
discipline from his father. It was a difficult adjustment for everyone.

Ervine's ambition to continue formal education had to be jetti-
soned, an early casualty of his 'family comes first' resolve. He had
wanted keenly to go to Queen's University, but when he realised that
the maximum grant was £48 a week, he knew that his wife and son
would suffer financial hardship if he were to go to Queen's and
believed that he had already caused them enough suffering.

He started work as a milk roundsman for Belfast Co-operative
Society immediately on his return from their short holiday together.

At that time unemployment in Northern Ireland stood at 14 per cent, but he was one of the lucky ones who had a regular wage and also, he thought, plenty of free time during the day to pursue his studies. However, as he discovered, when you work during very early hours in the morning, the need for sleep is not banished, but simply transferred to another time slot. He abandoned his A level evening classes in sociology and accountancy.

A job was advertised in the Co-op for an area controller with responsibility for thirty-eight milkmen in the east Belfast area, and he applied for it and got it. Nobody knew who he was. He just did his work and kept himself to himself.

Ervine was now an anonymous working father whose concerns were to get his job done and ensure that there was enough food on the table, a pressing reality because a second child was on the way, to Mark's delight. Jeanette says: 'Mark used to say he wanted a baby brother or a baby sister. "Either that, Mum, or a doggie." I said, "Son, you've more hope of getting a doggie." And then when I was pregnant and we told Mark he was delighted. He was going to have a baby brother or baby sister, who was Owen.'

Ervine had not been present at the birth of his first son, but he and Jeanette planned that he would be there when their second baby was born. Ervine was to discover that children can thwart their parents' plans, for Jeanette took ill a few days beforehand and was hospitalised with complications. The birth had to be induced at 9 o'clock in the morning. She kept saying:

> 'Get in touch with my husband. He wants to be here.' By lunchtime there was no sign of me going anywhere and I rang David, 'I'm still here,' for he had taken time off to be present at the birth. I should have told him, 'Come up right away,' but I said, 'You've time enough yet. I've said to everybody you want to be here.' I thought that somebody would contact him, but it didn't happen. The midwife said, 'Oh well,' and I cried, 'My husband should have been here.' 'Ach,' said the midwife, 'never mind him now.' And he didn't know until he came to visit me that night and the crib was beside me. He missed out.

Ervine had no contact with loyalist paramilitaries. There was no network of ex-prisoners who would congregate together every so often, no club which met every month. He was back into society, leading his own life, socialising, enjoying a pint in a local pub now and again, enjoying his natural environment. There was no active involvement in party politics, though his enthusiasm had not diminished.

Ervine used to argue frequently with his brother Brian about politics, as Jeanette often witnessed: 'At home we always had debates between David and Brian when he paid us a visit. David was just so interested in politics, in everything that was going on in world politics.'

Ervine was also keen to develop his career when opportunity presented itself. He moved on from management, where regimentation irked, and became a sales rep. for a personal hygiene company, for more money and increased autonomy. Then, after a year and a half, he returned to the milk distributing sector when it was reorganised under a franchise system, working as an independent milkman. He was his own boss.

Ervine's political voice was not only heard domestically. In the circles in which he moved, where people were undemanding of their unionism and 'activist' did not appear in the lexicon, his enthusiasm got him noticed, and he developed a reputation as a political 'talker'. 'My politics would have been no more than expounding my attitudes in a pub, or in work. At that point I was probably a bar-room politician.' And from that an invitation came in 1984 to become more than a vociferous political spectator on the terraces and get involved on the pitch:

> I'm minding my own business, sitting in my wee house in the afternoon as milkmen do, doing my book work, when someone knocked at the door. Two guys who I had never seen in my life before arrived, came in, and said they were from the Progressive Unionist Party. They were sent by Hugh Smyth [the PUP leader]. It seems that some stories had been doing the rounds – 'See yer man, the ex-prisoner! You should hear the things he's saying!' 'There's a fella over in the east, and you'd be as well talking to him' – that type of thing.

Hugh Smyth is well known and universally liked throughout Belfast for the reconciliatory nature of his tenure as lord mayor in

1994–95. He has spent a long time in local politics and admits that
public report played a minor role in Ervine's recruitment into the PUP.
Much more influential was the positive impression Ervine's political
talents made upon him. He explains the origins of the Progressive
Unionist Party (formerly the Volunteer Political Party):

> We were all independent unionists. In about 1978 there
> was a big push for independence, mostly from within some
> sections of the Ulster Defence Association, that an inde-
> pendent Ulster might be the answer. So we, as independent
> unionists, were scared of people getting us mixed up, and
> decided to take a political name. We searched the history
> books, and discovered there was a Progressive Unionist
> Party back in the 1920s, formed within the Unionist Party,
> for the same reasons we reformed. There were people, par-
> ticularly in the country areas, who felt that the Unionist
> Party had turned its back on the working class. Because of
> the social issues they raised, they were branded commu-
> nists, etc., and it fizzled out, disappeared.

The PUP was formally established in 1978. This reformed PUP,
which had sent two men to talk to David Ervine, had only one elected
representative, Hugh Smyth, sitting on Belfast City Council. He
admits, 'At that time I was the only [unionist] elected representative
who probably could have been close to the paramilitaries.' When
Ervine joined, in effect a new PUP was launched. Previously, in the
late 1970s, the PUP had had three elected councillors but had since
declined at the polls. It was then clearly a party of no importance com-
pared with the Democratic Unionist Party and the Ulster Unionist
Party.

Smyth, who had been at a few meetings at which Ervine had spoken, recognised his talents and realised that he had potential. In Long
Kesh, Spence had hoped that Ervine's political dynamism would thrive
in civic life, and Hugh Smyth would have been made aware of Ervine's
political bent through his paramilitary contacts. Spence had been trying to influence the loyalist paramilitaries on the outside. He used his
name to speak from a position of authority to the active UVF leadership, even though his views were not always accepted. Hugh Smyth
was aware of Spence's embrace of democratic politics and welcomed

that development. The fledgeling PUP wanted to attract political thinkers like Ervine, former loyalist paramilitaries or any other member of the public who wanted to take a political road but who were unsympathetic towards mainstream unionist parties.

There were no legions of party supporters to boost morale and no muscular party apparatus upon which to build. This was a party whose political appeal was to argue the case for unionism afresh, but it had a limited audience. There were only a dozen or so present when Ervine sat for the first time in a normal party political gathering.

In 1983 the Ervines moved house. In addition to David's milk delivery run, they went into business, buying a newsagents/local shop with a flat above. Before his arrest the Ervines were purchasing a house in Roslyn Street through a £1,300 interest-free loan from a local builder, which they were paying off at £2.50 per week. While Ervine was away Jeanette poured any money she had into the house, regularly paying more than the agreed weekly sum, and by the time Ervine came out most of the loan had been paid off. The purchase of the shop and flat, at 121 My Lady's Road off the Ravenhill Road in east Belfast, was financed through selling the house in Roslyn Street and taking out a mortgage.

As a shopkeeper Ervine made no attempt to hide his politics. Rather, he enjoyed the conversations with those customers who entered into the spirit of banter and debate, including young people of the district, who might have been more easily influenced by paramilitaries. As Jeanette says: 'There was always a debate going on in the shop, especially with young people who would come in. Maybe they'd have been inclined in other ways, but political talk was an ongoing thing.'

Those young people may have felt stronger tribal pressures propelling them elsewhere. On 2 October 1984, *The Irish Times* reported that, in the first nine months of the year, the IRA had killed twenty-two local Protestants in the security forces, six British soldiers, one Catholic ex-UDR man, one magistrate's daughter, one assistant prison governor, two alleged informers, and one alleged criminal. On 12 October, there were fatalities and injuries at the Grand Hotel in Brighton, which was devastated by an IRA bomb, including injuries to some British government ministers who were attending the Tory Party conference there. Against such a backdrop, a bald man talking

politics in a corner shop offered no counter-attraction to the paramilitaries.

Spence was released from prison on 13 December 1984. He kept
in contact with Ervine and also delivered his assessment of the Troubles to the UVF: 'I said, "Boys, grease the guns and put them away.
If the IRA have to be dealt with, let the security forces deal with
them." I was not quite *persona non grata*, but the paramilitaries
looked at me a little bit askance: "He's gone pacifist." Which was not
the case. It didn't make me very popular with the UVF; in fact it made
me damned unpopular with the UVF, and other paramilitaries, too.'

Spence's changed attitudes should not have been a surprise. While
in Long Kesh he had sent out political analyses to the UVF. One message in 1981 had been 'to start to embrace a more in-depth political
philosophy. Not to leave their politics to anyone else, but to engage.
And if they would not, then to recognise that myself and other UVF
prisoners in the jail had engaged politically and knew what we were
speaking about.' Spence believes that the scepticism of the UVF
towards his point of view originated in class prejudice, deep-rooted
in the unionist political psyche. 'The cult of the well-dressed man is
very well entrenched in Northern Ireland society . . . "Sure didn't he
go to Malvern Street public elementary school? He couldn't be
smart." . . . But when you prove you are as smart, and maybe even
smarter, then other people sit up and take notice.'

Spence was invited into the fledgling PUP in 1985. Despite its obvious inadequacies, for him its heart was in the right place. Anyway, he
could afford to be patient. There were those in Compound 21 whom
he had earmarked for the PUP. After their release, perhaps unionism
would be given an opportunity to recognise that 'smart' and 'well
dressed' deserved a wider social remit.

In 1985, local council elections were held in Northern Ireland. The
PUP decided to stand, and Ervine ran as its candidate in Pottinger
ward, in east Belfast, for the City Council.

For teenager Mark, his father's candidacy brought exasperation.
The first he knew about it was when he saw his father's face on a
poster in a shop window. He thought he should have been told beforehand. In the street Mark was nicknamed 'Councillor', which he hated
and got into fights about. Above all, like any typical teenager, Mark
hoped his father would not embarrass him, especially since his father's

opinions ran contrary to the predominant feeling in the neighbourhood: that the most effective response to republican violence was from
the barrel of a gun.

Jeanette had reservations about David's candidacy: 'I was reluctant
about David going forward because he was an ex-paramilitary, and
this campaign would get him noticed in public. I was afraid of him
being targeted.' Jeanette listened to her husband's arguments that this
was a lifelong commitment, not a passing fancy, and she resolved not
to deflect him but to work for him. The campaign went ahead at short
notice. They approached the election, called for 15 May 1985, without any experience or professional expertise: 'Within a matter of two
weeks we had to do all. I had cramp in my hand, writing. We didn't
have a typewriter.'

Insults were hurled by opponents from within the unionist community. The PUP were accused of being a unionist Sinn Féin – claiming they were politicians, whereas they were, said their detractors,
gunmen masquerading as politicians or, at best, puppets of loyalist
gangsters. The brief campaign was unsuccessful, but, says Ervine in
retrospect, not because of political slurs: 'Frankly, it was ill-conceived.
Because there was only a handful of us involved, we were inexperi-
enced to be honest, and the haste, written material didn't go out, and
there was no campaign fought. But in the little pocket that had a
polling station right beside where I lived, I got almost all my votes.'

David Walter Ervine polled 394 first-preference votes, coming ninth
on the ballot, and was eliminated on the seventh count behind the
heavyweights of the DUP, UUP and Alliance parties. There was much
to learn from this first electoral experience, disappointing as it was.
He had responded to the challenge, made an impression locally, and
enjoyed the political argy-bargy directed against him. It got him
noticed more widely and, maybe, showed that his opponents had been
worried about his chances.

Unfortunately, Jeanette's worst fears for her husband were soon
realised. First, one morning he had to give up permanently his milk
round in Ballysillan, an area which skirts north Belfast where the Provisionals operated, after the RUC informed him of an imminent threat
against his life. Next, one early afternoon after Ervine had loaded
weekly supplies for the shop into his car in the parking lot of a whole-
saler's, at Dargan Industrial Estate off the foreshore motorway leading

north out of Belfast, he was starting up when the windows of a car opposite wound down and he saw three guns aiming at him. By sheer good fortune another car, whose driver thought he was about to get a parking spot, stopped between them. The gunmen's view was blocked just for long enough to enable Ervine to make his getaway at full speed. Then, finally, in the shop a week or so later, his sister-in-law spotted a familiar face, a man from Turf Lodge, a notorious republican area, who had been on a course with her. She fetched Ervine from upstairs and he went to see who it was, but the man had bought a packet of chewing gum and left. The implication was that this was an IRA man on reconnaissance, or even perhaps a mission to kill. After that, Ervine was particularly careful and on a couple of occasions spotted strange people in vehicles in the area. So he decided to sell the shop and move home and family to another part of east Belfast. Ervine had no illusions about the IRA: 'I had to duck and dive because the Provos were going to kill me.' He could not be sure why he was being targeted.

On 28 February 1985, nine RUC officers were killed and thirty injured in an IRA mortar attack on Newry RUC station. In the same area at Killeen, just south of Newry on the road to Dundalk, four RUC officers were killed by a 1,000-pound IRA bomb on 20 May. There was widespread damage to the centre of Belfast after a 1,000-pound IRA bomb exploded on 14 June. So Ervine was small beer in the context of the Provos' war. It is likely that IRA intelligence knew of him from Long Kesh, his conversion to politics there, and his emergence as a party political activist. To get shot of Ervine would achieve two objectives: eliminate a former UVF paramilitary and a thinker who was trying to politicise loyalism and to reform unionism.

Public life now took a back seat for Ervine. Being on the run from the IRA was not a state that lasted for a few weeks or a few months. It became a way of life for the family for some considerable time. Fifteen-year-old Mark knew his father was in danger because the family had to sell the shop and an irregular pattern of house relocation started. His father sat down with him to explain the background and advise him of security precautions to take about the house and in his daily life. Naturally, this was upsetting for a young lad and brought added insecurities. At some stage, would he be moved away from his friends, without consultation? Would he have to change school?

When Jeanette is asked how long this second upheaval in their marriage lasted, she calculates in an unusual way: 'I'd have to count
houses. You don't count in years; you count houses. We're in this present house two years, three moves since we had the shop. I found that
hard to cope with. I suppose about eight years.'

An unstable existence, accompanied by a constant threat to his life,
did not detach Ervine from his commitment to politics. Although his
lifestyle was in a state of uncertainty, his determination remained
intact.

LOYALISM FINDS ITS POLITICAL VOICE

T HE DIE WAS now cast. In a perverse way, the Provos' threat
served as a catalyst to confirm to Ervine that he was a political activist. As his past had shown, bully him, patronise him,
and he will often surprise his adversaries by carrying on more
resolutely than before. On the run and rebuffed at the polls, he was
in politics to stay, now more than ever determined to convert those
intentions from Long Kesh into some political action that would work
towards a resolution of his country's seemingly intractable problems.
For now his work would have to be away from public view, in the
shadows, for the sake of his wife and children.

David Ervine got involved in politics because he enjoyed it, and
he enjoyed it because he was good at it, and he was good at it because
he could talk well, and talking politics well satisfied him intellectually and emotionally. He thought he had at least as much to contribute as many of the established unionist politicians. So he invested
his political capital in the PUP, which was in the business of propa-
gating a radically different unionism. He had a fervent desire to
ensure that the ordinary unionist people would never again be used,
and ultimately betrayed, by politicians who exploited their fears, and
for which they paid dearly. Underpinning all this was his strongest
motive: he had been in Long Kesh and did not want his sons to end
up there, too.

Ervine had no grand plan, except to rely on the personal qualities he had imbibed in east Belfast, the political enthusiasm nurtured in him in Long Kesh and the confidence summed up in his recurring refrain, 'Live your life!'

The PUP was small, but for Ervine the attraction lay in its policies. Though Hugh Smyth may have been its public face, former Northern Ireland Labour Party people played a pivotal role in formulating its left-wing stance. In 1977, the PUP had adopted a policy document, 'Sharing Responsibility', which had first seen the light of day in the UVF compounds in 1972 under Spence's influence. So, for politicised ex-UVF paramilitaries, the PUP was a natural focal point.

Spence and Ervine, along with party officers, directed their energies into consolidating the political organisation of the PUP. They had digested as one model of planning the British Labour Party's blueprint for setting up the Welfare State before its election in 1945. Local influences were strong, too, as Billy Hutchinson describes:

> Gusty pumped it into us that you must sit down and decide how you move forward. Analyse everything you do. We learned that. The Officials [IRA] said exactly the same thing. What we did in terms of politics, we learned from the people who were most successful; those who analysed and strategised. Look at what the Labour Party did just after the war in terms of trying to build the Welfare State. They had a strategy; they knew what they wanted to do.
>
> Among ourselves, we looked at local political figures who had broad appeal, and we found they came mostly from the Northern Ireland Labour Party, or from an independent unionist background. Their appeal was that they showed the people that they were with them. It was a question of you're electing me to work with you, not work for you. I think of people like Midgley on the Shankill and the Hewitts on the Woodvale, who were a big Labour family. They had a rapport with the people.

A PUP constitution was written in 1985, which included the original Clause Four of the British Labour Party constitution:

> To secure for the workers by hand or brain the full fruits of their industry and the most equitable distribution thereof that may be possible upon the basis of the common ownership of the means of production, distribution and exchange, and the best obtainable system of popular administration and control of each industry or service.

A first election manifesto was also produced, which in the first couple of pages dealt with conflict resolution and support for Northern Ireland's remaining as an integral part of the UK, as long as a majority consented, and then went strongly into social issues: education, housing, employment, the economy, policing, the status of political prisoners and a Bill of Rights. In addition, in the same year, the 'Sharing Responsibility' document, which had gone through several reissues, now appeared in an abridged form. It was subtitled 'An alternative to foreign involvement in the internal affairs of a region of the United Kingdom'. It had as its aim to 'enable representatives of all the community to contribute in a responsible way towards the enhancing of wider local government, and all the inherent stability that it offers'.

It is worthwhile setting forth some of the principal points made in a document so far ahead of its time that it must have appeared heretical to orthodox unionists:

> .. . this region is and will remain part of the United Kingdom so long as our people wish to remain within that constitutional position.
>
> The Northern Ireland Electorate would elect by proportional representation 153 persons to serve in an upper tier of regional government.
>
> In order to encourage all minority parties and groups to participate it is suggested that the absence of a cabinet style government could provide for a Central Committee.
>
> There should be a deputy Leader elected who must represent a minority party or group within the administration.
>
> The distribution of chairmanships should be done through the 'usual channels' with the principle of proportionality among the Constitutional parties in mind.
>
> There should be a Central Committee consisting of all the Chairmen and Deputy Chairmen of all the Committees. This

Central Committee should be chaired by the Leader of any constitutional minority party, with the usual voting rights.

The Constitution of Northern Ireland should embody a Bill of Rights along the lines of the European Convention on Human Rights which should include guarantees against discrimination.

. . . we have proposed that there should be a properly constituted North/South committee to discuss these matters free from the Constitutional arguing that has dogged all previous attempts at cross-border co-operation.

The committee formed would consist of Northern Ireland representatives (backed up by civil servants) and a similar number of elected representatives from the Republic.

. . . a serious commitment to open discussion on the whole question of persons convicted of politically motivated crime.

To Progressive Unionists also, the Union is of paramount importance but there are also other issues which we are committed to pursue seriously and resolve within it on behalf of the common people throughout all the community.

The PUP claimed to be the only socialist unionist party in Northern Ireland.

This document was first mooted in 1972 in Long Kesh compounds and first published by the Volunteer Political Party in 1974, before being adopted by the PUP in 1977. It was reissued in 1979, 1980 and 1984, and abridged to 'Sharing Responsibility' in 1985 by the PUP. Spence wrote the document.

Hugh Smyth was sympathetic towards Spence's goal of establishing an alternative unionism. The Volunteer Party, which Smyth joined, was founded by ex-UVF prisoners but received derisory support at the polls and disbanded. This failure did not surprise Spence, who had told them that to have any chance of success in representing their community, it was essential to incorporate the word unionist in the title of the new party. Hugh Smyth became an independent unionist. 'Sharing Responsibilty' was constantly ignored by the mainstream unionist parties before the PUP, in 1985, adopted it as party policy, albeit in abridged form.

This political pedigree scotches once and for all the notion that Spence, Ervine, Hutchinson and others are simply ventriloquist dummies manipulated by loyalist paramilitaries. Clearly the PUP formulated its own political thinking, separate from the body of the UVF.

From the start the PUP's agenda, as well as being conciliatory, was unapologetically left-wing Labour. Even during their time in Long Kesh, Ervine and Hutchinson's brand of radical unionism had caused them to be labelled the 'Red Brigade' by fellow loyalist prisoners. Many prisoners were sympathetic, though. The very few who would have been right-wing were generally religious and more than likely became 'born-again Christians'. With the PUP in the latter half of the 1980s, Spence and Ervine saw themselves resuscitating left of centre unionism, a casualty since 1969 of the one-issue policy of unionists – the 'Border'. Since the policy of the Labour Party in Britain favoured a United Ireland, unionists had decreed that socialism was a fellow traveller of republicanism, and therefore socialism must be anti-unionist. To reinforce the solidity of unionist votes against hostile external forces, the Labour tradition within unionism was suppressed; specifically the Ulster Unionist Labour Association fell into decline after the Stormont parliament was prorogued in 1972. The PUP perceived no contradiction between unionism and a Labour stance. On the contrary, they believed their prescription of diversity within unionism was essential for the health of the Northern Ireland state. In order to purge the plague of exploitation and the cancer of sectarianism, transfusions of class issue politics and inclusive policies would be vital.

They were setting out to offer a realisable alternative to the mainstream parties, whose every gambit served only to heighten already debilitating fears among the unionist electorate. These myopic parties had sought in vain for vision. They had historically succeeded in bringing about one humiliating defeat after another upon their alarmed people, who could see only an inevitable downward spiral of events. The PUP had a different perspective, steering towards possible agreements, based upon a programme aimed at achieving consensus across the community, prepared to use persuasion but ready to fight opponents with the force of argument in the political ring, and nowhere else. Their fundamental divergence from other parties lay in their espousal of the pluralism of unionism, declaring their right to provide a different voice and to challenge those who perceived themselves, or who were perceived by others, as being born to lead the unionist community.

Not all the contents of the abridged version of 'Sharing Responsibility', however, were prescient. On one issue the PUP document got it spectacularly wrong: 'With the exception of cross-border security the Westminster parties, and indeed governments international, give tacit acceptance to our submission that there really is no need for any grandiose Anglo-Irish pacts or agreements.' From a unionist perspective, this was an enormous miscalculation.

A matter of weeks after the PUP had adopted the document, the British and Irish governments signed the Anglo-Irish Agreement, on 15 November 1985, at Hillsborough, County Down, which gave the government of the Republic of Ireland the right to influence the decision-making of the government of Northern Ireland. The impact upon unionists was cataclysmic. They felt betrayed by their British government for imposing upon them an accord which, potentially, could cast adrift an allegiance they believed to be their birthright. They were dismayed that their sense of nationality had been used as political barter, to the advantage of the republican movement. They had hoped for better from an Irish government but, in their hearts, expected nothing less. Respect for authority was damaged at a stroke.

The unionist body politic floundered. All fifteen unionist MPs at Westminster resigned their seats on 17 December, which, in January 1986 when all the by-elections were held on the same day, forced what amounted to a referendum in the province over the recent diktat. Unionists managed to ensure that they were returned to Westminster minus one of their seats, lost to the nationalist SDLP. Thus, they had connived in weakening their own position.

Anxiety among the unionist population manifested itself in collective agitation. The early part of 1986 was characterised by civil disorder in the streets, made worse by intimidation. By 3 March, the unionist community was in such a state of turmoil that it responded overwhelmingly to a call from its politicians, the UUP and DUP acting in concert, to demonstrate their opposition to the British government's policy in a day of protest. The unionist people came out on to the streets in such numbers that they brought their own country to a standstill, ironically a desired outcome of republican violence which they had frustrated up to that point by a determined will to get on with their lives despite almost daily disruption.

The ramifications of that 'strike' were to prove decisive for loyalism. A '1986 Committee' of shop stewards, trade unionists and industrial workers was formed ostensibly to support unionist agitation against the Anglo-Irish Agreement. Ervine, representing the UVF, was invited to a secret meeting on the day that Molyneaux, leader of the Ulster Unionists, and Paisley returned from 10 Downing Street, where they had been in talks with the British prime minister, Mrs Thatcher. According to lunchtime radio reports, the meeting had gone satisfactorily for the unionists.

Initially, the '1986 Committee' was addressed by two DUP politicians, Peter Robinson MP and Sammy Wilson, at the DUP offices on the Newtownards Road in east Belfast, who said that the outcome of the deliberations in London would have been a sell-out for unionism, but, in the interim, they had been in contact with their negotiators and had stiffened their resolve. The assembled group was then asked to transfer to Unionist Party headquarters in Glengall Street for a secret meeting with Molyneaux and Paisley. The purpose of that meeting was to call a province-wide strike, but the two leaders had been informed that the only way a strike would happen was if they jointly called it.

The '1986' group was kept waiting downstairs in Glengall Street before the meeting. Eventually, Molyneaux and Paisley descended the stairs from the room in which they had, indeed, called jointly for a stoppage. Ervine listened: 'Paisley says, "This is a bad experience for the PM." I said, "Dr Paisley, I heard you on the radio at lunchtime, saying that this was pretty much all right, and that you were happy enough." He said, "It must have been the way they edited it." I said, "Dr Paisley, it was live." He blustered.'

For Ervine the interesting part had still to unfold. When the 'secret' meeting was concluded, they all made their way out, only to be met by a bank of cameras, television and newspaper reporters. The following day the pro-unionist *Newsletter* carried this report: 'Paisley revealed that he had warned Mrs Thatcher that if she could not reach agreement with loyalists, then any strike would be "like a Sunday school picnic in contrast to the opposition that would be provoked".' For many of its readers, this would have conjured up images of the

1974 Ulster Workers' Strike, which had brought down the devolved power-sharing Executive.

Ervine was furious, because the agitation had been a bluff from the start. He saw it as the usual unionist politician's ploy to the outside world: '"I'm a reasonable man, but I've all these hard men behind me." They hadn't even the common decency to tell the prime minister that it was a bad deal. They had to go through this ritual drama where the "hard men" were brought in, and, of course, it was a secret meeting.' Ervine is certain that the media had been tipped off by a unionist politician. Ervine's report back left no room for doubt about his conclusions. The days of being exploited were over: 'There's no way that these men have our interests at heart, or the country's interests at heart. I don't give a damn about what you say, but that's never going to happen to me again. This is a turning point. We have to fight for ourselves.'

During this turbulent period in the unionist community and through the smokescreen of burning vehicles, barricades, roadblocks and public demonstrations, the PUP perceived significant shifts in the republican movement. They noted that, on 15 October 1986, the Provisionals had come out in support of a policy of Sinn Féin members taking seats in the Dáil, and consequently, on 2 November, the Sinn Féin Árd Fheis had voted by a two-third's majority to end its abstentionist policy vis-à-vis the Dáil. Both events signalled a momentous shift in republican ideology. However, most other unionists failed to appreciate the significance of this departure.

Further events, in January and February 1987, illustrated a dichotomy in unionists' reaction to the Anglo-Irish Agreement. First, indicating a naivety in mainstream unionist political circles, unionists from Belfast City Council handed in to Buckingham Palace a petition signed by 400,000 citizens who were opposed to the Agreement. This 'loyal to Crown and empire' attitude was hopelessly out of date, despite evidence of impressive support. Did they really expect the queen to take action on their behalf?

Secondly, a document was published, from an unexpected source, which gave an appropriate political response. The UDA loyalist paramilitaries' think-tank, the New Ulster Political Research Group, published 'Common Sense', which advocated devolved government, based on consensus and shared responsibility. It went largely unnoticed.

Thirdly, in February, in an attempt to assert control over events, the leadership of the UUP and DUP set up a Joint Task Force to carry out a consultative exercise among groupings in the unionist community, to produce alternatives to the Hillsborough Agreement. By so doing, they exposed the unpreparedness of their leadership. From the start Gusty Spence was sceptical about the exercise, but he was canvassed for his and the PUP's views. When the PUP delegation met the Task Force, Spence expressed an opinion that the final report would be ignored by the established unionist leadership. In response, the three Task Force members stated how serious they were about the project. However, when they presented their report to Molyneaux and Paisley, in July 1987, no further action was taken. The accuracy of Spence's prediction was confirmed to him later in the year, while attending a Labour Party conference in England, by one of the same Task Force members. The leaders of both unionist parties would not countenance the enlightened findings of the Task Force report.

Unionists were now paying the price for decades of stultifying slogan politics. In plebiscite after plebiscite, they had electioneered under mantras like 'This We Will Maintain'. The Rev Roy Magee says: 'I don't want to be cynical about this, but I'm not sure that a lot of people knew what the "This" meant. They didn't have to think.'

Chris McGimpsey, a Belfast city councillor and member of the Ulster Unionist Party since his schooldays, explained the shortcomings of the largest unionist party and its inept response to the Anglo-Irish Agreement:

> It used to be if you joined the Unionist Party and did well, then by definition you did well in politics, because the Unionist Party always won elections. So, there is an undercurrent within official unionism that the way to do well in politics is to shaft other people in the Unionist Party. That's where the dynamics for success are. They're at the Al Capone station within the party, within a branch. If you've got fifty old dears, and if you can get thirty of them to think you're a great fellow, then they are going to vote for you. You can deselect the sitting councillor and get in. You know there is a solid unionist seat because everybody votes official unionist in . . . wherever.

So the first big hurdle is to get selected. The Mafia used to say, 'It's not personal, it's business.' Well, in the Unionist Party, 'It's not business, it's personal' . . . inside the party.

The Ulster Unionist Party is a party fuelled by internal jealousies, a party without a cohesive centre. In the absence of an effective parliamentary opposition, the dynamic to evolve further the party's philosophy, and argue it intellectually, was diminished to the point of enfeeblement in the mid-1980s. So come the Anglo-Irish Agreement, it was a party outplayed and outmanoeuvred.

PUP activists like Ervine, by contrast, were strategic thinkers, who made it their job to access, assess and utilise resources to further their cause. The basic raw material of their trade was information. It was gathered, weighed up and then put to use judiciously. They were working to reach a position either of exercising direct influence to produce positive, peaceful change in the community or, at least, to influence the larger parties. But they recognised from the outset that two elements were crucial to the realisation of their ambitions. The first was the imperative of political analysis. Ervine and Spence knew that analysis is to a politician what knowledge of the sea is to a sailor. Both needed as much relevant information as possible to allow them to navigate across unfamiliar tides. For example, Ervine wanted to know what was meant when, in 1988, a Sinn Féin Árd Fheis called for a pan-nationalist front. Was it a call for all nationalist organisations to get behind the military campaign, or did it signal a shift away from militarism towards democratic political activity? Ervine and his colleagues concluded that it was a move towards politics, because neither the SDLP nor the Irish government would support violence: 'So there obviously was a shift taking place. Gerry Adams was moving the ground, moving his troops to create a certain situation. We didn't fully know or understand what it was, and we began a process of evaluation.'

The second element was that a period of political stability was a prerequisite for progress. Without that, everything and everybody were insecure. With it everything was possible. Spence knew that the PUP could not make an impact until there was a reasonable period of political stability, because 'people will always vote for the safe bet when bombs are going off and guns are being fired'. While the behaviour of the rest of the unionist community manifested itself in a collective panic, the PUP was keeping its head and its counsel.

At the same time, barely perceptible yet profound changes had begun to emerge within the seemingly implacable body of militarist loyalism. A prominent UVF commander characterises this change: 'It had seemed for quite some time, for some four or five years from the mid-1980s in my own experience, where I saw a desire, by primarily my own community, to seek a different way. That way was obviously going to have to be a political way. There was no military way forward. In fact, there was no military solution to the problem from either side.'

The difficulty was to find people within loyalism who might have the acumen to undertake a political role. The military men knew they were obviously out of the frame, so they began a trawl to uncover potential politicians with the nous to develop and articulate the political voice of loyalism. The search began necessarily within the fold of the trustworthy. The UVF commander made approaches:

> . . . to individuals, probably the most notable was Billy Hutchinson, to literally 'give a hand'. I had known Billy most of his adult life, but didn't know David personally all that well. I knew that Gusty obviously was always going to be interested, and David was in the frame because of his ability to articulate. His ideas weren't any different from anybody else's, but his ability to communicate and to articulate were probably unique among the grouping. Spence had the same ability, but wasn't prepared to go as far forward in public, and neither was Billy. Davey was quite prepared to go and do whatever had to be done.

Up until that point, the UVF command had been content for the PUP, an autonomous party working to establish its political credentials, to agitate on peripheral matters affecting loyalist prisoners. Now in 1989, the militarists, seeking a political way forward but not knowing how to do so, decided to capitalise on the PUP talents. In turn, since the Provisional IRA seemed to be taking steps in a new direction, the PUP strategists felt that this was their opportunity to influence the political direction that the UVF was seeking. Ervine was chosen to be their liaison: 'It was felt that I would be the best person to liaise between the PUP and the UVF. I had the political attitudes, but I also had, to use an Americanism, "street cred". Those twin

attributes were seen as advantageous in talking to the UVF.' A structure was set up, as Ervine recollects:

> The UVF effectively created what was called a 'kitchen cab-
> inet', of which I was part. There were about four or five of
> us, and we met twice a week. There were two members of
> the PUP, and two or three members of the UVF on a constant
> basis. It was about a political analysis. It wasn't about vio-
> lence and what the UVF should do. It was, what's going on?
> What do we read into this? Why is that being said? Is there
> a change? Is there a nuance of a change? What has happened?

At this stage discussions probed how far the militarists were prepared to move, what they would accept. Spence was involved, and he
applied his usual penetrating, questioning style, testing the UVF representatives about their thinking, their objectives and what they
thought could be achieved. This was not always well received by men
committed to violence who had, in the past, viewed Spence's political
utterances with suspicion, even derision. Some saw him as a traitor,
some as capitulating to the enemy, and many as generally unacceptable. They had tried to blacken his name, calling him a communist,
for example. Anyone but Spence would no doubt have been banished
from the discussion rooms, but his views could not be ignored. He
persisted in putting forward his points in a reasonable manner in
response to those who disagreed heatedly with him.

The conjunction in the 'kitchen cabinet' of an ex-prison 'officer
commanding' driving a political agenda and an active paramilitary
commander seeking political direction bore fruit when the UVF commander took his understanding of Ervine and Spence's arguments
back to his comrades. The UVF commander explains:

> To be frank, we were looking for political direction. There-
> fore, it was important to know what Gusty and Davey
> wanted, and for me to translate that back in military par-
> lance, to get my analysis of what they were trying to do.
> Gusty and Davey could have made decisions at political
> meetings which, had they just been reported verbatim,
> might not have been taken up so easily. Because I was able
> to give a perspective on it from a military point of view, it
> was easier for them [the UVF command] to accept.

There were risks in liaising with the UVF, but if violence continued, the PUP would drown. If violence were prolonged by an isolated
loyalist side, then the wider community would suffer horribly. If the
PUP were to do nothing, the political cost to the very existence of
Northern Ireland could be disastrous.

A question must be asked at this point. Was David Ervine involved
with paramilitary planning or decision-making? He clearly states:
'No, it was for my political analysis that I was asked to be there. I
couldn't divorce myself from the UVF. I'm not going to do that. I'm
not going to say I wasn't part of the UVF, but specifically that political element was there.' The UVF commander is equally emphatic in
denying that Ervine and Spence had anything to do with the military
side of loyalism or that they were present when military decisions
were taken. When it is put to him that the terms 'military' and 'political' were merely words of convenience, he denies it.

There was much for Ervine and the PUP to ponder outside the
paramilitary bunker. Peter Brooke, then secretary of state for Northern Ireland, suggested, on 3 November 1989, that the British government might talk to Sinn Féin if the Provisionals renounced
violence, and he also admitted that the British military could not
defeat the Provisional IRA.

The pace towards talks between the constitutional parties and the
two governments increased in 1990. On 9 January, in a speech in
Bangor, Brooke launched a bid for inter-party talks to bring about a
devolved government.

On 18 March a Dublin newspaper, the *Sunday Tribune*, called for
Articles Two and Three of the Irish Constitution to be amended following the ruling of the Irish Supreme Court on 1 March, on the case
brought against the Irish government by the McGimpsey brothers.
Michael and Chris McGimpsey, members of the Unionist Party, had
challenged the legality of Articles Two and Three of the Irish Constitution which laid claim to the territory of Northern Ireland. The
McGimpseys had sought a ruling forcing the Irish government to
recognise Northern Ireland as part of the United Kingdom. The Irish
Supreme Court ruled that the Republic's claim to Northern Ireland
was not merely 'aspirational' but was a 'constitutional imperative'.

On 5 July, Brooke outlined the difficulty over setting up talks
owing to differences over when the Irish government would enter into

negotiations. Unionists insisted that there should be substantive progress made in discussions about internal government in Northern Ireland before progressing on to North-South dialogue. On 7 September, Brooke attempted to relaunch the talks in a speech in Ballymena, saying that he might have to 'set the pace and show the way'.

On 12 December, a Workers' Party resolution to amend Articles Two and Three was defeated by 74 votes to 66 in the Dáil. On 28 December, Brooke said in an interview with the *Belfast Telegraph* that in talks during the year there had been 'real advances, new thinking about difficult issues, re-analysis of goals, and re-evaluation of traditional aims in the context of the 1990s'.

In 1991 the confluence of influences continued to raise the tide of expectation. Garret FitzGerald, who had co-signed the Anglo-Irish Agreement with Margaret Thatcher, revealed in an interview in the *Irish Independent*, on 2 February, that he had considered a referendum on Articles Two and Three at the time but had decided that it was not worth the risk. On 14 March the Irish government consented to Brooke being the arbiter of when they could enter talks, and a new formula was presented to all parties involved, which was agreed by 25 March. The following day Brooke, in a speech in the House of Commons, described a three-strand process for the talks: internal Northern Ireland, North-South relationships, and an East-West dimension. He further declared that 'Nothing is agreed until all is agreed.'

Ervine and the others in the loyalist 'kitchen cabinet' were observing these public developments, seeing a correspondence with the steps Adams was taking to move the Provisionals in a new direction. As a consequence, change followed within loyalism. The Combined Loyalist Military Command (CLMC) emerged. Spence says that the UVF saw the neccessity for coherence between the separate loyalist paramilitary groups: 'They recognised that if they moved alone, they could be left exposed.' Moving together would avoid this and also provide political and moral strength from mutual support. Bringing people together eroded intransigence and encouraged dialogue. Individuals gained confidence from what others were saying to them. Meeting as a joint group facilitated expressing opinions that had been uttered only in private before.

On 9 April 1991 it was announced that, following the next meeting of the Inter-Governmental Conference of 26 April, there would be

Orangefield Under-14 soccer team (David Ervine back row, left).

Compound 18, Long Kesh, 1975 (David Ervine standing, third from right).

In Long Kesh, 1974 (David Ervine crouching, right).

Relaxing by the sea on release, May 1980.

*On a visit to Leipzig to see Glentoran play Locomotiv,
European Cup Winners Cup, October 1986.*

David Ervine in his shop, 1985.

David Ervine in the flat above his shop, 1988.

Brian and David Ervine celebrate Dolly's 80th birthday, 1991.

Jeanette, David and Dolly Ervine at a surprise 25th wedding anniversary party organised by Dolly, 1 March 1997.

Jeanette and David celebrating a friend's wedding, 1998.

Billy Hutchinson, Gusty Spence and David Ervine at the opening of the East Belfast PUP constituency office, 1997.

Meeting President George W. Bush.
[Harrison Photography]

a gap of ten weeks before another meeting, so as to facilitate discussions to take place in Northern Ireland under Strand One of Brooke's announced proceedings. This was a fudge to get unionists off the hook of refusing to comply with the workings of the Anglo-Irish Agreement.

Spence and Ervine argued in the 'kitchen cabinet' that now was an opportunity for loyalism to demonstrate its political weight. This was the first opportunity in sixteen years for constitutional politicians to talk to one another, and loyalists should not be excluded. Spence further advised that in the lead-up to the talks, the loyalist paramilitary groups should declare a unilateral ceasefire. He wanted to convince them of the political credibility they could achieve for the first time: 'The talks are about to happen. By calling a ceasefire you're showing them you don't want to continue with violence, unless it's absolutely neccessary. You will wrongfoot the IRA, the SDLP, the British government and the unionist politicians.' And it happened. A loyalist ceasefire was called. In the event, it was to last for only six weeks, but it was a beginning, a vital step towards the day when there would be a universal ceasefire.

On 30 April the talks process began with a new secretary of state in office, Sir Patrick Mayhew, but because of wrangling over a venue and who would chair Strand Two, weeks went by without any progress. With three weeks remaining before the Inter-Governmental Conference was due to reconvene, Sir Patrick Mayhew called a halt on 3 July. The following day the loyalist paramilitaries' ceasefire ended.

Ervine stated the reasons for the end of ceasefire: 'In their mind it broke down for two specific reasons: the talks broke down, but secondly, during the period of that loyalist ceasefire the IRA planted bombs in loyalist housing estates, shot a senior member of the Orange Order, did things that were about direct, straightforward provocation to loyalism.' Retaliation followed as the reality of war took hold again. But a more subtle process had begun to take shape. The loyalist militarists began to ask what the Provos were really up to. There was a need to know why the enemy was doing what it was doing. What did they intend to get out of their goading? What did they hope to achieve?

The frustration of the loyalist politicians was acute. In a distinctly unpromising situation, they had achieved what few had thought possible. They had succeeded in persuading the loyalist paramilitaries to desist from violence. Nevertheless, an opportunity had been squandered by mainstream unionists, who had failed to capitalise on a chance to engage with the Provisionals in open political argument and question republicans' motives, forcing them to defend their position publicly.

Yet for loyalists this period was significant. They had proved wrong the security pundits who mocked them as a bunch of thugs and gangsters who would never hold to a ceasefire. Ervine, Spence and other PUP people always emphasise that there have been two loyalist ceasefires. The forgotten ceasefire of 1991 was seminal for loyalism, for, though it had been temporary, its effect was more durable. It inculcated in the minds of loyalists the 'theory of ceasefire': that it was possible to end the war and win the peace by a strategic withdrawal from the battlefield and an advance to the field of politics. Loyalists could now argue that abstention from violence was a means to a positive end and not a self-destructive end in itself.

The individuals who argued for a political response felt vindicated. Their arguments had persuaded their militarist opponents to act upon their analysis, and the outcome was beneficial. Ervine recognised the conundrum that the militarists were facing: while they wanted to end the war, they were entering new territory. The recurring question of this time was, 'What the hell is going on?'

The ceasefire of 1991, an achievement against the odds, was one of the defining moments of Ervine's life as a politician. No one had believed the ceasefire would hold, but it did. The consequence was the birth of a political voice talking from a loyalist perspective: a voice of unionist self-confidence, separate and belonging, autonomous and not subservient, finding its own path and not in tow. Through their involvement in the 'kitchen cabinet', Spence, Ervine and Hutchinson had acted as catalysts for change among loyalist paramilitarists to find, as the UVF commander says, 'A credible loyalist voice, people who would deliver on what they were saying, and who would stick by their word.' Up to that point, the reputation of loyalist integrity was in shreds. While giving lip-service to the notion of rejecting violence, they did not desist. The general view of loyalists, especially on the part of nationalists or republicans, was that they could not be trusted. As the UVF commander admits: 'I think the results of the "Brooke talks" ceasefire was that, for the first time, it could be said,

"We're not sure whether they are men of honour or not, but at least they have kept their word on this occasion. They seem to be able to control what's happening.'"

The ceasefire induced a feeling of solidarity among loyalists. They considered themselves the community within unionism which had suffered most from the Troubles, who lived in areas which had borne the brunt of unionist hurt year after year. That sense of solidarity increased confidence among those loyalist paramilitaries who had begun to consider a political option. For the first time, they did not take their politics from their traditional establishment, nor follow the direction of its political leadership. There was a growing realisation that loyalists had been exploited historically by unionist politicians who cynically tolerated violence for the unionist cause and then preached law and order after the loyalists acted. Loyalist leaders had always been aware of this exploitation, but now, for the first time, they had an alternative, a political voice rising from within their own ranks. They realised that they could represent themselves. Ervine states:

> We were doing two things: establishing our own identity, our form of unionism, whether it was going to take on or not; plus, we were trying to find our way toward peace. Get a peace established, not just a temporary lapse in hostilities, but something that could be built on, perhaps towards a lasting peace. That's what the people wanted in both communities. And if anyone couldn't see that, they didn't want to see it.

For some among the paramilitary leadership it posed a challenge they wanted to respond to positively. For their 'men on the ground', it would be nothing short of revolutionary, and full of uncertainties. For Spence, Ervine and Hutchinson, it was the political shift for which they had been working. There was a determination to capitalise on this new dynamic and find some way forward out of the morass. They were new to the business, but were aware that in a political sea of sharks they had to learn quickly how to swim. They took the plunge. The loyalists entered the political process.

BOOTED OUT

For LOYALISM TO gear itself up politically and speak with its own voice, they needed someone to go out on to the highways and byways of the political world to forage around and bring back information, reliable or not, for analysis upon which loyalist policy could be formed and then placed in the public domain. Some head-hunting was done, and Ervine became the obvious choice. He accepted willingly, but the stakes were high. Now it was no longer just personal business; it was the political survival of a community.

Ervine was, as he himself says, 'booted out to find out what was going on'. He had to discover what the game was, what the rules were, who would be referee, if there was one, who the other players were, and at what level the game was being played. Sent on in mid-game, he would simply have to discover the rules as he went along.

As the UVF commander puts it:

> It was just a finding-out process. We had never been through anything like this before. We knew where we wanted to go, but we didn't know how we were going to get there. It was like walking about in the dark. We didn't know what we were going to find. We thought, well if we go down this way, that should be all right. Then, we bumped into a wall and had to turn round, go back and

go somewhere else. Basically that was what Davey was doing.

One reason the loyalists devoted little time, energy and attention to Great Britain and its government was because, since the signing of the 1985 Anglo-Irish Agreement, they distrusted the British. That was one reason why the UVF had been formed. Some of that mistrust was fuelled by perception rather than reality, but it was there nevertheless.

In contrast, infinitely more time and resources were directed to finding out what was going on in the Republic of Ireland, because, according to Ervine:

> The real problem was, as far as we were concerned, the republican war didn't emanate from mainland Britain. It emanated from the Republic. People, although I don't necessarily equate one with the other, equate republican violence with the Republic of Ireland, for less than factual reasons. Nevertheless, they do. So why not go to the seat of where it was perceived? That's the one thing you learn: perceptions are more important than truth. It was perceived that the Republic, if not totally sympathetic to what was going on in the North, certainly, on many occasions, showed a lot of acquiescence and reluctance to deal with the problem.

Unlike the overwhelming majority of his fellow unionists, Ervine had no pathological qualms about going South. He recognises that other unionists might have criticised him for this, but explains:

> If the Russians were to launch a pre-emptive strike on Britain, everybody would say, 'Why didn't the Brits know about it? Why didn't they have an early warning system? Where were their spies and what were they doing?' Countries have ambassadors all around the world for two reasons: one, to look after their interests, which is wholly selfish; and the other is to make friends and influence people, which is selfish as well. So when a Prod does something that is wholly selfish, he's called a traitor. That is unreasonable and ridiculous.

In the period 1992–94 Ervine travelled often to the Republic, at least ten or twelve times. He travelled the length and breadth of the country and talked with TDs from all the political parties and anybody or any group of influence, like Chambers of Commerce, trade unions, people in the hierarchies of churches. He also spent time in pubs, listening, picking up bits of information, gauging the mood. The loyalists used a multi-pronged approach. Indeed, as beginners, it could be said that they employed an any-prong approach.

On many of his journeys Ervine was accompanied by the UVF commander, for two reasons: firstly, so that he could hear for himself what was being discussed, and then with Ervine, whose reputation was impressive but had no clout in paramilitary circles, sell the findings to the Command back in Belfast. Secondly, he was there because neither Ervine nor the PUP had the total confidence of all of the UVF: 'At first I was there as the UVF's conscience. In other words, "Don't let David go too far." Which is technically impossible. If I'm sitting at a table, and David says something, I couldn't kick him under the table and tell him, "Don't be saying that." It was a false sense of security they were getting from my being there, but I was quite prepared to go along with that.' He kept himself very much to a minor role, leaving most of the talking to Ervine: 'As far as I was concerned, I was there to do a job, say as little as possible, listen as much as possible, intervene where necessary. That was about it.'

In this joint venture, unstructured though it was, the PUP politicians were not merely sleeping partners. They felt that the time was ripe to begin the task of politicising the wider loyalist community within Northern Ireland and to talk their brand of unionism to a wider public. Through the media, they exploited the opportunity of representing the UVF's constitutional position to boost their own profile, by repeating Spence's astute phrase: 'We are close to the thinking of loyalist paramilitaries.'

The paramilitaries, though wary, did not pull back from the uncharted political path Ervine was treading. He states unequivocally:

> They were completely genuine. I don't think you could have got the 1991 ceasefire had loyalism not been absolutely genuine in its desire to take us somewhere better. Of that I have no doubt. At times they were sceptical, but,

in real terms, they were the drivers as much as I was, as any of us were. They were as politically shrewd as we were. Without question, events could never have moved had the UVF not been committed politically. The initiative sprang from them. The UVF leadership wanted to end the war.

They were not journeying into the Republic just to bring back the state of public opinion and the political views of various influential groupings. They had a definite goal, which Ervine declines to reveal, other than to state that they were seeking 'more than opinions'. He is not being coy. For him to reveal more would betray people, meetings and negotiations which took place in confidence. However, we can assume that he was travelling with the 'Sharing Responsibility' document as his guiding philosophy, striving for its implementation. 'Sharing Responsibility' cries out for compromise. Ervine would be seeking people of influence whom he could impress with those views and to whom he could convey the message that loyalism had a brain and was thinking politically.

In early 1992, shortly after Albert Reynolds became taoiseach, Ervine travelled to Dublin as a community worker to speak at a private meeting organised by people close to Republican Sinn Féin and the Irish Communist Party, who wanted to hear authentic voices from the Protestant working class. Among others, the UVF commander was in the party, as was Chris McGimpsey, Belfast city councillor for Court Ward on the Shankill Road. They met at Central Station in Belfast, but a mix-up in arrangements delayed their departure. While they were waiting, Ervine approached McGimpsey and frankly outlined his background. As they chatted, McGimpsey found that they shared a left-wing unionist perspective and discovered they had met before:

> Ervine said, 'You know this is not the first time I've met you.' I said, 'Really?' and he said, 'I was your milkman. You live in a big flashy house out at Ballyhackamore.' I said, 'I do.' He had arrived at my house one Friday night to get paid, and I opened the door. He said, 'Milkman.' So I said, 'She's not in. We'll pay two weeks next week.' And before I could slam the door, he said, 'Middle-class house, working-class response.' Then I vaguely remembered him.

McGimpsey had invited a friend who lived in Dublin, Chris
Hudson, to come along to the meeting. Hudson is a trade unionist and
had been involved with McGimpsey in the Peace Train organisation.
Before the meeting started, McGimpsey took his friend aside and
enlightened him about Ervine's UVF connections. Hudson's interest
was aroused when Ervine spoke:

> I was impressed. I was totally disappointed in the attitude
> of the people from the South, who got up and harped on
> about their usual baggage, the 'victim culture'. Ervine retal-
> iated extremely well, saying that he wasn't going to be held
> responsible for seventy years of unionist misrule, never
> mind eight hundred years. I made a judgement that night
> that the man made good sense. I got up, said a few words,
> and to him that I was sorry the response he got from people
> down South was negative, in that all he got was a lecture
> on what had been done to Catholics in Northern Ireland
> by the Protestants, and that he should not feel guilty for it.
> I pointed out that he was speaking to a very select audi-
> ence, made up of people who had nothing but their own
> baggage, Republican Sinn Féin and the Irish Communist
> Party, who got annoyed with me. I said, 'It's a pity you are
> not down here speaking to ordinary working-class people,
> because I think the response would be very different. I
> think they would warm to what you are saying and under-
> stand what you are saying.'

A responsible trade unionist speaking in support of Ervine's coming to Dublin consolidated the confidence of one voice of the Protestant working class. Ervine was struck by Hudson's manner, nerve and
courage.

When the meeting was over, the participants adjourned for a drink
and a chat. Hudson remembers his conversation with Ervine: 'We
were talking generally about loyalist paramilitaries, and I made some
comments about things I had said on the BBC in the North. He said,
"Would you speak to those people if you got the opportunity?" I said
that I would, but I would tell them exactly what I thought of them.
So he said, "Maybe that could be arranged." I didn't pay much more
attention to that.'

Besides the Peace Train connection, Hudson has other links with Northern Ireland. His elderly mother is originally from Belfast, the daughter of a mixed marriage whose parents had to flee South in 1922 from their home on the Ormeau Road after receiving a death threat from loyalists of that era.

On their return to Belfast, Ervine and the UVF commander recommended Hudson to the UVF. The paramilitary leader explains: 'We were keen to have someone able to assist in explaining and understanding the loyalist position with the Irish government.' A few weeks later Hudson received a phone call inviting him to Belfast. He travelled up on 26 May, and Ervine met him. Hudson recalls:

> We went up to the Shankill Road. I met with what I was told were the top men of the UVF. I was nervous, as a Southerner with my accent, being brought up the Shankill Road. I didn't even know who David Ervine was. I had met him and made a judgement about him. This man had a quality that I could trust. When I went up, he said to me, 'Now, you might not like these men, but everything they say to you, it's the truth as they know it. They'll say things that irritate you, annoy you and upset you, but it's their truth.' I said I understood that concept.
>
> I said to them, at first, that I wanted to take five minutes to tell them what a shower of bastards I thought they were, because they had killed one of my best friends who played in the Miami showband, had planted bombs in the centre of my city which had killed a girl I used to know years ago. So I said, 'I'm sitting here talking to you, not out of anger but to find out why you did those things.'
>
> They retaliated by saying they could have done it a thousand-fold. They could have planted more bombs in Dublin, and if it worked for the IRA it could work for them. To hell with the Dublin government. You Southerners have done nothing to help the situation. You've been using the Provos as the cutting edge of Irish nationalism.
>
> The discussion went on for about two hours, lots of things, even things I felt they needed clarification on. One thing they did know which was cute. They said to me, 'By

the way, Chris, you come from a republican background. Your father was an old IRA man.'

I said, 'No, my father was never an old IRA man. He was a young IRA man. We call them the Old IRA now to make them respectable. Some day you may be called Old UVF men.' They understood that. After the discussion I walked out with David. He said, 'That was good.' I said, 'I don't think so. I think they think I'm some quichey peacenik.' David said, 'No, those guys are conscious you came up here on your own, you sat down, you spoke to them, and that was good.'

Hudson did not need to be told the purpose of the UVF's invitation: 'I believe at the time they were sussing me out. They needed somebody to talk to from the South, and David was given that job to do.' In the blind-man's-buff world of 'more than opinions', loyalists had stumbled upon a conduit to the Irish government, a crucial step in their strategy to make their presence felt on the political stage, to 'win friends and influence people'.

Hudson was one of numerous people with whom they talked. Not all contacts proved fruitful. In return, the UVF frequently received emissaries working on behalf of the Irish government, or the IRA, or perhaps both. All sides knew that the others wanted peace and were working to find out their conception of the mechanisms and logistics required to achieve it. In many instances there was mutual suspicion, often misunderstanding, and consequently those contacts evaporated.

In retrospect, the meeting with Hudson assumes great significance. Potential for the liaison with Hudson to develop depended on the impression the three key characters made upon each other. Hudson had obviously impressed the two loyalists, but what made him persevere? He had already demonstrated a commitment to the Northern situation and working with its people for peace; was familiar with the make-up of the Protestant community in Northern Ireland, and knew that it was not as homogeneous as people and politicians in the South thought; was aware of its diversity in terms of religious grouping and class structure. He was well placed to play a more effective role now as an unorthodox facilitator, in efforts to work towards a political solution to a seemingly intractable conflict. Hudson says:

I'm a proud citizen of this state. I'm a republican. I love my country, but I'm cheesed off with the way my country responds to issues in Northern Ireland. They don't always understand the sensitivities of how people operate in Northern Ireland. As one loyalist said, 'The best way to get rid of the siege mentality in the North is to lift the siege. If you lift the siege then we can start growing.' There simply is no siege from the South, but where the siege mentality comes in we propagate as if there is.

After the Shankill Road meeting, Hudson returned to Dublin not sure what, if anything, would develop. That evening, when reflecting upon the day's events, he was sure his first impressions of Ervine still held. 'I made an absolute judgement on him that the man is trustworthy. He has a brain, is intellectual. He is an honest broker. He has a vision that other people haven't got. I think I'm going to run with him, if he wants to run with me.' Significantly, Hudson had made the same judgement on the UVF commander. These important relationships, which played an integral part in bringing about an end to violence, were allowed to get off the ground and were held together by courageous men responding to intuitions of mutual trust and regard.

Hudson proceeded cautiously, waiting for an appropriate opportunity to sound out people whom he considered to have influence within the Irish political establishment. An opportunity arose when two members of the Unionist Party were sent South by its leader, James Molyneaux, to contact Fergus Finlay, adviser to Dick Spring, leader of the Irish Labour Party (which seemed about to enter government), in an effort to patch something together. Previously, the strongest unionist delegation ever to come to Dublin, with a working agenda, had been spurned by Albert Reynolds. Later, after the election, Hudson arranged a meeting, attended by the two Unionist Party members and Finlay and himself, where they discussed openly possible outcomes of Molyneaux's sending a letter to Spring, now tánaiste, to restart communications. During the meeting, Hudson mentioned that he had met UVF people, and Finlay asked him for his judgement on them. Hudson replied that they should not be written off as fascist and racist thugs, as influential pundits in the South tended to do. After the meeting, Finlay expressed satisfaction at the way it had gone and encouraged Hudson to continue his contacts with the UVF. He asked Hudson to keep him up to date on any progress made, but stated that, of course, the tánaiste would never know about the matter officially. Hudson assumed that the tánaiste would, indeed, be kept informed about his activities.

Thus, the UVF had achieved the desired step without which its goal, which Ervine has always refused to divulge, was unrealisable. It now had an indirect, but secure, conduit into the heart of the Irish government. For Hudson there followed a series of meetings with key people from Belfast and Dublin. During meetings with UVF military leaders, he wrote notes to keep a reliable record of the proceedings, which, upon return to Dublin, he handed over to Fergus Finlay in Dick Spring's office.

Ervine had many private and confidential talks with people in the Republic. He was trying to understand how respected figures in that society interpreted events, or what was likely to happen and what loyalism might do about it. These meetings were taking place against a backdrop of the continuing Hume-Adams talks and a gathering momentum between the SDLP and the Dublin government, a scenario that increased pressure on a loyalist political analyst to search widely for information, especially among those perceived as being antagonistic. The loyalists urgently needed to know what the implications for the Union were. 'There are many people who are not in a homogeneous group, of either all United Ireland or all United Kingdom, and, therefore, it was important we got out and found out what the reality was.'

Ervine shared his information with a closed group, the Combined Loyalist Political Alliance, which came into being in late 1992 or early 1993. It comprised representatives of the Ulster Democratic Party and of the PUP, whose job was to put together a political strategy. Much of it focused on trying to understand what the IRA was doing. As Ervine explains: 'We were expected to give analysis to the paramilitaries. It became a very frightening time, not physically, but from the point of view "Were we good enough?" This meant a lot. It was vitally important, and we daren't get it wrong.' Among the members of the CLPA were Ray Smallwoods and Davy Adams, both of the UDP, who gave political analyses to the Ulster Defence Association; Gusty Spence and Ervine; and one observer from each of the high commands of the UDA and the UVF, both of whom also sat on the Combined Loyalist Military Command. Ervine recalls that the Combined Loyalist Political Alliance fulfilled its analytical function for the military side by debating until the core issues had been identified. Then these were drafted by Spence and Smallwoods for the CLPA. When this joint body felt comfortable with a final draft, it would be given to the Combined Loyalist Military Command.

By establishing a working political think-tank, in early 1993 loyalism pitched itself into a race to catch up in the political stakes and compete with nationalist and republican strategies. But was there in loyalist ranks the talent to shape, as their desired goal, a political outcome that would satisfy their own needs, yet not be inimical to those of their opponents?

More than sheer guts and effrontery were going to be needed if the political establishment was to be persuaded to accept loyalists as negotiators in a lasting settlement. Loyalists knew that. The final battle was going to depend upon the power of their argument and persuasion. Levels of discrimination and diplomacy equal to that of their opponents would have to be acquired and applied.

As individuals, loyalists had been in worse situations before and surmounted them through mutual support, but nothing had been as daunting and as important to the survival of their community as what lay ahead. Encouragement came from the strength of their collective determination to succeed.

LOYALISM IMPACTS UPON REAL POLITICS

I N DUBLIN, ALBERT Reynolds, too, was determined. He had taken office on 11 February 1992 with peace in the North at the top of his agenda.

Just as Ervine does not fit the stereotypical unionist mould, wearing neither bowler hat nor Orange sash, so Albert Reynolds escapes the traditional Fianna Fáil image of a green republican. A successful, self-made businessman of some wealth before he entered politics, in his fledgeling entrepreneurial endeavours he had promoted showbands in Northern Ireland: 'The difference with me was, I did business up North back in the fifties and sixties. I used to take the Ulster Hall in Belfast. Years later, fellows would say, "Some of those guys must have been unionists." I said, "I couldn't tell you what religion they were, and I couldn't care less. Maybe they were all Protestants, Presbyterians, unionists, whatever. I don't know what they were. It doesn't matter to me."

That experience had taught him something about the nature of Northern attitudes:

> I felt I wasn't a stranger to people in Northern Ireland, whatever side of the political divide they came from. I said, right from the very start, 'These are people who are straight

talkers, and they respect people who give them straight talking.' They would have more respect for me, and more confidence in me, if I say and stand up for what I believe in and, at the same time, recognise what they stand up for and believe in. Let's try and deal on that basis, rather than try and do it in an indirect, behind-the-door situation.

That Reynolds could understand the directness of Northerners, where others might take offence and walk away, was of infinite value when he came to deal later with people like Ervine and Spence: 'I've always said that dealing with people in Northern Ireland, all my life I've a lot of good friends up there on both sides, I've known them to be people of their word. If they've given me their word, it's good enough for me. I don't need any other assurance.'

When he decided to enter politics, Reynolds opted for Fianna Fáil because, in his opinion, it was the party that could best serve the interests of small business. Surprisingly, particularly from a Fianna Fáil deputy, Reynolds shared with Ervine a distaste for the political *bête noir* of unionists. He had never liked the Anglo-Irish Agreement and had said so when it was unpopular to do so. Reynolds believed that not getting the unionists involved had been a major mistake. And like Ervine, Reynolds had noted a change in republican rhetoric, a shift away from intransigence. He believed that if he could reach the paramilitaries on both sides he would have a better chance, and he was prepared to take that risk.

The businessman in him had not lost his eye for a chance, and he had come to the conclusion that the conventional political approach had achieved nothing except to condemn another generation to more murder, killing and destruction: 'Everybody else had gone on with the politically correct way to do things: "Don't talk to anybody, don't meet anybody until everybody hands over their arms." It had been pursued for most of thirty years. It hadn't succeeded, and yet all we were getting was more people killed, and, by and large, a lot of them were innocent people.'

Politically speaking, Reynolds was a blank sheet as far as the 'Northern situation' was concerned when he entered office. It could be said that he was lucky to become taoiseach at a time of flux in Irish politics. During the briefing in the transfer of power from the previous administration, Charles Haughey told Reynolds: 'There have been talks going on between Gerry Adams and John Hume. John Hume has been trying to push for an initiative. It's up to you to make your own mind up when you come in as to whether you're going to pursue that or not, if it's going to go anywhere or not. It's over to you. That's all the information I have.'

Reynolds says that when he spoke with Hume about a week later, Hume assumed that the new taoiseach was fully informed about his private discussions, but Reynolds had to ask Hume to fill him in. Hume did so, but stressed that if the initiative were to go any further, then the two governments, Irish and British, would have to get involved. He suggested that Reynolds' personal relationship with John Major (they had known each other from the time both had been finance ministers in their respective governments) could be the key factor in developing the situation.

Reynolds tried to persuade the British prime minister to join with him to realise the potential of the work done on the Hume-Adams front: 'I rang up Major. We had the kind of relationship where I could ring him.' Major did not accept what Reynolds was saying. While genuinely keen to do something, Major could not see what he could do at that time. At their first meeting as heads of state, Reynolds recalls that Major said: 'I'll work with you. We'll work together. I don't want to condemn another generation in Northern Ireland to another twenty-five years of violence. Whatever we can do.' Reynolds promised to return as soon as something definite was developing.

As that revered footballing son of east Belfast, Danny Blanchflower, was wont to say, 'Funny, the harder you work, the luckier you become.' So credit where credit is due to Albert Reynolds, who did work at building something concrete. He had a good relationship with John Major, as, indeed, later he was to have with President Bill Clinton, which he cultivated in the interests of peace. Moreover, as taoiseach he was prepared to take, and to permit others in his government to take, irregular steps and risks in trying to find an agreement in the North. In Belfast the PUP was taking parallel risks.

For both parties 'risks' is not an exaggerated term. October to December 1993 was an unstable period, characterised by barbarity and black despair.

On the political surface, the tide of the Hume-Adams initiative was threatening to sweep all before it, even receiving the ultimate imprimatur of the time, the approval of Nelson Mandela. Hume met Reynolds and Spring in Dublin with the broad principles of peace agreed with Adams, untouched and unseen by any unionist. The Irish cabinet was briefed about it. At a rally in support in west Belfast, 2000 marchers turned out. In Washington, the US Congress gave its approval. Unionism was in real danger of becoming marooned and isolated.

On the paramilitary front, Northern Ireland appeared to be driving headlong towards disaster. On Saturday afternoon, 23 October, the Protestant Shankill Road was raped by a Provisional IRA bomb carried by two men into a busy fish shop where it exploded before customers could escape. Nine people were killed instantly and one died later. Locals tore with their bare hands into the piles of masonry and bricks, frantically searching for the crushed bodies of customers entombed beneath the debris. The IRA claimed later that their target had been a meeting of loyalist paramilitary leaders in a room above the fish shop, though evidently they were not there. Shock turned to anger, anger to rage, when media pictures showed Gerry Adams carrying the dead bomber's coffin at his funeral on the following Tuesday, 26 October. The Shankill was consumed in grief and fury. Hugh Smyth, the doyen of the PUP and a temperate man, remembers his crisis:

> I know one thing: from my own personal point of view, it was the lowest. I'm involved in politics twenty-six years, longest-serving elected member in Belfast, and it nearly wrecked me. It was the first time that I had to challenge what I was doing in politics. It was a very, very hurtful time, for a whole lot of reasons. My own chum – his sister, her young daughter and her husband were all killed, three out of the one family. So it had a major impact on me. The simplest thing would have been to go out and seek revenge, and blow this country into a complete war.

Smyth kept to politics. Paradoxically, the small PUP received an influx of recruits as a direct consequence of the slaughter. Community workers gathered on that Saturday evening in a centre on the Woodvale Road to discuss how to keep the situation calm. Many of them were former paramilitaries who had gravitated into community work after their release in the early 1990s. Eddie Kinner, along with Martin Snodden and David Ervine, were present. Among the constructive suggestions, somebody threw in the idea of starting their own class party. Ervine said, 'What's the point in that? The PUP is in existence.' He went on to argue that the PUP was the best vehicle to counteract violence, by channelling people's resentment. He convinced the dozen or so who were present to join the PUP, and the party just about doubled its numbers.

Yet, despite calls for calm, even the proverbial dogs in the street knew that retaliation was inevitable. In paramilitary ranks, a procedure was automatically triggered in the wake of an attack. The UVF's course of action was simple: all units were authorised to carry out 'calculated retaliation' within twenty-four hours. If they actually knew who had carried out the attack, then these people became the target; failing that, if they knew the area from where the attack had originated, that was targeted. As the UVF commander states, it was their way of saying, first to the nationalist population: 'These people claim to be your defenders and they can't defend you.' Secondly, to the IRA: 'If you carry out these actions, we're going to put it up you. Be in no doubt about that.' It was also a way of saying to them: 'Look, stop this! It's not making sense, because every time you do it, we can do it, too. If necessary, we'll do something that's even more atrocious than you have just done. Don't do it.'

Retaliation for the Shankill bombing was launched from different loyalist paramilitary units. On 26 October, two Catholic workmen were murdered and five injured at a municipal refuse depot in Kennedy Way, Belfast. On the 28th, two Catholic brothers were murdered near Waringstown, County Down. On the 30th, one week after the Shankill bombing, one atrocity was piled upon another when seven people were massacred and thirteen injured as they were relaxing in the Rising Sun Bar, in Greysteel, County Derry. It was a week that numbed the war-toughened people of Northern Ireland, and shocked the world. October 1993 was the worst month for casualties in Northern Ireland in seventeen years.

It was felt in some quarters, North and South, that risks had to be taken to halt the downward spiral. Ervine was approached by Ulster Television, the regional commercial station, to comment on the

Shankill bombing in its *Counterpoint* programme. There was some doubt about the wisdom of appearing. Jeanette Ervine was fearful about her husband's safety if he were to appear. The PUP weighed up the pros and cons. Nevertheless, Ervine decided to go ahead and appeared on screen in darkened profile. He did not voice the usual unionist mantras about letting the security forces deal with these thugs or sending the army and police into republican areas to root them out. Instead, Ervine challenged republicanism to put away its guns and use force of argument and persuasion. He challenged the IRA intellectually: 'Lay down your arms and represent your people. The only way out of this is dialogue.'

The *Counterpoint* broadcast impressed a great many people, who were surprised to hear a unionist, especially a loyalist, advocating negotiation. Amidst the carnage and mayhem, the impact of a loyalist voice advocating reason and tolerance was all the more telling. From out of that misery, a message of a hope that had seemed lost was stirring.

Hopeful steps of an irregular nature, approved by Albert Reynolds, were being taken by Fergus Finlay, advisor to Dick Spring, the Irish foreign minister and tánaiste. During the latter half of 1993, in an effort to revive the momentum of the aborted talks of 1991 which had sought a comprehensive political settlement, the British and Irish governments were preparing a document which would underpin and advance the peace process. However, the Irish government held off agreeing a final draft. It did not want to repeat the mistakes of the Anglo-Irish Agreement: rejection by the unionist community. This time around, Reynolds' administration was determined to be as inclusive as possible. Finlay was authorised to take the necessary steps:

> It was extremely important for us that we didn't make the mistake that had been made in 1985, which was to negotiate a document with the British government that we thought was inclusive but, in fact, excluded a whole section of the community of Northern Ireland. We made the classic mistake in 1985 – and I was part of that – of assuming that the British government was briefing unionism throughout the negotiations, and bringing them along, as we were in briefing nationalism. We were determined to try

to avoid that mistake in relation to the Downing Street
Declaration. That's why people like me were going around
and talking to any Protestant group that we could, and we
were doing it so that they wouldn't be surprised. Whatever
else was in it, they wouldn't be taken aback by it, because
we know from '85 that, if you surprise any section of the
community, the immediate consequence of that is they
don't read the document. They reject it outright and they
never read it.

Finlay would offer an analysis that would surprise unionists of all
shades and dismay nationalists. Since the outbreak of the Troubles,
successive Irish governments had tried to maintain a cordon sanitaire
between the unrest in the North and pacific social and economic
progress in the Republic, intent upon developing its strengths within
a European context:

Unity as a kind of national objective is essentially a dead
letter. The unity of Ireland is not a central feature of anybody's policy, and it hasn't been for twenty-five years. The
tacit underpinning of all Irish government policy in the last
twenty-five years has been, 'Whatever's going on in Northern Ireland, for God's sake let us not spread it down here.'
That's been the kind of imperative of policy, and unity has
receded further and further and further away from the
agenda with every day the Troubles has lasted.

Given oft-stated public concern in the South for the welfare of
Northern nationalists and Irish governmental demands, through the
Maryfield Secretariat, to have influence upon British policy in Northern Ireland, Finlay's comments expose an appallingly cynical attitude
of self-centred preservation at the heart of the policies of successive
Irish governments. On the other hand, it is what an informed visitor
to Dublin could have discovered in the course of normal social intercourse. But unionists had excluded themselves from that.

Reynolds' sense of fairness and equality propelled his administration's dealings with unionists. Finlay said that his aim was to get that
sense of even-handedness across to Northern Protestants, whether
they be Presbyterians, Methodists, or whatever: 'My mission, if you

would call it that, without breaking the confidence of the negotiations and without spilling the beans about what was in the Downing Street Declaration, was to try and persuade people, particularly those who would be most suspicious, that the Downing Street Declaration wasn't going to be something to be feared, and that it was going to be very even-handed.'

Finlay, towards the end of his journeying, in September and October 1993, met with Ervine and Spence in Belfast. It was a meeting which had enormous importance for loyalism, with implications for the contents of the Downing Street Declaration and the evolution of the peace process. Of course, there had already been contact through the work of Chris Hudson, but face-to-face communication changed the atmosphere and moved the relationship on to a participatory plane, a stage further in the loyalists' pursuit of 'more than opinions'.

The meeting took place in Belfast, amidst shadows of past deeds and half-remembered images. When he arrived, Finlay confesses: 'I got a bit alarmed because, in my stupidity, when Gusty's name was mentioned I somehow or other associated him with the Shankill Butchers. It was kind of hazy in my mind, except Gusty was a name from my childhood. I was sixteen when Gusty did what he did, and he was legendary in the South as a really hard man. I had a mental picture of Gusty in a balaclava holding a rifle.' Finlay was taken aback by this pipe-smoking, amiable, twinkly-eyed grandfather. 'There was a glint and a light in his eye that actually staggered me, and there was a humour about him, and about Ervine.'

They discussed the document that the governments were to publish jointly that December. Finlay briefed them on Albert Reynolds' government's intent. What the loyalist politicians heard must have encouraged them that this was not going to be a repetition of the Anglo-Irish Agreement. Finlay conveyed the aim of balance Reynolds sought to achieve and of the Irish government's commitment in the document to the principle of consent. Whether reunification of the island of Ireland would happen or not would depend on the wishes of a majority of the inhabitants of Northern Ireland. That was the message Finlay was anxious to get across to Spence and Ervine: a policy that would instil confidence among unionists commited to the 'Sharing Responsibility' document.

However, the proposals would not be sufficient for loyalists, who needed to ensure that Finlay's message was consolidated into binding legislation. The signal they were receiving was that the government of the Republic would be receptive to responses from unionists. Finlay was offering the opportunity loyalists had been seeking: to impress and influence people in authority.

Spence and Ervine had not come to the meeting merely to be receptive. They put on the table the political documents on which the Combined Loyalist Political Alliance had been working. Finlay's assessment of their paper was that the loyalists were in the process of developing a political philosophy. As he says: 'I'm not sure that you would say it was entirely original, but they went to great lengths to flesh it out and publish it in readable form. We talked quite a lot about that, and I was enormously impressed by the length they were going to, in terms of the development of their own party, their own political structures and their own political ideas. They were devoting an awful lot of time and effort to writing a constitution for themselves.'

Finlay suggested to Spence and Ervine that his political masters in Dublin would be very keen to see their ideas in print. The two Northerners were sceptical. What would be the point of sending their material South only for it to be ignored? However, Finlay's persuasion proved effective, and the thinking of the loyalists eventually made its mark upon the two governments' deliberations. On page four of the text of the Joint Declaration issued by the two governments, popularly referred to as the Downing Street Declaration, which was published on 15 December 1993, we read in paragraph 5 that, among other things, a political settlement . . .

> must, consistent with justice and equity, respect the democratic dignity and the civil rights and religious liberties of both communities, including:
> - the right of free political thought;
> - the right to freedom and expression of religion;
> - the right to pursue democratically national and political aspirations;
> - the right to pursue constitutional change by peaceful and legitimate means;
> - the right to live wherever one chooses without hindrance;

- the right to equal opportunity in all social and economic activity, regardless of class, creed, sex or
colour.

These would be reflected in any future political and constitutional
arrangements emerging from a new and more broadly based agreement.

Apart from the word 'sex', which Finlay added, those six principles
were written by the Combined Loyalist Political Alliance and approved
by the Combined Loyalist Military Command on the Shankill Road.

Furthermore, loyalists could read in the same paragraph '. . . it
would be wrong to attempt to impose a united Ireland, in the absence
of the freely given consent of a majority of the people of Northern
Ireland'. Reynolds' intent to deal in a balanced way had been delivered in print. The loyalists, though, were not lulled into political complacency and understood the semantics in the Northern Ireland
political grammar of an indefinite article 'a', in 'a majority of the
people', and not the definite article 'the', which would have indicated
the unionist population alone.

Ervine knew it was important to loyalists that they had made an
impression upon government thinking, in both jurisdictions. At a time
when there were rumblings of an IRA ceasefire, loyalists were still
apprehensive that attempts might be made to cobble together an
agreement only among the British and Irish governments and the IRA.
In the aftermath of the Downing Street Declaration, a clear message
had been sent to the Irish government, and through it to the Provos,
that loyalist thinking had to be part of any settlement. Strategically,
they had demonstrated their worth for future political discussions. To
people who had previously seen themselves as being patronised, mar-
ginalised or ignored, it was crucial to have had their opinions recognised. Failure to do so would have sent a very negative message to the
Combined Loyalist Military Command. Now there appeared to be an
appreciation and recognition of the things loyalism was saying. The
inclusion of the Six Principles meant that, as Ervine put it: 'We were,
at least, getting the core issues correct, and we were talking, to some
degree, the same language.'

Given what we know about Albert Reynolds' determination to
include paramilitaries from both sides in the peace process, the underlying neurosis of Southern governments towards imported violence

from 'up there', plus muted aversion to Irish unity among influential opinion formers and political agenda makers, the published thinking of the loyalists must have fallen upon Dublin like manna from north of the border.

The process which led to the incorporation of the loyalists' Six Principles into the Joint Declaration demonstrated a profound shift away from the way in which unionism usually conducted its politics to the use of 'civil society', which had been an integral part of politics on the nationalist side. For so long unionism had not felt the need to engage with 'civil society', by which Ervine meant unionist businessmen, churchmen, trade unionists, community workers and others, who could play significant roles as facilitators for loyalists. For the Combined Loyalist Political Alliance and the Combined Loyalist Military Command, civil society would ensure that their argument could not be ignored or put down without someone saying: 'That was unfair. That was unreasonable.' The arbiters of the integrity of the process were people of probity, like Rev Roy Magee and Church of Ireland Archbishop Robin Eames. As Ervine unequivocally states: 'That's vitally important, because there was no trust between ourselves and the British, or ourselves and the Irish. We must understand that. The modicums of trust were created not by us but by others. That's absolutely fundamental.'

The extent of loyalism's lack of trust in the wider body politic was indicated a few weeks after the publication of the Downing Street Declaration when, in late January 1994, loyalists held a private conference in the Park Avenue Hotel in east Belfast to consider their response. Through Roy Magee, private finance was arranged to fund a two-and-a-half-day conference. The original plan was for the conference to be held outside Northern Ireland, and that it be chaired by an English academic. The Combined Loyalist Military Command objected to both proposals.

Somewhere between twenty and thirty loyalists were in attendance, comprising representatives of the two main groupings: the Ulster Defence Association and its political spokespersons, the Ulster Democratic Party; and the Ulster Volunteer Force with its political counterpart, the PUP. Furthermore, there was a representative from the Ulster Unionist Party. On the morning of the publication of the Downing Street Declaration, John Taylor, a prominent UUP leader, had telephoned Ervine to say that his party 'could live with the document'. As a consequence of prior discussions that Ervine had had with eminent members of the UUP, the UUP leadership had concluded that change was taking place within loyalist paramilitarism, and Taylor's telephone call was to encourage the loyalists to make a favourable response to the Joint Declaration.

Importantly, several outsiders were brought in. A professor of politics of impeccable credentials, who had had previous contact with UDA leaders, had been persuaded by Roy Magee to take the chair. A local historian and a lecturer in constitutional law also accepted invitations. These outsiders were invited because the loyalists wanted to test their analysis against purported experts, to see if it would hold. It would also be an opportunity for the UDA/UDP axis to form their separate conclusion, though still in conjunction with fellow loyalists. A common stance at the end of the conference, as had been the case during the ceasefire of 1991, was the desired goal.

The loyalists needed assurance that the Downing Street Declaration, whose balanced tone both pleasantly surprised and gratified them, was genuine, and where potential for political skulduggery, if any, lay camouflaged beneath its language. Were the guarantees effective? They were afraid that the issue of consent might have a catch in it. They wanted to know where the IRA and Sinn Féin would fit into this scheme of things. They also were keen to know the British government's intentions about just how much legitimacy would be bestowed upon the government of the Irish Republic in the internal governance of Northern Ireland, before the loyalists were ready to enter into an as yet undefined relationship.

The academic noted of Ervine's performance: 'In terms of the searching questions he was asking, it wasn't about every minute detail of the Joint Declaration, it was about the wider political world. He was trying to survey the world of politics and not just, "How will this go down in east Belfast and the Shankill?"' Ervine wanted to test the analysis already reached with the PUP and to prove its bona fides to the UVF leadership. In turn, the UVF men tested what Ervine said to the limit; in particular, the UVF commander who had accompanied Ervine on his travels had the earnest intention of ripping apart, if he could find a flaw, that very analysis with which he was already familiar. He was examining the document minutely, using independent expert opinion, to find out just how accurate the PUP analysis was. Loyalism could not afford to indulge in a mutual admiration society. Some in the room played devil's advocate, while others expressed genuinely held fears: where does this take us? What does it really mean? Are we giving anything away?

The UUP position was explained, and the three experts gave their analysis, extrapolating the position of other unionist parties in relation to the document. Very incisive questions were asked. The document was taken apart, put together again, and evaluated at that conference. Participants were conscious that unionism was at a point of no return. The document was leading into new territory that was going to affect people's lives, and nothing would ever be the same again. The constitutional lecturer and the professor of politics were equally explicit, saying that this was just the beginning of a process of irreversible change. The document would be fleshed out by the two governments in the months ahead. Yet, the certainty that further developments would emanate from London, and Dublin especially, did not deflect the loyalists from their goals. The fluidity of future political circumstances was unsettling, but many in the room recognised that in the principle of consent lay the fulcrum of a potentially constructive future. Obviously, implementation of that principle would have repercussions for the republican movement. For the Provos to accept it, or have it forced upon them, would mean a serious ideological shift.

Collectively, the loyalist conference decided to go along with the Joint Declaration. Although the UVF leadership did not come out in active opposition, they were not enthusiastic, and the UDA was even less comfortable. However, the CLMC adopted a holding position and did not attack the Joint Declaration, indicating that the paramilitary leaders were still involved in the search for a political solution. Conscious of the deliberations of the conference, the Combined Loyalist Military Command would go away, consider a separate response, and deliver it in a matter of days.

The balance sheet was not unequivocally positive. Loyalists who supported other unionist parties were wary of growing PUP influence, and doubters were envious of Ervine's influence. This could spell trouble if things went awry. Yet dividends did accrue. Ervine emerged with his judgement vindicated after his analysis had stood up to rigorous examination by eminent figures, and his standing among loyalists increased. The UVF commander and some of his cohorts gained satisfaction from the outcome of a searching enquiry which confirmed both the validity of their decision to take political direction and their choice of emissary.

Loyalism could now move on, and with growing maturity and confidence: retaining misgivings about the motives of the British government while giving a favourable response to a policy which partly originated in the Irish Republic signified that. Ervine has no doubts about the importance of the Park Avenue Conference: 'It was extremely valuable. That conference was a way of lifting a barrier that allowed the political process proper to take off. If we hadn't got past that base, we were going nowhere.'

For loyalism, the Park Avenue Conference of January 1994 was the political twin of the military ceasefire of 1991.

CEASEFIRES COMING

THE MOMENTUM FROM war to peace gathered pace. The CLMC signalled its willingness to consider a ceasefire and engage in a political way forward when it released a statement shortly after the Park Avenue Conference that accepted as legitimate the aspiration for a United Ireland achieved by democratic and peaceful means. The UVF commander offered an insight into the loyalists' thinking: 'I would never have been in the position where I said to myself, "I don't recognise the right of those people who aspire to a United Ireland." If they want to, fine, as long as they don't do it with a barrel of a gun stuck down my throat. How can you take away a man's aspirations? He's going to aspire, whether I like it or whether I don't. I never had a problem with that.'

On 26 January 1994 the *Irish News*, Belfast's nationalist morning newspaper, reported that loyalist reaction to the Downing Street Declaration was to 'wait and see how it was implemented'. The following day in the same newspaper, Albert Reynolds was quoted as being 'reasonably encouraged' by the 'relatively positive response to the Declaration by the Combined Loyalist Military Command'.

On the last day of January, again in the *Irish News*, Reynolds was reported as saying that a three-month IRA ceasefire would not lead to renegotiation of the Downing Street Declaration. It is clear from his use of the word 'renegotiation' how ill at ease the republican movement felt with the Declaration. From the beginning Reynolds had set out his stall. He had played hard ball, through intermediaries, with the IRA and would not budge from the published text.

As he explained later:

> We built the alternative strategy. Forget about violence. Run this and you'll make more progress. I kept talking about a new accommodation for communities and people to live and work together. In time, let the new situation evolve, whatever it's going to be. The best foundation, I believed, would be built on consent because the unionist community was suspicious of the IRA. It would have to be consent.

That January there was much debate in the Irish, British and American media about whether or not Gerry Adams' request for a visa to visit the United States should be granted. The taoiseach manipulated the situation to show republicans the benefits that would accrue if they were to find an accommodation with his 'new strategy'. He phoned President Clinton personally to argue that, with strict limitations, Adams should be allowed to enter the United States. When Clinton granted the visa, it sent a clear signal to the IRA Army Council that joining the peace process paid dividends. On 1 February, Gerry Adams arrived in New York, his visit circumscribed by stringent conditions: there was to be no fundraising, he was confined to New York, and there was to be no moving outside the agreed agenda.

The Ulster Unionist Party, too, was stirring and had woken from its pre-Anglo-Irish Agreement permafrost mentality. James Molyneaux had claimed, in an interview with *The Scotsman*, that he had succeeded in getting rid of Dublin proposals for all-Ireland structures from the Joint Document, since Fergus Finlay had kept the Ulster Unionists abreast of developments, initially through Archbishop Robin Eames of the Church of Ireland; but the *Irish News* of 2 February carried a report in which the Irish government challenged his claim. In the same edition, the leader column called for an IRA ceasefire to be the next step in the search for peace.

Loyalist military leaders remained suspicious of the IRA and what they might do in the coming months. They needed to know if the republican movement was genuine in its search for peace. They gave Ervine a remit to test whatever emanated from the other side, analyse any utterances and statements, and to seek out any hidden meaning that might indicate dirty deals or betrayals. The leaders were serious about wanting peace, but needed to be certain that others were, too. They were determined to arrive at a maximum understanding of the nuances of diverse opinion within nationalism and republicanism throughout Ireland, which are fragmentary rather than monolithic, and, in return, to deliver the loyalist argument. At times they found themselves in a miasma of mistrust and insecurity, frustrating attempts to find a way out of the morass of guerrilla warfare. Where Ervine, Spence, Hutchinson and others found valid avenues, they pursued their objectives confidently and solidly, and shared knowledge among themselves, having garnered it from their independent explorations.

In March 1994, Ervine and others travelled to Dublin to meet Chris Hudson. Usually, Ervine travelled with the freedom to act as he saw fit, but, in this specific instance, he carried a message with the direct authority of the UVF leadership. He asked Hudson to set up a meeting with Fergus Finlay, at which loyalists would deliver 'the big prize': peace. The CLMC was prepared to call a ceasefire before the IRA. Hudson was sceptical that such a meeting could be arranged, since the Dublin government had refused to meet with the IRA before they had called a ceasefire, but he went ahead. He phoned Ervine back two days later to say that Fergus Finlay had agreed to a meeting. Then, to Hudson's uncomprehending frustration, the loyalists went cool for two months. He never found out why, though he suspected they may have felt that the meeting had been too easily achieved and that perhaps they were exposing themselves to manipulation.

The cause of loyalist disenchantment lay in the North. Based upon analysis which concluded that the IRA had nowhere else to go and from information received from an impeccable cross-community source, they knew the IRA was heading towards a ceasefire. However, loyalists also learned indirectly, from a church person whom they assumed had the ear of government, that the IRA was insisting upon one condition: they were going to go on a ten-day blitz. The loyalist response was, if that's the case, in any future scenario a loyalist ceasefire would only happen within a reasonably short time after an IRA ceasefire had been called and loyalists were satisfied that it would hold. Albert Reynolds received that message, both directly and indirectly. The IRA threat was interpreted as a deliberate gesture, treating with contempt the statement made in January by the CLMC which acknowledged the legitimacy of the nationalist aspiration to a United Ireland by democratic means.

Was the IRA threat genuine at such a sensitive time? The UVF commander had his doubts, and his speculations are symptomatic of the potential for treachery that inhabited the neurotic world of negotiations. Perhaps the British government wanted to delay a ceasefire, or certain government agencies working to their own agenda may not have wanted a ceasefire at all. Which is why Ervine, Spence and Hutchinson, with the valued back-up of trusted and responsible people in civil society like Roy Magee, had to go to extraordinary lengths to cross-reference information, then double-check to eliminate any possibility of a mistake, at every stage on the journey to peace.

Nevertheless, loyalist analysis of the inevitability of an IRA ceasefire held up, and planning for its eventuality continued. Its timing was uncertain, but loyalism's reaction was going to be pivotal to the future of the Union. The PUP put this argument to the military side: who was going fight for the Union when unionism ran away from negotiations following a ceasefire? Was it to be left in the hands of Albert Reynolds, John Major, John Alderdice of the Alliance Party and Gerry Adams? Loyalism needed to establish the terms on which the IRA would stop the war. Loyalists had to be sure why the Rolls-Royce of terrorist machines, as Ervine termed the IRA, was giving up the armed struggle.

There was no trust between loyalists and the IRA, but Ervine and the other PUP politicians were in the business of trying to evaluate how much trust could be placed upon the Provos' intentions. A series of discussions followed, which would have caused consternation had they been placed in the public domain at that time. On most occasions communication was made indirectly with the Irish government. Unionists did not do such a thing, but loyalists did, to find out what was going on. Fergus Finlay was on the phone 'a lot, and talking a lot' with Ervine. Finlay met with Gusty Spence. Subsequently, Finlay met other loyalists. Roy Magee had a direct line of communication to Albert Reynolds. The UVF commander spoke with Chris Hudson, who forwarded the UVF's messages to the Irish government and then communicated back. In this way, through a network of contacts, information was cross-referenced by the loyalists in order to discover what, if anything, would be given to the IRA in return for their calling a ceasefire.

An indication of loyalists' thoroughness was when Gusty Spence dispatched himself to Dublin to meet a former Fianna Fáil leader, a hate-figure among unionists for over a decade, 'to hear', as Spence said, 'old, respected attitudes', whose 'commentary on the situation didn't cause any consternation'.

Local sources in Belfast were not neglected. In one attempt to hear what the Provos were thinking, the loyalists had some contact with Clonard Monastery on the Falls Road, the headquarters of the Redemptorist Order, which had an honourable history of using its resources to broker a cessation of violence. Moreover, Ervine ventured into west Belfast to see a group called Cornerstone, on the Springfield Road, formed by both Catholic and Protestant clergy in the area, to try to understand what was going on there. As all those discussions were taking place, loyalist politicians were at the same time trying to analyse and interpret the daily deluge of incidents and utterances, while going through a process of consultation with the UVF. As Ervine said, it was a time when time was a scarce commodity: 'A twenty-seven-hour day would not have been long enough, but a twenty-four-hour day had to be enough.'

They were working hard to be prepared for a peace that a Provos' ceasefire would herald, but when and how that ceasefire would come about presented the problem. Would the Provos take their bow with a 'spectacular' or the rumoured blitz?

Chillingly, the military wing of loyalism got its retaliation in first, as if to warn the Provisionals off. On the evening of 18 June 1994, as most of Ireland was settling back to watch a long anticipated World Cup soccer match between the Republic of Ireland and Italy, in the USA, a UVF unit entered O'Toole's bar in Loughinisland, County Down, and mowed down six innocent Catholics. It was a lethal demonstration of the UVF's intent to 'be more ruthless and determined' than its enemies.

Ervine's fears about an IRA 'coup' were confirmed on 11 July, the eve of the central day in the unionist calendar. The Provos assassinated Ray Smallwoods, the man who had been attempting to politicise the UDA in much the same manner as Ervine was doing with the UVF. To them Smallwoods' execution was an act of provocation which confirmed to Ervine a core tactic of the republican movement's political strategy: 'Loyalism, as far as the Provos were concerned, was not meant to be part of the situation. We were not meant to be an issue.' Ervine knew that the IRA Army Council regarded itself as 'the legitimate government of the island of Ireland. Their enemy is the Brits.'

Ervine believed that republicans expected the scenario to be:

> Adams and his cohorts would all go to talks on the future of Northern Ireland because unionism would be reticent, run away from ceasefires, run away from the countenance of change, run away from dialogue, jump up and down and pull their hair out as Prods killed Taigs, while Gerry Adams swanned the world's stage as a peacemaker. The British prime minister would stand at the despatch box and say, 'We must move to crush unionists' unreasonable attitudes towards the peace.' That was what was envisaged by the Provos, believe me.

Ervine's analysis, which he put to the UVF, was that if that were to happen, then it would be the beginning of the end for unionism. The UVF had also accepted Gusty Spence's tenet: 'Any opponent who is predictable is doomed to failure.' So loyalism refused to react according to republican expectations.

Even more urgently for Ervine, his name was on the hit list alongside Ray Smallwoods'. The IRA had demonstrated that it did not want leaders from the Protestant working-class communities to play a role in post-ceasefire negotiations. On the day of Smallwoods' murder, Ervine phoned Chris Hudson to say that he believed the IRA wanted him dead, too. Hudson agreed. 'David Ervine was probably, for the Provos, the biggest hate-figure for a fair bit of time, because this guy is articulate, looks good, puts across a Protestant working-class point of view, is generous, is putting out the hand of friendship, yet spent time in prison and is close to the UVF.'

Being a target was nothing new for Ervine. This time, however, there was no full-scale family evacuation. Precautions were taken, but their effectiveness was necessarily limited, because he now moved in a semi-public arena. At first, Ervine stayed sometimes in other people's houses, while Jeannette remained at home. Her great fear was for the two boys.

A recurring nightmare was that one of them would be mistaken for his father and shot during a night-time raid. Really, there was nowhere else for Ervine to go. He was not complacent, but would not do the Provos' work for them by absenting himself. So he returned home to protect his family and continued his work, albeit with prudence.

During this period, Sinn Féin was holding a series of 'peace commissions' around the country to maintain cohesion among its membership by canvassing opinion about ending the war. Hudson attended one: 'I made a submission. "The loyalist paramilitaries have learned so much, so well, from you people. Everything you do this week, they'll do three months later. Mark my words, they have the ability to do it. I know they will make horrendous judgements on how to retaliate to your war." Somebody from Sinn Féin said to me, "How do you know this?" I said, "Trust me that I know."'

Hudson knew because he had expressed his abhorrence of loyalist atrocities to UVF faces and been told.

> I know from talking to UVF people. They said to me that the decision to take out Catholics in large numbers is wrong, but they weren't going to blow up a street, shoot policemen. They wanted to hit the soft underbelly of the nationalist community, so the Provos could know that, though they could bomb London, shoot an RUC man, could wipe out three or four soldiers, their community would pay the price.

In Dublin, in early August, Albert Reynolds was now facing a problem which threatened to bring his peace edifice crashing down. The IRA held a special conference in Letterkenny to discuss their conditions for calling a ceasefire. Republicans disputed the interpretation of proposed referenda in the Downing Street Declaration. The two governments had declared for two separate referenda, North and South, which could not be aggregated. Loyalists agreed, since it ensured that nothing could be implemented without the public assent of unionism. Republicans saw a discrete referendum in the North as being tantamount to a unionist veto and clung to their preference for one combined referendum on the island of Ireland. A negative response was relayed from Letterkenny to the Irish government.

Reynolds determined to hold his ground. Indeed, he sent a clear message to the IRA that if they did not call a ceasefire, the whole thing was off. John Hume and Dick Spring were pessimistic. As August drew to a close, the IRA announced they would be on ceasefire from midnight on 31 August.

The loyalist politicians and leading militarists took a benign view of it. For a start, a ceasefire is never refused, and they were ready to take the IRA at its word. Ervine, accompanied at times by Billy Hutchinson, at others by a member of the Orange Order or by the UVF commander, had visited unionist politicians in their homes to explain how loyalism intended to deal with the expected IRA ceasefire. Ervine had held telephone conversations with John Bruton, leader of Fine Gael in the Dáil. Roy Magee had been in shuttle diplomacy with Albert Reynolds, and Ervine was privy to that communication. Through Chris Hudson, Fergus Finlay and others they had become acquainted with the views of the Republic's government and politicians of all parties and knew future policy towards the North would be driven by the principle of consent. They were confident that a rapacious Southern state was a figment of unionist imagination, summarised in Hudson's description of the concerns of the man in the Dublin street: 'There is no great desire down here for a United Ireland. We do not lie in bed thinking, "Oh my God, when are we going to get a United Ireland?" We lie in bed worrying about our mortgage, worrying about our jobs. The historical image of a predatory South, nurtured from generation to generation by unionists, had not stood up to loyalist scrutiny. Now many, like Ervine, recognised that the Republic was not the problem.'

Ervine's opinions were not widespread among unionists. A feeling of betrayal pervaded their community, not least because they did not trust their own British government, nor the secretary of state, and most certainly not the Northern Ireland Office, which was nominally in charge of their welfare. When the IRA announced its ceasefire, unionists concluded they must have been betrayed: 'They must have given in to the IRA.' Demands were made of loyalists to make a violent response. Instead, they moved to quell the response upon which they believed the IRA ceasefire was predicated. When men came into the PUP office on the Shankill Road looking for guns, they were given pots of paint to go out and write on the gable walls: 'The Union is safe.' If they were expected to react irrationally and go on the rampage, they would not. Instead, they wrote on a gable wall: 'The Loyalist People of the Shankill Accept the Unconditional Surrender of the IRA.'

It was critical, too, that loyalists 'talked up the Union'. Billy Hutchinson's coming out the next day and saying, 'The Union is safe and nothing to worry about' had immeasurable significance in preventing a violent reaction. His opinion carried weight. Ervine, Spence and Hutchinson were saying to their people: 'Hold on a minute. It's not as you imagine.'

Was Ervine's analysis of republican expectations the product of a fevered imagination? Hudson does not think so. He met Ervine's view among media intelligentsia sympathetic towards republicans in the South, who, in their treatment of the IRA, expounded its intelligence and vision. However, when they turned their attention upon loyalists they were scornful, dismissing them as reactionary thugs and unthinking blockheads. They forecast that when the IRA called a ceasefire, the loyalist thugs would go on killing Catholics because that's all they knew how to do, had no real leadership and would wipe out their own so-called new thinkers.

A couple of days after the announcement of the IRA ceasefire, Hudson met Ervine and others in Belfast. He had with him a note from Fergus Finlay which said that there were no secret deals with the IRA. In response to Albert Reynolds' even-handedness, the loyalists told Hudson that, in time, they, too, would call a ceasefire. They could not yet name a date, but it would happen. Like the republicans, they would require a period of time to convince everyone.

In September 1994 a period of consultation took place within loyalism. It was slow because loyalism, more often than not, is a factional and fractious organism. Ervine was a pivotal figure in this necessarily protracted procedure: 'We had to be very slow, extremely deliberate, to make sure the consultation process had taken place, and no one was left out. It was hard work. I was travelling the countryside going everywhere and anywhere, no question unanswered, and made clear: "If you have a problem, ring me. I'll come and see you, whatever." That's the way it had to be done.'

The process was not without complications. Ervine's door was accessible to anyone. Near the end of September, Billy Wright, in charge of the Mid-Ulster Brigade of the UVF, arrived on Ervine's doorstep and demanded a ceasefire, as if it were in Ervine's gift to deliver. Ervine explained to Wright that there was a process going on and it would take time. Wright, passionate about the matter, unwittingly created problems when he spoke to journalists whose newspapers carried his story. It created difficulties because the UDA was angry that somebody was talking when nothing had been agreed. The UDP was in immediate contact with Ervine. A lot of people in different areas were involved, and not just the UVF leadership. The UDA and the Red Hand Commandos all had difficulties in selling a ceasefire to their members.

In a delicate process, Wright was not the only person to rock the boat. James Molyneaux spoke publicly about the longing for a loyalist ceasefire. This, too, had the effect of hampering the leadership in its attempts to explain and educate paramilitaries about the benefit of a ceasefire. By one stage, Ervine had compiled a twelve-page dossier which documented proposals about the ceasefire. So fraught had the situation become that, to counter internal opposition and security forces' agents, and for the sake of his own health, Ervine had to secrete a single page in each of twelve separate houses.

Against this strained and nerve-wracking backdrop, Ervine sought to put in place the final part of a case that he could sell to the UVF with absolute certainty in his own mind. Once that could be resolved, a loyalist ceasefire would be imminent.

In Dublin, a familiar emissary from the North arrived again in Albert Reynolds' office:

> The guy came in and sat down in front of me. He says, 'I've a message from Gusty Spence.'
>
> 'What's the message?'
>
> 'He wants to know what you're going to do for them, now that you know what you're doing for the other crowd.'
>
> Says I, 'What's he want? What's he expecting me to do to gain their confidence? What does he expect me to do?'
>
> He says, 'I don't know. I'm delivering a message.'
>
> I said, 'That message is so vague, it's no good. I want to know.'

And he said, 'Maybe I'll go back.'

'No,' says I, 'here you are.' And pushed him over the phone on my desk. 'Here you are. Ring Gusty Spence and I'll listen to him.' This is before they had any ceasefire or anything.

So he [Spence] says, 'What are you going to do for us?'

And I said, 'It's as simple as this, Gusty: I'm talking to you now when you have no ceasefire. I didn't talk to the other people before their ceasefire. I'll meet you tonight, tomorrow morning. I'll talk to you and meet you before a ceasefire, because I want you to understand that I'm doing something I shouldn't do. I didn't do it for the others, and I shouldn't do it for you. I think I'm entitled to go the extra few steps along the way to make sure.'

And he says, 'You want to fix a meeting?'

I said, 'Yes. I'll have it tonight, tomorrow morning, tomorrow evening.'

He said, 'No, I can't.'

'Well,' I said, 'OK, you name the day.'

He said, 'Saturday morning.'

'Where?'

He said, 'Halfway. Dundalk or Newry, or somewhere.'

'No, Gusty. No Dundalk. No Newry. Dublin.'

And he said, 'Ah now, you're pushing it on. You're making us go the whole way. You won't even meet us halfway.'

'I'll tell you why and then you can change your mind if you wish. If I go to Dundalk or Newry, or anywhere else, everybody'll know. I don't have any problem with going to either of those places, and my security people will be trailing. I have a back-up car. Every member of the security forces, around Dundalk and along the way, are going to be notified. So it cannot be a private meeting.'

He said, 'Well, how are you going to shake them?'

'If it's in Dublin, I'll give you the name of a hotel where you can drive into the basement. You can come in a lift to the very top floor, where nobody'll see you. I'll either walk, or be driven down there personally. There'll be no security. Security won't even know where I am. That's the best I can

do. If you want it to be made public, it'll be made public.
If you want it quiet and private and nobody knows, this is
the way to do it.'

He said, 'OK.'

'See you at eleven o'clock on Saturday.'

That was it.

Spence and Ervine drove to meet the taoiseach in a hotel in Dublin.
What was Ervine seeking that was so vitally important that he would
leave the North at a tense and nervy period for loyalism? Albert
Reynolds explains:

> I'll tell you what he was clearing up. The main thing he
> wanted was the principle of consent. I told him that I'd made
> it clear to the nationalist and republican movement that
> everything was predicated on the principle of consent. I laid
> it on the line. 'I'm not going one inch forward unless you
> stand over the principle of consent.' They thought I wouldn't
> carry it through my own party down here, because no
> taoiseach, or Fianna Fáil leader, had ever laid it on the line.

So that's what they went back with: the principle of consent.

Ervine's phrase 'more than opinions' now takes on greater defini-
tion. He had achieved a guarantee for the democratic continuation of
the Union. It was at the outset an audacious ambition for working-
class unionists, but they had, indeed, secured to their satisfaction the
Union with Britain through contacts with the perceived enemy, the
government of the state they considered to be the antithesis of empire,
of commonwealth, of their Britishness.

When the contents of this meeting, of which Ervine disclosed neither existence nor detail, are laid out before him, he states:

> People were very friendly and very reasonable, but that
> wasn't why I went. It was so that I could get guarantees,
> and those guarantees were achieved. You can't sell cease-
> fires on a nod and a wink. Unfortunately, I think Adams
> did sell his ceasefire on a nod and a wink, and that's why
> it didn't last. The loyalist ceasefire was not sold on a nod
> and a wink. The loyalist ceasefire was sold on copper-
> fastened guarantees, from me.

Gusty Spence stated that Ervine was 'pivotal' in bringing about the loyalist ceasefire. This view receives conditional support from the UVF commander: 'Very impressive, very articulate. Something that hadn't been in existence as far as we were concerned.' However, in the final analysis, the UVF used its own judgement, though the commander does admit that Ervine 'certainly would have had more than his fair share of influence. They were quite happy with his analysis of the situation, what he was prepared to do for the UVF, or say for the UVF. And, obviously, quite happy with his ability, which couldn't be faulted.'

On 13 October 1994, the Combined Loyalist Military Command announced a universal loyalist ceasefire of all operational activities as from midnight. Importantly, at the insistence of Spence and the PUP, a 'no first strike' policy was attached. Republicans would have to break their ceasefire before loyalist paramilitaries could resume operations.

MEETINGS HERE, THERE, AND OVER THERE

WHY WERE THE PUP initiatives successful? Ervine's ability to influence people lies in his talent to tackle the essentials of an issue with generosity, and a flair for words and images. He has a knack for the apt phrase. Roy Magee recalled an Ervine riposte when he had been criticised for talking to Sinn Féin: 'Republicanism is not contagious.'

Fergus Finlay was impressed by Ervine's direct simplicity: 'The first time I met Ervine, he said to me, "I would never expect you to feel less Irish in order to make me feel more British, but, by Christ, I never want you to ask me to be less British so that you can be happy to be Irish." I must say it had a profound effect upon me. I haven't even quoted it as well as he said it. It seemed to be one of those obvious remarks, where you say to yourself, "Why didn't I think of that?" '

Albert Reynolds appreciated a civil and courteous directness with no flannel: 'They told me straight out, "Look, there's areas we wouldn't agree with you, but there are areas where we all have common ground." They agreed that people have a right to live where they wanted to live and have a right to pursue any religious persuasion they wanted, that they had no problem with equal opportunity and equal treatment for everybody, for they weren't even getting it themselves.'

Reynolds found that straightforward approach conducive to negotiation: 'Ervine's an honest guy. He puts it all out on the table, and
that's what he did with me the first time. First of all, we saw we were
only interested in peace. Let's see what talking and dialogue bring.'

Still, there were occasions when the loyalist politicians had had to
be forceful and persistent in demanding their right to enter discussions
and make their voices heard. In August, a few days before the republicans declared a ceasefire, an Irish-American delegation led by former
Congressman Bruce Morrison visited Belfast. They held a three-hour
discussion with Sinn Féin but could find no place on their agenda for
talks with loyalists, who pestered them for a meeting. They were
finally offered an appointment at 7 a.m., on the last day of the visit.
Spence and Ervine arrived well before the appointed hour at a hotel
in the Queen's University area. Loyalists reminded members of the
delegation that to ignore the unionist case was to renege on a core
American concept: impartiality. The loyalist politicians were listened
to over a long breakfast discussion, during which new and favourable
impressions were made on both sides.

One negotiator has an interesting opinion about the psychology
which motivates Ervine, Spence, Hutchinson and other ex-UVF paramilitaries, which may explain their often-remarked-about positivity:

> There's a striking difference between them and the kind of
> Provos I've met. It's in the eyes. Spence, Ervine and
> Hutchinson have the same kind of light in their eyes. And
> they are all men who, in my opinion, have gone through
> some kind of personal inner redemption. They've come to
> terms with whatever they've done in the past, or whatever
> they've believed in, and they've learnt from it, where the
> Provos haven't. The Provos have been killed by it. In them
> you see kind of dead pools, nothing there at all, like a light
> gone out in the soul. It's what convinces me, more than
> anything else, that these are men who have been damaged
> by the things they have done. There's some kind of spiri-
> tual destruction.

With the loyalist ceasefire in place, the PUP was poised to capitalise
upon a long-awaited opportunity to make an impact on the political
developments which were likely to follow. Billy Hutchinson had long

held the view that loyalists needed some way of gaining widespread sympathy and understanding, something that would catapult them into the political arena the way the hunger strike had done for Sinn Féin. The declaration of their ceasefire did that by providing an opportunity to expose a new side to loyalism, arousing interest in its politics.

Loyalists entered a busy phase and went wherever they thought they could make some difference. They made a breakthrough with the first of several visits to the United States, in October 1994, shortly after the ceasefire announcement. The invitation was a dividend from the constructive encounter in Belfast with Bruce Morrison's Irish-American group. From their knowledge of Irish history, the PUP delegation, which included Ervine, knew that Irish republicanism, and also Irish nationalism, had always drawn its money and armaments from America. What they had to do was to try to counter the long-held perception by Americans that the IRA was not only fighting for the freedom of Ireland, but was fighting for civil and human rights as well. Ervine and the others wanted to make clear that the IRA 'was fighting not only the security forces, but also the unionist population'.

Bill Flynn, one of those influential Irish-Americans challenged by the PUP to demonstrate American fairness and impartiality, prepared the itinerary and opened doors. He and his staff arranged meetings and seminars for the PUP delegation. They went to Harvard University, spoke to the Foreign Relations Committee of Congress, went to Capitol Hill and spoke to senators and their staffs, even to Teddy Kennedy's aide-de-camp. They also met the key figure in the State Department responsible for Northern Ireland. They got their story across. After that, American perceptions began to change.

Interestingly, the UVF commander, also in the PUP delegation, saw an unexpected opportunity while in the US. Their visits could be a way to send messages to republicans at home. Obviously, loyalists would not talk directly to the IRA or Sinn Féin, but they knew that the Americans they met were in touch, and any fears or ideas they had could be fed through the Americans to republicans.

Ordinary working-class Protestants articulating their own views played a significant part in opening American eyes to a more complex Northern Ireland political situation than they had previously considered. Loyalism started to influence some mainstream perspectives. Government circles included the loyalist perspective on the Irish

peace agenda. Some influential Irish-Americans respected that loyalists had a case they had never heard before, and media circles treated
their views in a balanced fashion. C-SPAN television channel, for
example, broadcast live the loyalists' address to a meeting at the
Catholic Boston College.

The UVF commander, and especially Ervine, gained credibility in
US political circles and dispelled many misconceptions. However, they
knew full well that they could not undo centuries of history and were
not going to dislodge Irish republicanism's position in the States.
What they had sought, and achieved, was an opportunity to present
fairly their side of the case and, in the process, to advance their own
position. Repeat invitations were to follow in succeeding months.
Once political America heard a reasonable and articulate unionist
case, its instincts moved to include this fresh voice from a significant
section of the 'Irish' population.

The entry of loyalist politicians in October 1994 into US policy
matters revived a potential line of communication, discarded by President Clinton in 1992. During his first presidential campaign, Clinton
had indicated some sympathy for Irish-American clamour to send a
US envoy to Ireland. Albert Reynolds had told him that it was the
wrong time, mainly because mainstream unionism was not yet prepared to talk peace with an outsider. Besides gaining credibility for the
unionist cause in the USA and winning acceptance as a bona fide political entity in their own right, the loyalist visit opened a way for Americans to become involved positively in the search for a peaceful
settlement in Ireland.

While loyalists focused on transatlantic matters, the Forum for
Peace and Reconciliation, in Dublin, set up by Albert Reynolds to
encourage republicans into the democratic process, began its public
sittings at the end of October. The PUP stayed away on the grounds
that the Forum was being held in a foreign jurisdiction. At that stage
they could not be seen to give a submission in public to a body that,
as unionists understood it, was holding the hand of republicans. For
the PUP alone to have attended would have damaged its prospects as
a unionist party. In any case, sympathetic parties in Dublin supplied
them with all relevant papers.

Yet, on their return from the United States, such is the way politics
works, one of the first tasks of loyalists was to travel privately to

Dublin, where John Bruton had replaced Albert Reynolds as taoiseach. This time, Billy Hutchinson accompanied Spence and Ervine. His job, as a fresh mind, was to assess Bruton, to test for his adherence to commitments already given by Reynolds' government. Ervine explained Hutchinson's role as 'trying to get a read of the man, and where exactly the practical issues were. I would have talked a lot, whereas Billy's job was to intercede where I would have missed gaps and, also, to make sure he was reading the man. We just couldn't make a mistake.' The loyalists found no reason afterwards to be vexed.

Bruton was impressed by the PUP delegation, particularly when Ervine told him: 'The unionist people represent, in themselves, the British presence in Ireland. It's not the British state that represents the British presence. It's the unionist people.' In their not relying on the British state to underpin who they are lies the originality of the PUP's intervention into unionist politics. It was a significant departure from reliance upon childish slogans, patriotic flags and simple posters to state an identity. The PUP behaved like grown-ups who, after mature reflection, chose responsibility rather than dependence. As Bruton also saw: 'I think, equally, what David Ervine has come to terms with is the fact that the British edition of the document reads "no selfish strategic or economic interest in Northern Ireland". There is a valid argument put by unionists about the position of the word 'selfish', which appears before 'strategic' in the British statement, and a following comma, which Southern politicians tend to leave out, but essentially Bruton's point about Ervine is sound.

Secondly, Bruton found: 'Ervine has the capacity to express unionism in a sense that is genuinely trying to understand the fears, concerns and identity of nationalists. He doesn't see nationalists as "others". He sees them as people with whom he must coexist.'

Ervine's contribution also placed a large question mark against the nationalist, and in particular the republican, conception of what the Northern problem is about. For Bruton this is:

> . . . very challenging in a fundamental way to nationalism,
> because the traditional nationalist view has been that it's
> the British state that is 'holding on' to Northern Ireland
> against the wishes of the Irish people. This focus on the
> British state has meant that nationalists have avoided

coming to terms with the existence of the unionist people
and their simultaneous Irishness and Britishness. David
Ervine was one of the first unionists, actually, to be able to
put the thing in those very strong and clear terms.

Bruton contrasts this fresh, original thinking with that of republicans, whom he characterised as being obsessed with the issue of
British sovereignty: 'They have not revised that view at all, and have
not come to terms with the point that David Ervine has made, that
the real British presence is the unionist people.'

From Dublin, the PUP returned to a domestic scene which, over the
next busy twelve months or so, saw for them an incremental gain in
political respectability on several fronts and a move into the mainstream of politics in the North. In December, for the first time, loyalists were invited to exploratory talks with civil servants from the
Northern Ireland Office. Ervine and Hutchinson were the PUP delegates. It was not the first time either of them had had dealings with NIO
officials: they had dealt with them in Long Kesh. Memories remained
of unreasonable and devious bureaucrats, so the two men made sure
that they had prepared themselves thoroughly. The PUP held a planning meeting and drew up a list of issues they wanted to talk about:
socio-economic matters, prisons, constitutional issues, formal talks
(including with Sinn Féin) and, above all, setting a timetable to get into
those talks. Then Ervine surprised everyone by suggesting that Hutchinson lead the delegation to Stormont. He said: 'I'm not abdicating
responsibility, but David Ervine isn't the PUP. It can't be a one-man
party. We need to have somebody else.' All of the NIO officials whom
Ervine and Hutchinson knew would be present had had dealings with
Hutchinson at one time or another, either in negotiations in the prisons to get men out or to end special category status, or in fundraising
for community projects. So Hutchinson was the right man for the job;
he would gain more experience and the party would grow a little.

For characters who are not short of self-confidence, even Ervine
and Hutchinson had nervous second thoughts right up to the night
before the meeting. By their own account, their trepidation was banished once the meeting got underway and they realised that this job
was well within their capacity. Afterwards Ervine and Hutchinson
were walking back out along a corridor at Parliament Buildings when

suddenly Hutchinson slapped Ervine on the back and said: 'These people are easy meat. I thought they were Las Vegas card sharks, but they're not.' The civil servants had revealed everybody's plan to them, with the exception of Sinn Féin's, and the PUP men could see that the established unionist parties did not have a clue where they were going.

Hutchinson took the media conference on the steps of Stormont. When he was asked where the PUP received its mandate from – they had only one elected local councillor then, and neither Hutchinson nor Ervine had yet been elected anywhere – he answered in a memorable phrase: 'Our mandate is the silence of the guns.'

For a party that had developed from tiny to small, those first exploratory talks proved to be an enormous boost. The internal leadership of the PUP and their public profile were strengthened.

After five months without violence, the 'Frameworks for the Future' document, published by the British and Irish governments, appeared on 22 February 1995. Its stated aim was to 'carry the Talks forward to a new beginning'. The talks referred to were those aborted in 1991, whose agreed aim had been 'a new beginning for relationships within Northern Ireland, within the island of Ireland and between the peoples of these islands'. The Frameworks Document stated that the main political objective was to bring about 'a comprehensive settlement', based upon 'the principles in the Joint Declaration of December 1993'.

The Frameworks Document caused consternation among unionists, who in the main rejected it as meeting nationalist needs to the detriment of Northern Ireland's constitutional position within the United Kingdom. It was also a huge obstacle for Ervine and the peace strategists of the PUP. Loyalists who had been persuaded by the Joint Declaration in 1993 were now vehemently opposed to the 'Frameworks'. Billy Wright visited Ervine and demanded an immediate end to the ceasefire, because 'loyalism had been shafted'. Wright said, according to Ervine, 'that the game was up and that it was all about a United Ireland'.

Fergus Finlay explained away unionist rejection by claiming that unionists, in the main, did not bother to read the document. If Finlay believed that is what happened, then the Republic's government had just repeated its self-admitted folly of the Anglo-Irish Agreement of

1985. If the Downing Street Declaration was the door to their political future, the Frameworks document opened it, and unionists were repelled by the decor. Just to read one extract, on page 17:

> . . . there would be a new North/South body or bodies, an interparliamentary forum, an administrative support unit to service the body (or bodies) and the forum, and day-to-day North/South co-operation and communication between Departments, and between counterparts with relevant executive authority at the political level. The source of their authority would stem from the administrations in Belfast and Dublin. . .

This was enough for the unionist man in the street to shy away from this offer of new political accommodation, and it cast suspicions over possible Dublin hypocrisy about good faith in previous dealings.

Ervine rebuts Finlay's allegation. The document was analysed line by line by the PUP itself, and then in consultation with the UVF leadership. Together they worked through the document, 'throwing out, as far as we were concerned, bits that we couldn't live with, identifying bits where there was a requirement for clarification and understanding, and therefore further analysis'.

PUP credibility in the process was reflected in meetings during 1995 at increasingly senior levels. On 22 March they, together with the UDP, had a meeting with Michael Ancram, minister of state in the Northern Ireland Office, followed by another a week later. On 12 September they met the secretary of state, Sir Patrick Mayhew. The agenda at the meetings centred on a battery of issues submitted by the PUP and UDP, as mentioned by Ervine above. Spence was well aware that the British government had met everyone else involved in the process, even the IRA, before meeting the PUP, and he could not fathom why their own government had not spoken to the people who could have offered valuable political analysis of UVF thinking.

There were publicly announced meetings in the North between the PUP and visiting delegations from parties in the Republic. On 15 May, Bertie Ahern, then leader of the opposition in the Dáil, met the PUP. On 23 October, Dick Spring, minister for foreign affairs, met them. Southern politicians were recognising publicly the regard Dublin had for the small unionist party in the unfolding political process.

Perhaps the stamp of approval most noticed by the unionist people occurred on 25 June, when the Prince of Wales, Prince Charles, arrived in Belfast for a round of engagements. During a visit to the Shankill Road, he shook hands with Billy Hutchinson. That common gesture brought into sharp relief Hutchinson's suitability to move among the highest in the community, his obvious talent to represent his people, and his ability to conduct himself graciously during public duties. The significance of this handshake was widely recognised by unionists in Northern Ireland, bestowing a kind of 'halo' effect on Hutchinson and elevating the working-class PUP politicians to a new status of respectability. By a delicious irony, on that same day, the Ulster Unionist Party resuscitated its Unionist Labour Group in an attempt to appeal to the working class.

While in public the PUP was weaving itself gradually into the political fabric of Northern Ireland, its politicians still had to operate at a clandestine level to some degree. They had taken personal risks to test further the requirements agreed with Reynolds and confirmed by Bruton. Loyalism now had to apply those tests at the extreme end of the nationalist spectrum. If a loyalist unilateral ceasefire was predicated upon loyalist paramilitary cohesion, then, equally, an eventual universal peaceful settlement demanded republican and loyalist understanding of fundamentals. Otherwise a move towards peace would likely fail. During 1995, Ervine, accompanied as usual by a colleague, had two separate secret meetings in the Republic. For him it was becoming extremely dangerous, since he was now better known. They met two people who purported to be able to speak on behalf of the Provisional IRA, but who, as Ervine cryptically described them, were not of an age and a demeanour that one would expect of active members of the IRA.

Ervine accepted the danger involved because he did not want to make a mistake in his analysis to the UVF. If extreme elements of republicanism were not involved, then the process would be flawed. Ervine realised that the republican movement is a broad church, broader than it is usually given credit for. The agenda was wide-ranging, responding to unpredictable events, on the basis of 'What comes next?' in times of change. He discussed with republicans or their agents commitment to issues like the principle of consent, the capacity of the republican movement to carry its supporters and a whole raft of issues relating to 'the pain of the violence we had gone through, and the pain we could potentially go through again'. Ervine and his colleague collated their information. They concluded that, although loyalism would find comfort in it, the principle of consent was going to be a major concession for republicanism, an outcome which had been implicit when Reynolds first introduced it.

The public round of talks continued into 1996 when, first, the Workers' Party from Dublin and then the SDLP met with the PUP in January. Through its distinctive voice, the PUP demonstrated diversity within unionism, despite serious suspicions and rivalry within its own community. However, to their dismay, Ervine, Spence, Hutchinson and others discovered that their party's unionist identity seemed to be disregarded by those in high places in Dublin, with consequences of almost catastrophic proportions for Ervine.

A PUP delegation, after a meeting on 6 February with Sir Patrick Mayhew, in which they discussed how talks could be moved forward, left late in the afternoon for Dublin in response to an invitation from the Irish Department of Foreign Affairs to dinner at Iveagh House, hosted by Dick Spring. Previously, both governments had been struggling to find a way of bringing all the Northern parties together into talks. The Ulster Unionists refused to sit down with Sinn Féin, and in frustration Dick Spring had privately proposed to Sir Patrick Mayhew that they should move forward by adopting 'proximity style' talks – where hostile parties are brought to one building but do not meet face to face and negotiate via intermediaries – which the American administration had used to achieve the Balkan peace accord at Dayton, Ohio, in 1995. Spring gave the British secretary of state a week to consider the matter, after which he would then 'go public'. The week of reflection was nearing its end as the PUP delegation – Ervine, Spence, Hutchinson and others – arrived at Iveagh House for a 'getting to know you evening'.

Afterwards Dick Spring and his officials considered things had gone very well. To begin, they had a meeting where Dublin was acquainted with some of the fundamentals which inform Ervine and the PUP's politics. Fergus Finlay remembers being struck by:

> . . . the class nature of his [Ervine's] politics, the fact that his politics were inextricably bound up with jobs and welfare,

and it wasn't just about the national question. All those things are extremely important to him, and to Gusty Spence. They are a point of departure in terms of their analysis of unionism because, again and again, they come back to the point that a working-class loyalist was never treated any better than a working-class 'Taig'.

The second thing that struck me was his confidence about his unionism, about his Britishness. He's at ease with it. He expects you to be at ease with it, and, once you are, you get on like a house on fire. You then talk about other things.

Finlay categorises the dinner afterwards as having been a great success: 'I have to say it was most convivial and delightful – great crack!' Clearly, the Irish considered things had gone very well.

That is not how any of the PUP delegation remembers the occasion. They were unanimous in their assessment of the evening: it was a disaster. One delegate, the UVF commander, was astounded by the attitudes of the Irish government people he met. He considered their opinions and arguments as simply 'lambasting unionism', especially David Trimble. He felt their Dublin hosts behaved as though the PUP was not a unionist party, thinking the PUP delegation would go along with them. The Dublin people appeared to have no notion that expressions like 'paymaster Britain' were anathema to the PUP. This inability to understand the loyalist position by people living 'only one hundred miles away' was to the loyalists a manifestation of the mono-culturist nature of Irish nationalism, which expects unionists one day to realise they have been deluding themselves all along, and that their nature as 'true' Irishmen will assert itself.

Ervine remembered it as a 'bad meeting'. He was offended at Dick Spring's opening arguments, with expressions like: 'The unionists will have to understand . . .' He thought this extremely insensitive, although he did not think Spring was aiming his remarks directly at them. Ervine felt the Dublin people went from the one extreme of patronising the loyalists to the other of admonishing unionism, without appreciating that they themselves were unionists. The loyalists felt the meeting was serving no useful purpose and that the Irish government people were just rehearsing hoary old arguments.

A contentious issue arose about the election of delegates to a forum to conduct negotiations. This was one proposal in a report by Senator George Mitchell, which had been elevated by John Major to the next essential step in the process. Northern nationalists and the Irish government wanted a speedy entry into talks by the political parties. The PUP agreed with Major, but sat in near silence while their hosts criticised this move. When Ervine asked five times what the alternative was to elections, Spring replied, 'Just call talks.' Things were bad up to this point and got worse as the meeting was coming to a conclusion. According to Spence, at the very last moment, when Finlay was helping him on with his coat, Spring's advisor confidentially dropped the bombshell that Spring was going public the next day with his Dayton-style proposal to get talks started in the North.

What rankled with the PUP was that when their delegation got back to Belfast the following day, they found themselves confronted by a media scrum, demanding answers on the Dayton proximity talks plan, when this had not been discussed at the Dublin dinner. They felt the Irish government had acted in bad faith and left the PUP looking foolish.

Ervine decided he would deal with the fuss head-on, and two days later, during the afternoon of 9 February, he fulfilled a speaking engagement at a grammar school in north Down. His last words to the sixth formers were, 'It is my belief that the war is over.' Afterwards he had arranged to deal with the fallout from the Iveagh House dinner and gave his account to the UVF. At 7 p.m. he received a telephone call that a massive bomb had been detonated at Canary Wharf in London. The IRA ceasefire was over.

On Monday of the following week, two community workers close to the PUP, who were in Dublin on business, robustly accosted Finlay about the events of the previous week, describing in clear terms the level of PUP dissatisfaction. Finlay insisted that he had, as a matter of fact, informed Spence of the specifics of Spring's announcement. The two men related this account when they got back to Belfast. Things then got very nasty for Ervine, 'to the point that elements of the UVF believed that I was playing dirty games'. Graffiti reading 'Who does Ervine think he speaks for? He doesn't speak for the men on the ground' were plastered all over part of the Shankill. Ervine concluded that someone wanted him dead. He did not believe that the

Irish government had 'set him up', just that their stupidity had confirmed the suspicions of him harboured by certain elements within the
UVF:

> I was in big trouble. At a meeting to thrash the matter out,
> I was going to be taken away and my head blown off. There
> were those who certainly wanted to do it. I was seen to be
> close to elements in the UVF leadership, but there were
> other elements rumbling in the background. This paint-pot
> stuff had been done with high ranking authority within the
> UVF. What happened was that the top man, and people like
> him, moved over and stood beside me, more or less to say,
> 'We dare you.' And they faced the opposition down. It was
> scary. I had a visit from the Special Branch to tell me the
> UVF were going to do me in. I let the UVF deal with it. It
> was bloodless. It was a question of people being faced down
> and a proper explanation of the situation given.

Political relationships are a brutal business. After Iveagh House, the
political initiation of the PUP was over. Relations with the Irish
government cooled to icy. Silences exist today. The Canary Wharf
bomb shattered buildings, ended two lives, changed attitudes and sent
shock waves through Reynolds' edifice for peace, leaving it teetering
towards collapse. A chastened Irish American, on hearing the news,
exploded in anger: 'Those guys have shafted my president.' But a
pragmatic PUP leadership doggedly resolved that loyalism would not
be deflected from the political struggle for a settlement.

WATERSHED ELECTIONS

P ROGRESSIVE UNIONISTS, AND key figures in the UVF leadership, too, knew that a violent response to the Canary Wharf explosion would inevitably blow away their hopes for an influence upon a political settlement. Their original analysis – that the republican movement had nowhere else to go but down the political path – still stood, even though as a consequence of Canary Wharf the Provos had excluded themselves from the political process.

In a paper entitled 'SCENARIO, For the Attention of the Combined Loyalist Military Command', which the PUP delivered as part of its political analysis to the loyalist paramilitaries in April 1996, an absolute commitment to the democratic process is stated:

> What is so wrong about democracy being the firmest and ONLY rebuttal to violence as well as the unswerving adherence to a principle which has stood us in good stead during many traumatic years?
>
> The PUP sees no contradiction when comparing democracy with justice, decency, honesty, and equality since they each are component parts of the other and the non-application of these human principles are anathema and the antipathy of democracy. So beyond any shadow of a doubt, the UNION IS SAFE so long as the majority of the

people of Northern Ireland so desire it and as the unionist population constitutes the greater number of our citizens that principle will not change and can at any time be re-enforced in any subsequent Referendum.

The PUP reiterated their warning against a return to violence, which would not only bring the security forces down upon their heads, but would also discredit loyalists' commitment to politics. It would also provide the IRA with an excuse to carry on its military campaign. The ultimate danger would be if 'a British Prime Minister stood at the Dispatch Box and explained to the United Kingdom population that there really is nothing he can do with the unionist people, and why he had mobilised the security services to crush union-ist and loyalist opposition to peace'. Later in the document, the PUP alerts the CLMC that loyalism will have an opportunity to prove they genuinely desire peace and not war, dialogue and not destruction: 'A general election is on the horizon.'

From before the two ceasefires and during the comparatively long period when violence was absent from the streets, the PUP had seen its position consolidated by talking its politics and had received pos-itive responses from civil society within the unionist community. They were not prepared to see those advances jeopardised. Importantly, they were aware of an imminent opportunity to make further progress. The PUP looked forward to elections to get into formal talks, the elections that Dick Spring had been so negative about.

Spence, Ervine, Hutchinson and other ex-prisoners like Snodden and Kinner were inextricably wedded to the political path. Violence as a panacea for all their political ills was a fake. They had suffered because they had resorted to violence. The social fabric of their work-ing-class, urban community had been degraded, its self-confidence left in shreds; it was friendless, without influence and increasingly iso-lated after decades of violent retaliation against perceived nationalist physical force. Suffering formed part of the daily diet. Comfort and a sense of security were scarce commodities. Everyone in Northern Ireland experienced pain to a lesser or greater degree, but among the unionist population it was felt most acutely in loyalist, working-class strongholds. The loyalist politicians were resolute that an alternative to such waste and destruction had to be found.

The CLMC accepted the PUP's political analysis, although it was difficult to rein back those hotheads in the UVF who desired to retaliate. While the well-rehearsed argument that loyalist violence was the Provos' ally held sway ('Why do the work of your enemies?') the critical factor came down to location. Quite simply, if the bomb that destroyed Canary Wharf had exploded within Northern Ireland, it would have been impossible to contain demands for revenge.

A first step towards the possibility of a more optimistic future presented itself in the shape of an election to a Northern Ireland Forum. The Ulster Unionists had argued that the ballot box was a prerequisite to their participation in all-party talks. They required a fresh mandate to enter into negotiations which would include republicans. Without an election, in their view, they would be handing over the mantle of unionism to Dr Paisley and the Democratic Unionist Party. The Irish government was opposed to holding elections, and the SDLP considered them unnecessary, a sop from the British government to David Trimble and the Ulster Unionists.

This election presented a formidable hurdle for the PUP from within the broad unionist constituency. Not the least of their problems, given the PUP leaders' background, was unionists' generally antagonistic attitude towards 'gunmen'. Was not scorn from her neighbours one of Jeanette Ervine's first fears when her husband was arrested? As Roy Magee explains: 'Among the working-class people, there is a tendency to believe their politicians should have clean hands, completely clean hands. In contrast to the republican community, where attitudes are quite different. In unionism they actually ostracised the people who took up arms.'

In the local media many unionists directed a spiteful word-game at the loyalist politicians. In radio phone-ins and across the letter pages of newspapers, correspondents declared that the sincerity of PUP politicians in wishing to bring an end to violence was bogus and that they must be rejected by all right-thinking people unless, like their critics, they used the C-word. The rolling controversy centred on the refusal of loyalist politicians to use the word 'condemn' when interviewed about terrorist beatings, bombing and murders. Besides being, for ex-paramilitaries, a core matter of self-respect, violence had been condemned for decades by various people, and that had not had the slightest effect on preventing it. Ex-paramilitaries were never going to lie down in public and bare their inner selves to those they considered self-righteous, as seemed to be demanded of them. It was too private a matter. The ex-paramilitaries were now trying to do something to improve the situation by acting politically, as they believed their vociferous critics should have been doing for decades. Some PUP activists took the view that it would be hypocritical to condemn actions which, at one time, they themselves had committed or had been prepared to commit. So to condemn was an easy and negative reaction. A more positive response was required. Loyalist ex-paramilitaries considered public demands for 'condemnation' from them as an evasion of responsibility by the very public which had created the conditions conducive to violence in the first place. Loyalists took a cynical view, too, of those unionist politicians who stridently exhorted loyalists to 'condemn' as engaging in patent exercises in political self-promotion.

The controversy affronted Ervine, who refused to ingratiate himself into a smug community: 'I'm pretty good with semantics. I'm good with language. I could go on and convince people that I'm condemning. I could actually use the word "condemn" and probably not do myself that much damage with the paramilitaries. But we measure on the basis of what is good for the argument that gets this society to accept responsibility for itself.' Ervine probably underestimates the effect his public use of 'condemn' would have had upon fellow loyalists.

Ervine has pointed out that just as he, and others, underwent a painful process of self-analysis in Long Kesh, so the wider unionist community needs to do likewise: 'We have to do it communally and individually. I'm sickened by the honeyed words of 'I condemn', but I hear no words of awareness of what society has done and its responsibility. It's always somebody else's fault, or somebody else's responsibiltiy, and that's why our critics get themselves into bellicose rantings. Nothing changes, of course. We're all complicit in this society. And the fear is coming to terms with the fact we are all complicit.'

The public seemed impressed by what they saw and heard on television and radio, or at least by the manner in which Ervine, Hutchinson and party leader Hugh Smyth presented themselves in the media, even though they intended to vote mechanically for the two traditional unionist parties. Allied to civility and courtesy, the PUP politicians looked well and could actually talk engagingly about political issues. They did not regurgitate the negative, cliché-ridden utterances churned out *ad nauseam* by the habitually grumpy faces of conventional unionism. They struck audiences as able, enjoying what they were doing and at ease before the microphones and cameras. The image was not false. What the audience saw and heard was honesty.

Edna Longley contrasted the media-friendly impact of the 'new' unionists with the exasperation caused by representatives of traditional parties: 'I do think that image and self-esteem are tied in together. It's quite extraordinary the insensitivity of some unionist politicians to this fact. Every time they go on national television they can't get this through their heads, whereas David Ervine can.'

The PUP, firm on the Union with Great Britain, left-leaning (with Clause Four of the old British Labour Party constitution written into its constitution) and conciliatory, positively welcomed its opportunity to debate unionism on two fronts.

First, it challenged unionism from within. A programme emphasising social policies, education, the health service and housing differed radically from the single issue unionism, 'the Border', which governed the outlook of the established parties and where tradition was master. The PUP considered that that mentality had led to an unthinking outlook, incapable of devising means to fashion changing circumstances. There was some humour when opponents labelled them 'card-carrying communists' again! The PUP policy-makers believed that the body of unionism had deteriorated to a vulnerable monolith which needed reform, through debate, to be able to describe better to itself what it stood for.

The PUP rejected the view that unionism is a political philosophy. Rather, it is a statement of identity: 'I am a citizen of the United Kingdom, without anti-Catholic or anti-Irish baggage.' Perhaps that was not the most effective sentence ever designed to garner traditional unionists' votes, and when Ervine was accused of not being unionist enough, he replied: 'The electorate has the right to evaluate our policy, but we, the Progressive Unionist Party, have the right to make the policy.' The PUP's conciliatory approach challenged the confrontational manner of the DUP. In addition, its class influence, summed up in Spence's phrase 'to create a caring society', challenged the middle-class attitudes which informed the UUP.

Secondly, the PUP challenged unionism to face up to the political task of devising a future for a divided Northern society. As Hugh Smyth said: 'There are half a million people who live in Northern Ireland who don't believe in the link with the United Kingdom and who are going to have to be accommodated. So how do we go about it?'

Determined upon an inclusive agenda, equality of rights and equality of opportunity, the PUP saw itself as a party of reconciliation and dialogue, committed to talking and negotiating with its partners in Northern Ireland. In this way, it sought to tackle the core problem felt by many fellow citizens: mutual antagonism to communities and their institutions. Acknowledging the real difficulties, they determined to move towards integration into an agreed society.

John Bruton described accurately the position of Ervine and the PUP: 'If you were to locate him in terms of the extent to which he is trying to reach out to the other side, you would have to put him very close to the Alliance Party. On the other hand, in terms of his identity with traditional unionist feelings, he's not too far from the heart of unionism.'

On 30 May 1996, the PUP placed itself before the electorate for the Forum. Constituencies were on the Westminster election pattern. The mainstream Ulster Unionists received over 180,000 votes and the Democratic Unionists over 140,000. The cross-community Alliance, with 49,176 votes, polled almost twice as heavily as the PUP, which received 26,082 votes, a mere 3.5% across Northern Ireland.

But the exercise was invaluable. Ervine and Hugh Smyth took seats in the Forum under the 'Top-Up' system devised to ensure the representation of small parties. The PUP qualified because they ranked seventh place in the first ten parties, which also included, below them, the UK Unionist Party, the Ulster Democratic Party and the Women's Coalition. The PUP was now in a position to exercise what it sought dearly, influence, though they had no delusions about exercising power. During the campaign they had been encouraged by a quotation, unattributed and heard on radio in a different context, with which they identified closely: 'Going out on a limb is where the fruit is. The fruit does not grow too close to the trunk.' A tangible return could now be shown to sceptics and enemies within loyalism.

At the beginning of June, the Northern Ireland Office extended invitations to nine parties to attend talks at Stormont (Sinn Féin was excluded because the IRA was still active) under the chairmanship of former US Senator George Mitchell. He had been opposed originally by both the UUP and DUP, but after discussions the UUP had relented, much to the venomous disgust of the DUP.

Ostensibly, the aim of the talks was to arrive at a political settlement agreeable to the blocs of nationalism and unionism. This objective was based on the assumption that there were mature politicians who would negotiate seriously and inclusively, but a culture of self-indulgence, nurtured under Direct Rule, had relieved many local politicians of the habits required for decision-making, persuasion and compromise, the real business of politics.

In June, outside negotiations, tension in the streets mounted. An active IRA was doing what it does best to exert influence, and a contentious Orange Order march at Drumcree loomed. The day after invitations to talks were issued, the Provisionals reminded everyone that 'decommissioning' was not possible before a political settlement. On 10 June, the talks opened at Stormont; four days later the Forum, which was to run in parallel, opened in Belfast on a discordant note. The DUP disputed who should be in the chair, and unionists argued that the union flag should be flown when the Forum was sitting. The next day a Provisional bomb demolished the Arndale Centre in Manchester, injuring 200 people, and on 28 June the IRA fired mortar bombs at a British military barracks at Osnabrück in Germany.

In July tension continued to rise, exposing the fragility of the peace process. On Sunday 7 July, after a church service, the RUC prevented a banned Orange Order march from going down the Garvaghy Road into Portadown. Nationalists saw the routing of the march, past a nationalist housing estate, as provocative. The Orangemen feared that the agenda of nationalist protest was to rid Portadown, close to where the Orange Order had been founded, of its last remaining Orange procession in the town. A four-day stand-off ensued, with widespread disruption and hundreds of illegal roadblocks by Orangemen and their supporters. Many towns and villages were cut off among scenes of violence and intimidation. Drumcree is inflammatory because it is symbolic of competing tribal prejudices: staunch traditionalists confronting cynical reactionaries, or vice versa.

Ervine saw Drumcree as a question about the right to free assembly, about what constitutes opposition, and how much opposition there needs to be, and what determines the circumstances in which there cannot be free assembly. While he condemned the Orange leadership which created the problem, taking the Northern Ireland community up a political cul-de-sac and playing into the hands of those who planned to destroy it, what struck Ervine most was the depth of pain in a community of essentially decent people, in fear of those who hate and would subvert its culture. Accommodation is required, but since Orangeism offers no leadership, violent nationalism is comfortable with that hurt and actively strives to exacerbate it. As Ervine recalls, in the words of Gerry Adams, 'These things do not happen by accident.'

When the Orange Order is unhappy, it is prepared to hold a public protest, and happy then to go home, leaving its hangers-on to take responsibility for the inevitable disruption and destruction. Ervine believes Orangemen and unionists are trapped in their idea of morality: do not talk to opponents because they are tainted by their republican paramilitary past; let others deal with them. This is an abnegation of responsibility. And the Orangemen certainly will not speak to Ervine. If they are reasonable with him, there is an obligation to be reasonable with republicans.

Ervine advised the UVF, through the CLMC, to step back and not let itself be seen as the cutting edge of Orange culture. Getting involved in actions led by the Orange Order could offer only defeat. Ervine went to Drumcree, where he expounded the merits of the peace process to groups he spoke with, including Billy Wright, who unleashed a diatribe against the UVF leadership, and Ervine himself, whom he mistakenly considered a UVF leader. Ervine's influence at Drumcree was peripheral for it was an Orange Order affair. In mitigation, he says, the unionist community was angry, living in fear and ripe for exploitation by those who were determined to have a stand-off. So why get involved?

> Decent people, just thirty miles away, in the heart of my community, are trying to make a peaceful protest out of fear, and I'm supposed to turn my back on them? Whilst I do have difficulty with how Orangeism handled it, do I refuse to acknowledge, refuse to accept the hurt and pain of unionism, because those unionists are people who know the manipulation that is going on from the other side?

Billy Wright's perception of Ervine's power, and his place in the UVF hierarchy, was misplaced. He is ex-UVF, a former paramilitary. Republicans are sceptical, for Sinn Féin and Provo leaders are often the same people. Ervine became politicised in jail and evolved into a loyalist politician: 'All my life has been uncharted waters. I had never been there before. You deal with what you have to deal with, the best way you can.'

On 8 July 1996, the UUP, DUP and UKUP pulled out of the Stormont talks in support of Orangemen at Drumcree. On 13 July a bomb exploded outside an Enniskillen hotel, and the SDLP announced that it was withdrawing from the Forum. Finally, on 16 July, the Ulster Unionists reported the SDLP to the talks chairman for an alleged breach of the Mitchell Principles, accusing Mark Durkan of the SDLP of inciting violence at a riot in Derry, and the next day the Alliance Party called for suspension of the Forum. It seemed that Ulster society had become unhinged in a frenzy of summer madness.

On 29 July, with the annual 'marching season' drawing to its close, those same politicians in the talks at Stormont steadied the situation somewhat when they announced that they had reached agreement on procedures to carry the talks forward, but they were not able to agree on plans for the 'decommissioning' of paramilitary weapons. The talks had survived a tempestuous period, but the poison from the events of the summer seeped into them. In September the DUP and the UKUP unsuccessfully attempted to have the two small loyalist parties, the PUP and the UDP, ejected. This was because the Combined Loyalist Military Command issued a death threat against two loyalists in Portadown on 28 August. Even the original advocates of talking and conciliation, the Alliance Party, caught the bug and cited first the PUP and UDP for the same death threat in Portadown and, secondly, the UUP and DUP for remarks made over Drumcree.

Outside the talks, the PUP had urgent repair work to do after the UVF and UFF prisoners in the Maze (Long Kesh) announced that they were withdrawing their support from the peace process, blaming 'IRA activity and politicians' inactivity'. The prisoners were important in paramilitary circles, because these were the men who had 'served' their community and were paying the price. All paramilitary prisoners exercised pivotal influence on the organisation outside prison. So, if loyalist prisoners were moving away from the peace process, it was more than likely that the CLMC ceasefire would collapse.

Ervine and a delegation entered the Maze on 7 October to persuade the UVF prisoners to continue their support. The task was not made easy when they could see and hear, from the prison car park, the explosion of an IRA bomb wreaking death and destruction at Thiepval Military Barracks in nearby Lisburn. Before the end of the month Mo Mowlam, then the Labour Party's spokesperson on Northern Ireland, and David Trimble had paid the loyalist prisoners separate visits. The broad unionist population may have been scandalised by this attention paid to paramilitary prisoners, but without their support it was more than likely that the CLMC ceasefire would collapse.

Decommissioning of the Provisionals' weapons continued to dog the multi-party talks throughout the autumn. The UUP issued a paper, 'Addressing Decommissioning', outlining conditions for Sinn Féin's entry to the talks. The decommissioning issue exacerbated existing rivalry between the UUP and a DUP/UKUP axis to the detriment of moving the talks forward. The fundamentalist DUP/UKUP stance excoriated Sinn Féin, and, as usual in the interminable struggle for the soul of unionism, the UUP kept glancing over its shoulder, afraid of being outflanked. At Westminster the Queen's Speech announced a decommissioning bill before Christmas. In November the PUP and UDP warned British Prime Minister John Major at Downing Street that the loyalist ceasefire would be in jeopardy if the talks were held up in the decommissioning impasse.

The PUP addressed the issue pragmatically. Decommissioning was not going to be offered or conceded by either set of paramilitaries in negotiations, and certainly not as a precondition to entry, since their political representatives were already in receipt of a mandate from the electorate. Therefore, a process of negotiation must continue and thus reduce progressively any claimed justification for violence. In those changed conditions, the use of guns would be redundant and decommissioning made more likely. Ervine argued that the public shared his view. He regarded decommissioning as a red herring politically and was exasperated when Ken Maginnis, Molyneaux, Trimble, MacCartney and Paisley kept saying that the unionist people must have it.

Ervine recognised the moral imperative for decommissioning, but believed that 'making it a precondition to everything else merely perpetuates the pain, the suffering, the difficulty'. This interpretation of the public mood of the time was confirmed when, in a *Belfast Telegraph* poll on 7 April 1997, people were asked, 'what Northern Ireland thinks about decommissioning'. Those polled were asked to respond to each of two statements in one of four ways:

A. Stop talking until decommissioning is solved.

B. Do not stop talks. Let a sub-committee deal with decommissioning.

The findings were:

	Preferred	Acceptable	Tolerable	Unacceptable
A.	31%	15%	12%	42%
B.	69%	10%	10%	11%

The multi-party talks dragged on, lapsing into a boring routine of long, occasionally learned speeches. Nothing of note was achieved. Just before the Christmas recess, reflecting mounting election fever, David Trimble said that it would be difficult to continue serious talks until after the expected British general election in 1997. Towards the end of February, the SDLP launched its general election campaign, even though a date had not yet been set. On 5 March the multi-party talks were adjourned until 3 June, an agreed time-scale compatible with those statutory requirements for the imminent general election, which John Major had called for 1 May.

The PUP desired to make a difference; difference is achieved through influence; political influence grows in proportion to the impact made at elections. The PUP considered elections its business, opportunities to test and grow. Each election counted as an opportunity to build on the Forum performance.

The PUP approached the general election with the same outlook it had been endeavouring to engender among the unionist community during the Stormont talks: 'Have the confidence to use your talents; your only guarantee is your talents.' During the campaign, the party emphasised the label 'confident unionists'. It was unusual to hear a unionist speaking positively, sounding upbeat. The longer this 'confident unionism' could sustain itself, the more likely people were to look and listen. For a unionist party, the risks already taken by the PUP in the talks had been substantial.

Ervine prepared the ground:

> It was clear that the unionist people must come to terms
> with where they wanted to go, based upon argument only.
> People knew what really had to happen; issues arising had
> to be faced honestly, and with integrity, i.e. sharing a
> devolved regional government, equality agenda, cross-bor-
> der co-operation. Northern Ireland, Sinn Féin and all, had
> to come to terms with the real world, and could not go on
> living in splendid isolation, incubating parochial attitudes.

Ervine's strategy was to post clear red, white and blue water
between the PUP and the two larger unionist parties: the DUP, which
yearned for the calm certainties of an unquestioning yesterday, and
the UUP, which seemed reluctant to lead towards tomorrow.

To constitutional nationalism the PUP posed a reasonable challenge to negotiate a place in the sun for all in Northern Ireland. To
Sinn Féin, the party asked a simple question: 'Do you still think of
unionists as "boat people" who should be repatriated back across the
Irish Sea?'

Ervine was expected to run in the East Belfast constituency, which
everyone assumed was his natural political home. He took out nom-
ination papers for East Belfast to encourage opposition politicians to
think that, too. However, his capacity to surprise surfaced once again.
After internal party discussions, Ervine decided to stand in the neigh-
bouring, more affluent, leafy-avenued South Belfast constituency. It
was a tactic designed to contrast the policies of the PUP and the UUP:
the innovative with the well-worn, the courageous with the timid, the
defined with the woolly, the forward thinking with the stick-in-the-
mud, as personified in the public images of the two contestants – a
young and dynamic pretender and the stalwart, stolid incumbent, the
Rev Martin Smyth of the UUP.

Elsewhere, the Progressive Unionists did themselves no harm by
advising the unionist community to vote for Trimble's UUP where no
PUP candidate was standing, a shrewd move which capped accusations of causing splits while stating their own inclusivity.

Ervine fought a combative campaign on two fronts. While his election literature was printed in strident red, white and blue with a
'Great Britain' and 'Northern Ireland' draped together in the union
flag, he also stressed the bread and butter issues which heavily

impinge on ordinary people's lives: 'Economic regeneration – Employment and the lack of it – National Health Service – Written Constitution – Bill of Rights – Education and Youth – Conflict
Transformation – Energy and Fuel costs – Victims – Agriculture – The
Beef Industry – Housing – Environment – Policing and Police Authority – Equality for Women – Human Rights – Prisoners and Justice.' A
hard-hitting, unmistakably left-inclined, socially conscious and untyp-
ically wide agenda for a unionist, and one critical of what unionism
had become.

Anticipating that his programme would provide stick-in-the-mud
unionists with material to question the integrity of his unionism,
Ervine wrote in his campaign leaflet: 'We are in the forefront of
enlightened unionist thinking. We see our task as redefining Unionism as an honourable and legitimate political proposition and as a
rebuttal to cynical manipulation.' He made no attempt to soften his
message: 'Give Yesterday's Men the Message – Retire!!'

However, when the election results were declared, the world was
not waiting on tenterhooks for the PUP results. The media headlines
were dominated by the successes of Gerry Adams in West Belfast and
Martin McGuinness in Mid-Ulster, both Sinn Féin. Yet eyebrows did
arch in surprise when the number of votes of the three PUP candidates
were declared and none lost his deposit. In East Antrim, Billy Donaldson received a fraction over 5 per cent, and in South Antrim, Hugh
Smyth had taken 8 per cent; a modest percentage, but self-respect and
dignity were maintained. In South Belfast, Ervine polled 5,687 votes,
over 14 per cent, and got third place. The hoped-for impact had been
achieved. The party's public profile was enhanced and potential support for unionist risk-takers demonstrated. Within loyalism, while the
level of success vindicated self-reliance in political leadership and won
wider respect among those paramilitary foot soldiers who were unde-
cided about the wisdom of treading a separate political path, it
increased resentment among those who were hostile.

Straightaway, campaigning had to start for the local council elections three weeks later. The PUP had been laying the groundwork for
some time. The party had studied American electoral techniques and
had been out in the streets responding to people's needs and complaints, encouraging them, especially women, to use their votes,
reminding them that votes counted in a democracy. Such an

approach had paid off for Sinn Féin, and the PUP wanted to emulate that success.

But, whereas Sinn Féin had fertile soil, the PUP was on stony ground. Gusty Spence explained: 'You can be assured that in the IRA man there's a Sinn Féin supporter, and not only is he a Sinn Féin supporter but he supports Sinn Féin policies. The UVF was never like that. We had the ironic situation, at the general election, where members of the UVF worked for other political parties in opposition to the PUP.'

The PUP hammered away at their local election theme to build up the self-belief of a demoralised community. The theme of confident unionism was epitomised by Billy Hutchinson as he and his workers canvassed the hilly streets that wind up and down his Oldpark constituency, in north Belfast. Hutchinson recognised that there was no point in going to people saying, 'We've been sold out. We're beaten.' That had been the problem with mainstream unionism. What unionist voters wanted to hear was: 'We're young, we're vibrant and we've got a new message. The PUP message is, "Get off your knees. You don't need to be on them. We aren't beaten. We're winning." We're winning by coming to an agreement with the other people in Northern Ireland, who don't share our unionist philosophy or nationality.'

That message could be read in an election leaflet for the PUP candidate in Victoria Ward, east Belfast. First, since the PUP promulgates a distinctive brand of unionism, its allegiance to the Union is unambiguously stated:

> The Progressive Unionist Party is fully committed to maintaining and strengthening the present constitutional position of Northern Ireland within the United Kingdom. The Party will actively work by all democratic means to ensure there will be no constitutional changes which either diminish the constitutional position of Northern Ireland as an integral part of the United Kingdom or which dilute democratic structures and procedures within Northern Ireland.

Union flags seem to shimmer across the page. The statement seems strident, but everything revolves around the phrase 'democratic means'.

Secondly, negotiation with the aim of reaching agreement with opponents follows: 'The PUP is fully committed to the development

of a new era of PEACE and stability in Northern Ireland based upon
democracy and consent.'

Thirdly, the social issues already stated in Ervine's recent general
election literature are highlighted.

What did the voters think? The headlines on the front page of the
evening newspaper, the *Belfast Telegraph*, trumpeted: 'ERVINE LIFT FOR
LOYALISTS. Fringe loyalists the Progressive Unionists moved centre
stage today as they gained seats on Belfast City Council.'

There was more than some satisfaction among the PUP that they
could now lose that media-inspired prefix 'fringe', which had irritated
them for some time.

Twenty-three PUP candidates had contested ten wards in the
greater Belfast area, and five were elected, with Hugh Smyth overwhelmingly topping the poll in Court Ward. Ervine was elected on the
first count in Victoria, and Billy Hutchinson topped the unionist vote
and eventually reached the quota in a nationalist-dominated ward,
Oldpark. In the city council the PUP gained 9 per cent overall, almost
equalling the Alliance Party's vote, and 20 per cent of the total
unionist poll, only 3 per cent less than the DUP. In Newtownabbey, a
further candidate was elected, and in North Down another two. The
point is fairly made that inroads were mostly confined to the greater
Belfast urban area, but nevertheless the PUP had achieved another sat-
isfactory success. Roy Magee, when asked afterwards to comment
upon these gains, suggested that people were prepared to give the PUP
a try at local Council level.

Within twelve months, after three ground-breaking election campaigns, despite resentment fanned by the two established unionist parties and doubts among those opposed to inclusive political dialogue,
the PUP was celebrating the public's acknowledgement of its emphasis on social and economic issues coupled with principles of even-
handedness in a sectarian society. They now had a growing
constituency base.

However, an incident after the election counts in Belfast seemed to
put a dampener on the PUP's success. There was public revulsion,
also expressed in wider unionist circles, in response to a celebratory
cavalcade waving UVF flags from the City Hall, through the city
centre and up the Shankill Road. This was a spontaneous demonstration. As PUP people at the count observed that it was going well

and that three of their candidates were going to be elected, word had spread outside and supporters arrived to celebrate. For some voters of the PUP this electoral success had a more profound meaning. As one former paramilitary prisoner who lives on the Shankill said, it was 'our coming home'. His community had reconciled itself to him by voting for a party with its origins in paramilitarism, the same party which had become, for people like him, a vehicle to replace the war machine. Until that evening he had felt disowned by his own community, his part in the Ulster tragedy ignored, with not the slightest recognition of the price he reckoned he had paid for protecting his people.

The PUP did not move to distance itself from the cavalcade. That revealed something significant about the nature of its leadership, as defined by Ervine: 'A leader's job is not simply to say, "Here's the direction we are going." It's to educate and it's to mould opinion.' The PUP had set out a list of policies with the aim of rebuilding a normal society where all talents would find expression. They neither exploited sectarianism among the working class nor pandered to the incoherent anger of the comfortably off. They made clear their respect for, and the legitimacy of, the views and aspirations of their Catholic and nationalist neighbours. The celebratory cavalcade, which included some who previously would have bombed and murdered to oppose such a programme, was a vindication of Ervine, Hutchinson and the PUP leadership.

In a political stalemate which needed unionist imagination and drive for a resolution, the PUP had energy and ideas. Ervine's talent for articulating PUP policies in an open-minded manner made his language fresh, ear-catching and appealing. The perceptible shift among some sections of the electorate towards them showed that fertile ground existed.

The strategy was related organically to what Spence had begun in the compounds of Long Kesh.

AGREEMENT REACHED

THE TALKS AT Stormont, parked in neutral during the election, moved into gear at the end of May 1997. All the parties were flown for a short visit to South Africa, whose resolution of its political problems, though not identical, appeared to have lessons for Northern Ireland. All did not fly out together since, to avoid potential arrest in the UK of one of its delegation, Sinn Féin flew direct fom Dublin. The other parties flew together via Heathrow.

This 'corporate' two-day stay had several purposes. One was to create conditions which might lead to improved relationships between the various parties by having them spend all their time in close proximity, cut off from the outside world, to engender an atmosphere conducive to discussion. Given that the UUP had consented to travel on the strict condition that they would never be in the same room as Sinn Féin because the IRA campaign was still active, that aim seemed forlorn. Equally important and more realisable, the Northern Ireland politicians would have an opportunity to talk with their South African counterparts, who had resolved a seemingly intractable political situation through personal relationships and continuing commitment, despite formidable ethnic rivalry, internal opposition and public cynicism.

Talks resumed on home soil on 2 June. Sinn Féin was still barred. Tony Blair, the new British prime minister, had stated in an article in *The Irish Times* on 28 April that an IRA 'genuine ceasefire' and Sinn

Féin's signing up to the Mitchell Principles, a commitment to 'democratic and exclusively peaceful means of resolving political issues', were prerequisites for their entry into talks. On 24 June, British/Irish proposals for decommissioning were presented at a plenary session of the talks. The next day, to a great deal of unionist consternation, Blair announced that he was putting a definitive time limit to the talks. Substantive talks, with all options on the table about future governance, would begin on 15 September and be completed by the end of May 1998. During the summer, that September date hung over the Northern political firmament like a pole-star by which political ships navigated.

Many, mostly unionists, considered Blair's move ill-conceived, putting unwarranted pressure on participants. They thought the timescale was too short for people to become acquainted and begin to build confidence and trust in each other, especially with an event like Drumcree about to recur. Fears about the consequences of another confrontation were justified, though this time it was a nationalist eruption over a banned Orange march being allowed, with RUC protection, which cost millions of pounds' worth of damage. Yet nationalist and republican politicians remained in the talks in spite of the Orange march going ahead.

Blair's edict signalled the end of indulgence and the start of business. Almost a year had passed since rules of procedure for the conduct of the talks had been fairly quickly agreed, and for months politicians of all hues had been repeating, mantra-like, in the media, 'Everyone knows what has to be done.' It was time to draw up a framework instead of focusing piecemeal, for an inordinate amount of time, on a specific issue like decommissioning to the detriment of an overall settlement. Decommissioning had dazzled the unionists and continued to hold them in its hypnotising light. The two governments' report on the issue was presented 'to the talks' on 1 July. When it was discussed on 16 July, the UKUP walked out because the government would permit only one question. The following day Trimble met Blair to state that the report did not go far enough towards his party's wish for actual decommissioning during the talks. On 21 July, when Trimble again met Blair in Downing Street, the prime minister said that there was no need to amend the report. The government's view was: 'There must be decommissioning during negotiations.' On the same day, at its first meeting, an Anglo-Irish governmental conference expressed full confidence in the decommissioning report. On 23 July, a majority of those attending the talks rejected the report. At the end of August, with the start of substantive talks looming, the two governments signed an agreement to set up an Independent International Commission on Decommissioning (IICD), as suggested originally by Ken Maginnis of the UUP, which would work within the talks.

Sinn Féin's re-entry had been signalled by the Provisional IRA's announcement of 'a complete cessation of military operations from 12 midday, Sunday, 20 July 1997'. Entry was confirmed when the secretary of state, Mo Mowlam, made a determination that entry was conditional upon a six weeks' 'decontamination' period of total absence of paramilitary activity. Mowlam's determination created a storm among unionists. On 21 July the UKUP left both the talks and the Forum, this time conclusively. The DUP quit the talks, but remained in the Forum. Trimble embarked upon a period of consultation among the wider community, including a meeting with Roman Catholic Archbishop of Armagh Sean Brady, on 1 September, before he would commit his party one way or another.

The PUP was agitated, too. Given the recent violence and murders committed by the Provisionals, a period of six weeks appeared lenient, and on 26 August the party publicly accused the secretary of state of appeasement. The next day Billy Hutchinson said on BBC local radio that the talks offered nothing to loyalists and that he would be voting against participation. The following day, Mowlam turned the screw further on unionists by seeming to dilute the notion of consent in an interview in the *Belfast Telegraph*:

> I understand consent to be that it is that the wishes and support of the people that a conclusion or accommodation or outcome is reached. I don't define it in numbers terms, necessarily. I don't necessarily define it in a functional geographical sense, because those could change the nature of the outcome as both sides are very fearful. Consent means a willing accommodation. I think there is a willing accommodation for a peaceful outcome by many people in Northern Ireland.

A PUP delegation led by Ervine and Billy Hutchinson met with the secretary of state on 29 August and elicited an assurance in a written reply:

> The Government remains fundamentally committed to the principle of consent in all its aspects, as set out both in United Kingdom law in section 1 of the Northern Ireland Constitution Act and in the Downing Street Declaration.
>
> This means that the constitutional status of Northern Ireland as part of the United Kingdom will not change without the consent of the majority of its people. Moreover, we are committed to putting any agreed outcome to the negotiations to the people of Northern Ireland for approval in a referendum.

While what the PUP had established was important, equally as important was the manner in which it had been achieved. They had not left the talks, but had fought their corner with tenacity and respect for the system. There are occasions when a politician is like a plumber called out to inspect a toilet which is broken. He does not give a report and then leave. He is expected to restore it to working order. Similarly, politicians may have to sink their arms up to the elbow in muck to solve a problem. Unlike those unionists who criticised, and then upped and left the talks, Ervine and the PUP were prepared to do that.

The six weeks' decontamination period for Sinn Féin passed by with an absence of all republican paramilitary activity, and, on 9 September, the party signed up to the Mitchell Principles.

The date for the start of substantive talks, 15 September, was imminent, and Trimble's consultation exercise had not given a firm indication of intent. The PUP desired to enter talks, but without the UUP's inclusion it would be futile. At a joint meeting held in the Glengall Street headquarters of the UUP, the PUP argued the case for entry. So interested was one senior UUP negotiator that he sat and completed a crossword puzzle while the PUP put the argument. Interestingly, the UUP produced a document they had received from the British government, detailing plans for moving the talks forward. This document was news to the PUP, a fully paid-up participant in the talks. It was agreed that liaison between the two parties should continue through Ervine and Reg Empey of the UUP.

On 13 September, after a prolonged meeting, the Ulster Unionist Council executive delegated tactics on the talks to Trimble and his negotiating team. This was not a negative signal, but rather the manifestation of a feeling of self-confidence which had been increasing in the wider unionist community for some months. They felt that they ought to take on their enemies in negotiations and no longer adopt a defensive stance.

On 15 September, at the recommencement of talks, a statement was issued by the British prime minister and the Irish taoiseach which, among other matters and 'from which no outcome is of course excluded or pre-determined', wished to clarify two crucial issues. First was that 'consent will be a guiding principle'. The second was about decommissioning, which was said to be an indispensable part of the process of negotiation and confidence-building. Both governments wanted to see 'the decommissioning of some paramilitary arms during negotiation, as progress is made in the political talks'. Such a stance was at odds with the stated positions of Sinn Féin and the IRA.

Ulster Unionists took some satisfaction from the confirmation of consent as a guiding principle, but had difficulty with a diminution in the requirement to decommission.

On 16 September the PUP, together with the UDP, met the secretary of state to clear up some doubts about re-entry: the issue of consent; fears that other parties would make some conditional linkage between decommissioning and the release of prisoners; and, in the light of recent revelations in discussions with the UUP that the government did not distribute all papers to all parties, that the PUP should receive relevant documents as of right and not by second-hand. So, on 17 September, the UUP, PUP and UDP surprisingly stage-managed for the world's media an entrance into talks at Stormont worthy of the best PR efforts of Sinn Féin. Trimble, with Ervine and Hutchinson at the head of the PUP delegation, led the unionist groupings in, stating that these unionists were 'democrats', thus conferring establishment legitimacy on the loyalist political parties.

On 24 September 1997, a procedural motion was moved by the two governments at a plenary session. Item 2[b] repeated the two premiers' desires about decommissioning. Also contained in the proposal was the imperative that all parties had to work with the Independent International Commission on Decommissioning. If a party failed to cooperate, the Commission would bring this to the attention of the plenary session. Separate liaison subcommittees were proposed to deal with decommissioning and confidence-building measures. Sinn Féin opposed this item.

Item 3 proposed adopting 'as the comprehensive agenda for the negotiations' the outline proposals tabled on 15 October 1996 by the Ulster Unionist Party, the SDLP and the Alliance Party. Items 4 and 5 formally launched the talks. Unbelievably for many, after the decades of anguish, the talks were under way.

The PUP sat easily with the agenda and a defined time-frame. Their outline policy had already been framed via an updated version of the 1991 'Sharing Responsibilty' document, which included arguments for cross-border bodies, and their 'Reasonable Compromise' document of January 1996, which sought a 'Road to Peace and Reconciliation and the Ending of Conflict'. Underpinning their determination to get into negotiations was the knowledge that any final outcome must be submitted to a free-standing referendum of the people of Northern Ireland. Consent was no longer an issue. It had been secured.

They drew confidence from the private assurances of Albert Reynolds, who had told Ervine and Spence, 'Let's park the constitutional fundamentals.' And after the initial conversations with Fergus Finlay they accepted that the goal of a United Ireland was not on the Irish government's agenda, even though a new Fianna Fáil taoiseach, Bertie Ahern, who had been installed on 26 June, let it be known that he was taking on himself the leadership of nationalist Ireland. Ahern's gesture, rather than a rekindling of the pan-nationalist front, long regarded with foreboding by unionists, was a manifestation of a Dublin government starting to gear itself up to negotiate seriously in its own self-interest with unionists. John Bruton explained the problem from a south of the border perspective:

> I think that the government in the Republic, and this will probably be true of all governments, is always one step away from actually engaging unionism in serious dialogue. Partly because we have a lot to lose. There is, I think, at a certain subliminal level, an unwillingness on the part of the people here to put what we've achieved at risk, either for the sake of Northern nationalists or for the sake of an

understanding with Northern unionists. We're not sure
what it's all going to lead to, what it's going to cost, what
type of things we'd have to give up in terms of control over
our own affairs in order to reach an accommodation. I feel
that neither nationalists north of the border, nor nationalists south of the border, have really thought through the
implications of North/South bodies, or North/South development. North/South development means the Dublin government giving up power. It means the Dublin government
having to accept that some of the things it now does, it will
have to do with the agreement of unionists in Belfast.

With consent secured and a United Ireland postponed, Ervine was
not complacent. He knew that in negotiations the 'devil is in the
detail'. One eye viewed British government intentions with suspicion,
while the other watched for Irish government duplicity. Also, if the
negotiations were to arrive at a meaningful conclusion, the PUP knew
that a settlement had to be inclusive, with nationalism in the North
winning as well.

The PUP continued to force debate within unionism and promote
their distinctive policies. Tactically they may have appeared to ally
themselves with the party of 'those who considered themselves born
to rule', but submissive they were not. The PUP held to its strategy
that vibrant argument within unionism was a necessary tool to unlock
the door to a shared future, while recourse to tribal solidarity would
block it.

On the questions of equality, human rights, cultural expression
(including that of ethnic communities) and in progressing the three-
strand negotiation, the PUP pressed their policies originating from
'Sharing Responsibility'. The PUP welcomed the fact that the UUP
were active in formulating a policy on North/South bodies. However,
much persuasion had to be done on prisoners' issues. Ervine argued
that the prisoners had played an integral role in actively promoting
the peace process and that the risk in early prisoner releases was minimal, as statistical evidence demonstrated that the rate of recidivism
for paramilitary prisoners was extraordinarily low.

The PUP were equally keen to challenge the motives behind the
bloody campaign waged by republicanism against the unionist

community, which Ervine reduced to one question: 'What is so awful and alien about the notion of a British way of life that makes you want to kill people to achieve the opposite?' As a democrat he recognised, and accepted, Sinn Féin's place in the talks because of the party's electoral mandate. Ervine and the PUP went into the talks with the working assumption that Sinn Féin also wanted to negotiate peace. If Sinn Féin was not serious about this, or did not convince the unionist community that it was serious, then the talks were futile. For Ervine a fundamental function of the talks was to test the sincerity and vision of the republican leadership, to find out 'whether they are real or not'. What Ervine sought was 'the opportunity to begin the dialogue that, once and for all, makes people realise that the war is futile, that the war can't be won by one side or the other'.

John Bruton, then leader of the opposition in the Dáil, welcomed this 'rethinking' from the 'military end of loyalism', but was sceptical about reciprocation from the republican side:

> If you look at Sinn Féin's submission for the Talks, it is just a re-presentation of their antique view that the problem is the British Government's claim on Northern Ireland, the whole thing is all down to British sovereignty.
>
> They have a very significant leadership who have been lionised by the world's press and world politicians, who have been given a political status and respect which cannot easily be replaced and who, therefore, have a capacity to do things within Republicanism that they wouldn't have if they hadn't been lionised by the Americans, for instance. The test for them is, how are they using that? Are they using that to change republican thinking? Or are they using it simply to recycle old wine in new bottles?

For constitutional nationalism, led by people of vision and of the highest calibre, like Hume and Mallon, who had had the courage to set Northern Ireland on the road to necessary reform, the challenge as Ervine saw it was to move from criticising the stewardship of a community into taking the levers of power, and to share in reclaiming ownership of society. He regretted that 'someone with the skill and ability and talent of Seamus Mallon, for example, had never made an executive decision'. Ervine believed that the PUP was challenging the nationalist leadership to choose between permanent opposition, which may have its comforts, and taking responsibility for administering society and making decisions for the common good.

Ervine, with his talent for seeing both the wood and the trees, reduced the principle that governed his approach within the talks to one simple proposition: 'antagonism or integration'. Society in Northern Ireland had been directed towards antagonism. This had led to conflict and violence. The challenge was to redirect society towards cooperation and compromise. Hence his desire to negotiate with other unionists, as well as with his nationalist and republican neighbours.

As negotiations progressed into the autumn of 1997, intermittent 'noises off' and clashes inside the talks reflected both the need of some participants to massage their own nervous constituencies on the outside and the gap between confrontational positions that required reconciliation inside. On 5 October, Martin McGuinness carried a militant message to a rally in Coalisland, County Tyrone. He made no bones about Sinn Féin's objective in the talks; the leadership's intention was 'to smash the Union'. His uncompromising message bolstered those republicans who harboured doubts about the wisdom of going into talks. On 21 October, in the lead-up to parties' tabling their proposals for Strands One (internal NI) and Two (North/South), the Irish minister for foreign affairs, David Andrews, with typical hauteur, let it be known that the timing of a review of the contentious Articles Two and Three of the Republic's Constitution, as an inclusive element on the table, would happen at the instigation of the government in the South, and at its convenience alone. This was a perfectly proper stance for a sovereign government to adopt, but Andrews' imperious manner in these delicate negotiations infuriated the UUP, who staged a temporary walk-out in protest on this occasion. Claiming that Dublin was stalling, David Trimble said, 'Mr Andrews was talking as if the issues of Articles Two and Three would not be tackled until after a final settlement.' Andrews defused the situation by issuing a statement which made it clear that Dublin was quite prepared to 'discuss proposals for change in the Irish Constitution as part both of balanced constitutional change and of an overall agreement'.

Although the PUP saw Andrews as pompous and officious, the minister had not put the issue of the review in question. A week later, along with the other parties, the PUP put their own proposals on the table for Strands One and Two, at a meeting which was characterised by clashes over Andrews' attitude.

On 4 November Martin Mansergh, *éminence grise* of successive Dublin governments' policies on Northern Ireland, in a speech at Conway Mill, a republican centre on the Falls Road in Belfast, invigorated traditional republicans when he stated that deletion of Articles Two and Three (long and fiercely criticised by unionists for promoting claims upon their country) from the Republic's constitution was not on the table for negotiation. He urged his audience to continue to work for a United Ireland in their lifetimes.

A month later, Andrews provoked another cacophony of protest. In a statement which seemed to disregard totally the essence of negotiations, in terms proprietorial he declared on BBC Radio Ulster that North/South bodies would have a secretariat with 'strong executive functions not unlike a government'. To unionists of all shades, this reeked of colonialism bedecked in the Irish tricolour, and unanimously they berated Andrews for his views. In an effort to defuse unionist hostility, Bertie Ahern, on 3 December, retracted diplomatically when he issued a statement which said that Andrews' comments went 'over what is our own line'.

The politicians and parties in the talks were working industriously, but to their own agendas and without cohesion. Senator Mitchell, also on 3 December, to give focus and move the process forward, proposed that a list of six heads of agreement be drawn up between the party leaders, plus one other from each party, to be finalised by 15 December.

In preparation, the PUP had updated its submission, in a paper called 'Sharing Responsibility 2000', and subtitled 'Into the New Millennium'. Its stated aims were:

> To secure peace and reconciliation within this region of the United Kingdom.
>
> To establish a local Parliament in this region, representative of all interested parties and groups.
>
> To work actively for political, social and economic advancement to secure a better life for all our people.
>
> To secure the termination of the Anglo-Irish Agreement through the introduction of new agreed structures, within an elected devolved government.

To pursue new and established policies through a
broadly representative Committee System of Government,
i.e. sharing responsibility.

Some excerpts indicate the flavour and intent of the thinking which
expressed itself in policy:

The Progressive Unionist Party will not miss this opportunity nor sit idly by while others hatch their selfish plans.
Democracy is for all our people regardless of creed or class.

Freedom from fear and violence, social deprivation in all
areas; negations of basic human rights and many other
issues have not received the emotional public attention that
they so richly deserve.

Now we have to move away from the negative
entrenched positions; accept that the answers must be
found among ourselves. Accept that the problems are created to a great extent throughout the whole community
and resolve to end them.

The Parliament would have Legislative powers as well
as consultative and deliberative in other non-legislative
matters. The Parliament would have Tax Varying Powers.

The Constitution of Northern Ireland should embody a
Bill of Rights along the lines of the European Convention
on Human Rights which would include guarantees against
discrimination.

'Sharing Responsibilty 2000' dealt with a problem which was
intractable for unionists and fundamental to nationalists:
North/South bodies. In it the PUP accepted the symbolic importance
of such bodies to nationalists, stating its belief that the bodies could
work for the good of both states on the island and did not threaten
the Union. For the PUP, cross-border cooperation would work if policy emanating from the cross-border bodies were ratified by the
respective elected bodies, both North and South. In Northern Ireland, a common policy could be worked through at committee level
in a Northern Ireland Assembly, but be referred to the full parliament
for ratification in all cases. First, this would reassure unionists that
cross-border bodies would not become vehicles to transfer them into

a United Ireland surreptitiously. Secondly, nationalists would see that cooperation was a reality and had unionist support. Finally, to ensure that the bodies would thrive and mutual confidence grow, it would be vitally important that all should take place within the context of transparency, ratifiabilty and accountability.

To most unionists, adopting a policy of legally binding cooperation with the Republic was anathema. Ervine and the PUP argued for coming to terms with the modern world as it existed, in relations with the European Union for example, and a recognition that much could be achieved through cooperation to promote the economy and the well-being of people. In the PUP arguments lay a recognition that cooperation would not always run smoothly. Northern Ireland competes economically with the Republic, and there would be clashes of interest. Down the line, Ervine argued, if cooperation did not work or consent was withdrawn, then it would cease. However, the real hope was that utilitarian bodies might become institutions of trust and develop something that would lie beyond the realm of legislation, and help 'to secure peace and reconciliation within this region of the United Kingdom'.

A necessary balance for unionism was advocated in the next section, which dealt with East/West relationships, which were as important to unionists as North/South relationships are to nationalists. It proposed a supra-regional consultative body, consisting of all the regions of, and islands around, Great Britain and Ireland, in which there would be a coming together on issues: 'such as industry and energy, construction, trade and development assistance, employment and the working environment', and other relevant matters. The party suggested that the name IONA, the Islands of the North Atlantic, be adopted for this body.

The PUP proposals concluded: 'This document is offered as a reasonable and honourable compromise. Moving from our established traditional and legitimate position, with all its attendant aspiration of total integration into British mainstream politics, we have compromised a great deal. It is time others followed suit.'

A crunch meeting on the six Heads of Agreement, on 16 December, failed. The sticking-point was Sinn Féin's refusal to countenance any reference to internal bodies. All afternoon Ervine, Spence, Hugh Smyth and others on the PUP delegation sat and wrestled with a formula of words to reach out and satisfy Sinn Féin's requirements, but they were rebuffed. The question which Ervine had posed at the outset needed an answer after four months of talks. The PUP now had worrying and serious doubts about Sinn Féin's desire to come to a genuine settlement. The talks broke up for Christmas in crisis.

Frustration at Sinn Féin's intransigence the PUP could weather. Mowlam's and Andrews' *faux pas* the PUP could put right. But early release by the Dublin government of nine Provisional prisoners from prison in the South, as a confidence-building measure, without routing the measure through the process at Stormont, the PUP found unacceptable. Yet again, they were being left out of the loop. On 18 December, loyalist prisoners in the Maze (as Long Kesh had been renamed) went on the rampage immediately they heard the news through sources other than the PUP, whom everyone at the talks, including Senator Mitchell, understood were their representatives. The loyalist prisoners wondered what kind of deal had been struck between republicans and Dublin outside the negotiation process.

By ignoring them, a government minister had once more put the PUP in a difficult situation. Again, they had to react forcefully and immediately to preserve credibility and defend political territory.

Ervine retaliated the next day by stating that he was pessimistic about the chances of the PUP returning to the talks after Christmas. Loyalist prisoners then announced, on 23 December, a review of their support for a talks process which was following, so they said, a 'republican agenda' and gave 'concessions to republicans' while offering nothing to loyalists. Mowlam met with the PUP and UDP leaders the same day, and on Christmas Eve David Andrews announced to the PUP that he would meet with them in the New Year.

They met at Hillsborough Castle on 6 January. Andrews said that he wished to open the meeting with an announcement. To assure loyalists of his good intentions, he brought good news. He had obtained money from his government for the Boyne. The PUP delegation sat in uncomprehending silence. Then, after a few seconds, Billy Hutchinson asked what he meant. Andrews looked at Hutchinson with surprise. 'You know, the Battle of the Boyne, 1690, King Billy. Orangemen and all that.' Hutchinson pressed him on the relevance of the matter, and Andrews replied that the Irish government was going to develop a heritage park on the site, commemorating 'Orangemen and Orange culture'. Hutchinson and the others found it difficult to believe their ears. This was surreal.

Hutchinson eventually leaned forward and asked, 'Minister, are there any Orangemen on your side of the table?'

'Why, of course not, Billy,' replied Andrews. 'Why do you ask?'

'Cause there's damn all of them on this side,' said Hutchinson. The PUP had come to discuss a situation that could have resulted in bloodshed, yet Andrews' proposal was put forward in all seriousness.

Andrews then set out the reason for the meeting, stating that his government accepted that confidence-building measures needed to be dealt with within the talks process itself, but added, 'As a matter of policy, it will be discussed within the confidence-building committee, but, operationally, it will be entirely a matter for the government.' In other words, as the government of a sovereign state with a written constitution, it was not in a position to dilute any of its powers, even when it might desire to do so in the interest of better relations. The PUP accepted this position and looked forward to being better informed in future by the Irish government.

That gap in understanding characterised Dublin's dealings with loyalists, to their consternation. The PUP delegation, which included the UVF commander, could not believe that a minister in a government which claimed sovereignty over them could know so little about them. Among themselves, the loyalists talked about how the Americans could arrive in the North and quickly pick up on the nuances of the situation, but the Irish cabinet, from only a hundred miles down the road, had even less of a clue than the British representatives sent over from Westminster.

So sensitive and decisive was the issue of prisoners that the secretary of state tore up the book of protocol on 9 January and visited the Maze to have negotiations with loyalist prisoners, to the dismay of wider unionism. Mo Mowlam had previously visited as shadow secretary of state, but this was the first time that a minister had gone into the prison to talk to inmates.

On the matter of prisoner releases, the PUP also had made representations to the British government which, in a reply to Ervine's question at a meeting in Parliament Buildings at Stormont on the day following Mowlam's visit, stated that it was committed to having all confidence-building measures discussed in the talks process at committee level, clearing the way for negotiations to continue. Loyalist withdrawal from talks would have meant that less than 50 per cent of unionists would be in attendance, thereby prejudicing the legality of any outcome. Political pressure had been judiciously applied to make governments mindful of the PUP's proper place in the talks set-up, and the party's integrity was restored.

The Dublin and London governments determined on an initiative to move the talks forward in the New Year. On 12 January 1998, when the talks recommenced, each participating party received two documents. The first, entitled 'Joint Statement by the British and Irish Governments', stated that the governments were putting forward, without prejudice, proposals to move discussions on, based upon 'the views of all parties on the various issues'. In the second, 'Propositions on Heads of Agreement' (see Appendix One), the parties were invited to discuss issues such as balanced constitutional change, democratic institutions for Northern Ireland, a new British-Irish Agreement, a North-South Council, and related matters. In effect, the proposals contained in the document enshrined partition of the island of Ireland.

Yet Sinn Féin did not withdraw. This document contained a great deal that the party did not like and had blocked earlier when it showed it was prepared to concede nothing, even if a crisis ensued. But opportunity existed: 'Effective and practical measures to establish and consolidate peaceful society, dealing with issues such as prisoners, security in all its aspects, policing and decommissioning of weapons.'

The PUP viewed the governments' documents with equanimity, for their updated policy harmonised with many of the issues treated: consent, local assembly, proportionality, cross-border bodies responsible to a local assembly, a raft of rights legislation, prisoners/security/policing matters.

While the participants to the talks were reconvening inside Stormont to digest the two governments' paper, as happened so many times before, an all too familiar atmosphere of dread descended on the streets. After the assassination of LVF leader Billy Wright in the Maze prison by INLA prisoners on 27 December, loyalist terrorists embarked on a vengeance-inspired rampage, murdering a succession of innocent Catholics who were easy targets.

The talks moved to Lancaster House, London, for three days, 26–28 January, to deal with Strand Three, East/West measures. Much of the time was taken up in arguments about expelling the UDP from the talks. The UDP were politically linked to the UDA, the loyalist terror group associated with the UFF, which acknowledged in a statement that their ceasefire had indeed been broken, but was now restored. In effect, the UFF admitted its culpability in the murders, so dishonouring the UDP's commitment to the Mitchell Principles. The UDP realised that expulsion was on the cards and walked before they were pushed. Only a small amount of progress was able to be made in discussions about East/West relations. However, because the two governments wanted 'a fully inclusive talks process', and if evidence could be shown which 'continued to be consistent with a complete, unequivocal and unqualified ceasefire by the UFF', the UDP would be invited to rejoin talks on 23 February.

Discussions on Strand Two, the North/South dimension, moved to Dublin and were due to take place from 16–18 February, when the chief constable of the RUC ruled that the Provisionals were culpable of involvement in the murders of Jim Guiney, UDA commander south Belfast, at Dunmurry, and Brendan 'Bat' Campbell, an alleged drug dealer in Belfast, earlier that month. Sinn Féin, under threat of expulsion, attempted to pre-empt the governments' decision by contesting the matter, in vain, in the Republic's courts, and most of the time was lost. The session proved disappointing.

The PUP had already offered constructive input to Strand Two negotiations, as Liz O'Donnell, minister of state at the Department of Foreign Affairs, confirmed: 'On the issue of cross-border bodies, the PUP adopted a cautious approach based on pragmatism. They wanted assurances that these bodies would not be "Trojan Horses" for Irish unity but were prepared to consider them provided they could be shown to bring economic or social benefits. I regarded their contribution as positive.'

In any case, Ervine would not have been able to participate. He was unwell, and Dr Joe Hendron, former SDLP Westminster MP for West Belfast, diagnosed a flesh ulcer and had him hospitalised immediately. His political partner, the military commander of the UVF, attended social gatherings at Dublin Castle, mixing anonymously, mingling, hearing and seeing. Ervine and he did not now consort as formerly. When the talks had opened at Stormont, it was safer for the Irish government to be talking to Ervine and the PUP, who were now both coming into their own. Nevertheless, his views continued to be relayed diplomatically to the Irish government, via his usual channels.

Immediately upon their returning to the North, the governments applied pressure with the aim of reaching a comprehensive settlement by the Easter deadline. A requirement to include all participating parties in that agreement was evident in a joint press statement issued by the secretary of state and the minister for foreign affairs, following their determination to exclude Sinn Féin. Their statement said that if it could be demonstrated that the IRA ceasefire was intact contemporaneously, and were this to continue, then Sinn Féin could return to the talks on 9 March.

Further weeks passed and negotiations continued. Bilateral meetings were held, and papers were submitted and circulated among parties for discussion, in an attempt to close gaps in positions; but those gaps remained. The politicians were essentially dancing around the issues. Then, on 25 March, Senator Mitchell exercised his powers as chairman when, in trying to galvanise the parties to get down to the nub of negotiations, he announced a deadline for the end of the talks. Participants would 'eat and sleep' if neccessary in continuous negotiations, in an all-out attempt to reach a comprehensive final agreement by 10 April.

As the tempo increased, the PUP continued to conduct its dealings as decided collectively from the outset of talks: to get the best possible deal for their country consistent with their policy stated in 'Sharing Responsibility 2000'. They had met with suspicion and accusations of dubious character from some other delegates, but had remained focused. They had won trust and influence, were scrupulous in dealings with Senator Mitchell, and were as open and honest with all parties as they dared be: 'whether it be in plenary, bi-lateral, in corridors, in toilets. We felt that was the way we needed to be,' remarked David Ervine.

A further week of talks began with the political temperature soaring. Ervine counselled people to 'hold their nerve', for it was 'an historical and not hysterical time'. Everyone, talks participants and the public alike, were expectantly awaiting Senator Mitchell's production of a draft document, outlining his assessment of the best hopes for a political agreement. Once in the hands of the politicians, real business would begin. Prime ministers and government ministers, civil servants, Trimble and Hume were all engaged in frenetic to-ing and fro-ing to Downing Street and Chequers. Slanted soundbites from local politicians via the media outside Castle Buildings fed an impatient public's appetite for developments. On 31 March it was hoped that Mitchell's document would appear by Friday, 3 April, and the deadline was brought forward to 9 April, the end of the following week. By Friday doubt existed that Mitchell's document would appear over the weekend. His document, 'Draft Paper for Discussion' (see Appendix Two), was at last presented at 12.30 a.m. on 7 April, leaving two days for a deal to be struck. It launched an immediate midnight crisis. When they had read it, all shades of unionism felt alarmed. This was not the discussion paper they had been led to expect.

The PUP found much that it liked in the proposals in Strand One, 'Democratic Institutions in Northern Ireland', and in Strand Three, East/West relations. They looked forward to discussions on these items. However, they found proposals in Strand Two repugnant. Under a new British/Irish agreement, a North/South Ministerial Council would develop cooperation on matters of mutual interest and reach agreement on the adoption of common policies on agriculture, education and training, health, industrial and trade matters, marine and waterways, energy and transport, and the environment. All internal initiatives 'could be developed under the aegis of an all-Ireland Council', where the appropriate cross-border body would 'have a clear operational remit, to implement, on an all-island and cross-border basis, policies agreed in Council.' A Northern Ireland Assembly would be subservient to the North/South Ministerial Council. Even a party like the PUP, which was in favour of North/South bodies, in which mutual trust could grow and lead to increased cooperation and amplification of joint policies, refused to support the proposals for Strand Two contained in this document.

John Taylor, a leading UUP negotiator, said he would not touch the proposals with a long bargepole. John Alderdice, then leader of the moderate Alliance Party, said that if the British prime minister were coming to town, he should come now. He was criticised by some in his own party for taking up a unionist stance.

The truth of the matter was that no unionist politician, even one of Ervine's enlightened hue, could contemplate signing up to a deal containing the proposed Strand Two. He said at the time: 'Under no circumstances. Never a chance of us accepting this. Everything, as far as we are concerned, has to be routed through a Northern Ireland Assembly.' Unionists wanted to know why the proposals were so hardline and why the agenda presented was so emphatically republican/nationalist. The PUP suspected the work of Dublin civil servants, obeying their constitution's imperative to strive for administrative responsibility for the whole island. Ervine feared the Irish were out-manoeuvring their British counterparts. He wondered if the British had read and agreed to this document, and if so was Perfidious Albion revealing its hand? What the PUP had expected was the conciliatory tone of a Dublin government seeking agreement, but it saw only hypocritical Dublin's underhandedness.

The PUP needed to know whether or not this was the final text. Ervine and the other party delegates had long and serious debates, mostly with the Irish government, but found that ministers were 'woolly, to say the least' in their interpretation of what was meant. The civil servants, they found, were clearer.

There was a political Everest to climb if any agreement were to be reached by Tony Blair's deadline in two days. Cynics suggested that the finality of tone was deliberate, meant to provoke a crisis that could be fixed only by the heroic intervention of Blair and Ahern.

After serious internal debate, the PUP approached the chairman. Ervine told the senator that he could not believe that he, personally, had placed in front of them a Strand Two which was so alien to what they were capable of accepting. Mitchell admitted at that point that the document was not his. The public assumption was that it was his work, his series of proposals, but they were the work of the British and Irish governments.

The PUP retreated into a period of calm reflection to mull over the situation and decide on a way forward. Gusty Spence led the discussion. They asked themselves: 'What does this mean? What is actually happening to us here?' After thinking it over, Ervine and the others concluded that what had happened was that gaps existing between politicians after the previous months' work could not be closed, so a Strand Two had been constructed which would impel participants to move away from what had been set before them and negotiate towards an agreement thrashed out between themselves. The PUP calmed down after this, but realised that they would have to be vocif-erous and very firm in their arguments against the things they could not accept.

Ervine perceives two imperatives in negotiations: what you want and what you need. You negotiate between those two obligations. What you want may go beyond the needs of the people across the table, so your demands are reined back, adjusted. But your needs are basic, and if they are not achieved as a minimum, then the business is not worth the candle. The PUP's stated preference, their want, was for total integration into their nation's political system, but that was unattainable because it disregarded the needs of nationalists. But, equally, what the two governments' 'green' document was now offer-ing fell below the needs of the PUP, which required two things absolutely. First, every decision emanating from every cross-border body must be approved through a Northern Ireland Assembly before its enactment; divorce from a British legislative environment was not on. Secondly, prisoners must be brought into the equation.

Dismayed as they were by the Strand Two document, the PUP felt acutely that its aspirations for a peaceful settlement were in trouble if pressure to agree, arising from an imposed deadline, meant it were adopted quickly. PUP delegates could not negotiate further if no capacity existed to move away from the proposals set out. At this crit-ical juncture, they found solace in all parties' total compliance with Mitchell's request for confidentiality, which Ervine believed demon-strated willingness to negotiate further.

A palpable sense of urgency reinvigorated everyone as they realised this marathon was not yet spent. Ervine says that it was a very edgy and testing time. On the surface they were businesslike with the other parties, but internally, 'There was a great deal of strain because we were going to the wire – make-or-break time.' The well-practised for-mat of successive series of structured bilateral meetings was ditched as a huge increase of energy surged through the rooms and corridors of Castle Buildings.

Ervine remembers: 'There was anger. There was annoyance. There was not knowing. All kinds of emotion flooding on all sides. We ate in the canteen and, as usual, it was packed for there were so many delegates. There was nowhere you could go that was devoid of people. You spent a lot of time walking around the car park, talking. If you wanted to talk privately, you went round the car park. The atmos-phere was electric.'

Wednesday, 8 April, twenty-four hours after the appearence of the Strand Two document and twenty-four hours before the deadline was due to expire, the two heads of government arrived. The parties in effect began to negotiate by proxy. The Ulster Unionist Party, which had never spoken directly to Sinn Féin, spoke to Tony Blair, who in turn spoke to Bertie Ahern, who was talking to the SDLP and Sinn Féin. On the one hand, Sinn Féin, not having negotiated in any of the strands, was caught on the back foot. Its delegates could not believe a deal was going to happen, to the extent that they spent a long time with the Alliance party acquainting themselves with the details of Strand One. On the other hand, the UUP were stalling, but when Blair got into the fine details the UUP delegates were faced with the fact that the deal before them was for real.

Gusty Spence was a steadying influence, keeping Ervine and the others on track. Ervine was 'getting very angry, very frustrated at the prevarications, at the refusal almost to accept the reality'. He was angry at the UUP, but he also knew that they 'were under tremendous pressure from Paisley and McCartney'.

At the same time the PUP, in the person of Ervine especially, was never going to find favour among Ulster Unionist negotiators. Their long-standing antipathy had not been dissipated, even though, osten-sibly, they had been negotiating for many months on the same side. He had learned during the course of the talks that many unionists hated him more than they hated Gerry Adams. Ervine understood why: 'We were alien in so much as we were "breaking the line". Wee working-class boys, such as us, are not expected to have opinions that are, certainly, out of step with the Grand Democrats. But, above all, Gerry Adams can't take their votes.'

In a situation requiring no losers, some Ulster Unionists could not or would not see an outcome compatible with shared success. Ervine felt keenly that that was what he had to achieve, precisely because of his party's origins. The PUP negotiators had been the butt of snide politically motivated criticism in inner-city unionist areas of Belfast, where they were derided as 'men in suits', local sarcasm for talentless social climbers. On the other hand, a wider constituency had given some consideration to 'Sharing Responsibilty' when they had cast their votes in local and general elections, and the PUP had an equally urgent need to respond to them.

Discussions under the aegis of the secretary of state took place about the prisoners issue. Gerry Kelly of Sinn Féin approached Ervine to propose that the PUP and Sinn Féin agree a timetable for prisoner releases. The British government was proposing three years, Sinn Féin one. At the time, Ervine said that he would refuse but, nevertheless, would take the offer to his party. He realised that Sinn Féin was offering an alliance on an issue of mutual interest, but it did not take the PUP long to decline. In the context of reaching an agreement that could be sold across the unionist community, as well as to loyalists, letting prisoners out too soon would jeopardise everything.

The lack of progress by late Thursday even got to the normally upbeat George Mitchell. A hint of weary pessimism marked his demeanour. At one point, he asked Ervine how he thought things were going. Ervine replied, 'We're going to do it, Senator.'

'I hope so,' said the senator. 'If we do, I'll get you a case of champagne.'

In the final round-the-clock, adrenalin-fuelled, sweating, fatiguing, continuous rounds of negotiations, from late Thursday night into early Friday morning (when Ervine could grab some sleep only by stretching out upon a desk, using his briefcase as a pillow), the consummate skills and talents of Blair and Ahern made lasting impressions. Ervine had dealings mostly with Blair. At 4 o'clock in the morning, Ervine was asked to go talk to Blair. Half-asleep, he went to the toilet to splash water on his face and then walked to Blair's office. 'He was sitting in his white shirt. It was crumpled, but he wasn't.' Blair was 'as fresh as a daisy' and in command of his brief. Ervine was impressed that he talked about the Agreement 'without deferring once to a civil servant'.

The deadline of Thursday midnight had passed, but the negotiations had generated sufficient momentum to push aside that hurdle. Ervine was not involved, but the bushfire of gossip carried the news. 'A meeting took place between the SDLP and the Ulster Unionists in the early hours of Friday morning, and it went well. That looked like we were going to vote. And we were pretty certain of the Agreement. That was it. We'd got it. We were home in a boat.' That, as it turned out, was not it, yet. Despite the optimism abroad, knowledge of the decision-making structures of the Ulster Unionist Party aroused scepticism about its ability to come to a decision that was both unanimous and rapid.

The PUP looked likely to accept the Agreement arrived at, because it essentially matched the PUP's remit, 'Sharing Responsibility 2000'. Strand One and Strand Three were to the PUP's liking, and Strand Two now allowed for a more benign model of cross-border institutions designed to promote mutual benefit, and for working towards eminently sensible means of consultation and cooperation in crossborder bodies, with common legislation and action where mutually desirable. It would be responsible to the new Assembly and to the houses of the Oireachtas, and therefore, from a unionist viewpoint, routed through the Northern Assembly. This would provide a means of building trust and confidence between the citizens and legislators of each jurisdiction.

A North/South Council remained the cornerstone, its make-up and format unchanged. The Council would 'identify and agree at least six matters for co-operation and implementation' in each of two categories where, first, existing bodies were the appropriate mechanisms, and second, where the cooperation would take place through agreed implementation bodies on a cross-border level. The thrust was to add to what already existed, and, for unionists, the tone was more mellifluous. Imperatives had softened to exhortations based upon mutuality.

Crucial for the PUP was the inclusion of a 'three-legged stool' concept. If the Northern Assembly were not to function, then all three strands would fall.

Annexes A, B and C, which had formerly been prescribed in Mitchell's document, were now excised and replaced by one Annex, which was emasculated and stated at the outset: 'Areas for North/South co-operation and implementation may include the following:' and gave a list of twelve possible areas.

The emphasis lay in choice. It was up to the representatives to provide others that they might think to be more appropriate, and choose them instead.

The following matters, which had appeared previously in the three annexes of Mitchell's document, were not included in the Annex of the document being put to all the parties to conclude a comprehensive agreement: industrial and trade matters, energy, culture, heritage and arts, sport, science and technology. In addition, joint bodies for the following were no longer obligatory: Irish language, trade promotion and indigenous companies, arts, waterways and tourism.

To Ervine and the PUP's satisfaction, the document confirmed: 'It is understood that the North/South Ministerial Council and the Northern Ireland Assembly are mutually inter-dependent, and that one cannot successfully function without the other.'

For nationalists, much potential for North/South co-operation lay in the Agreement, but it is difficult to argue against the notion that a 'green' document was transformed from the 'wants' of nationalism to the 'needs' of unionism. But would nationalists sign up? The PUP's collective approval contained several provisos. On the victims and the equality agenda, the Agreement would be painful, so financial provision would have to be put in place for the families of all victims. There needed to be recognition of their continuing existence, without resorting to a hierarchy of victimhood (i.e. guilt/innocence). The PUP also wanted the incorporation of the European Convention on Human Rights into a Bill of Rights for Northern Ireland, to be overseen locally through a human rights commission in Belfast.

The PUP delegates did not go to a local hotel to get some sleep like representatives of other parties did; they stayed in Castle Buildings, still running on adrenalin: 'We talked and talked, talked more, and assessed and analysed, and talked again, and revisited. I suppose in some ways, back into my old carpet fitter adage: "Measure twice, cut once." '

While the rest of the expectant population were having breakfast and going off to work, the PUP heard that Trimble was seeing Blair. That could only mean that the Ulster Unionists were having problems. It was intimated to the PUP that those problems now lay with Strand One. Everyone was put on stand-by for an announcement at lunchtime. It did not happen. Despite the optimism abroad, inside there was scepticism about the Ulster Unionist Party's ability to reach a decision.

During the afternoon, the PUP learned of Blair's letter to Trimble, assuring him that if the mechanism for removing ministers from the Executive did not work, in the matter of decommissioning for example, it could be reviewed in six months' time. Trimble interpreted the letter as meaning that if a party, i.e. 'Sinn Féin /IRA', had not decommissioned, this would be enough to put them out of the Executive.

For Jeffrey Donaldson, an influential member of the unionist leadership and implacable opponent of sharing government with Sinn Féin before the IRA's arsenal had been publicly destroyed, Blair's assurance was not sufficient. Sinn Féin could be in executive government without decommissioning beforehand. Donaldson walked away.

If Trimble needed a letter from the prime minister to copperfasten the UUP's acceptance of the Agreement, that was fine by Ervine and his PUP colleagues. They were not then aware that the contents of Blair's letter gave to David Trimble a personal assurance that went beyond the deal his government had negotiated. There was speculation that Trimble had gone directly to President Clinton, who, in turn, put pressure on Blair to write the letter. But that afternoon, some Ulster Unionists were interpreting things very differently. Their row was witnessed by Ervine and all the other negotiators, who were reduced to bit-players standing with growing concern in the wings as UUP bickering blocked the finale due centre stage. Many more Ulster Unionists started to arrive. As they were having their discussions, Ervine could hear them getting louder and louder. The PUP's room was just up the corridor, in a building renowned for its thin walls. The Alliance Party members, who were even closer, were extremely agitated, because not only could they hear the noise, they could hear what was being said. John Alderdice, the Alliance leader, confronted the UUP group, and there was quite an altercation in the corridor between the Ulster Unionists and the Alliance Party.

The PUP representatives wondered what was going on. They knew this was a real crisis, which, Ervine believed, 'was really bad, and the carpet was coming out from under Trimble's feet'. They spoke to Mitchell, who replied, 'We've just got to wait. What can I do? Just got to wait.' Once again the PUP found themselves asking what was going on. There were fears that the Agreement was not going to work. Then, about a quarter to five, Mitchell got a phone call from Trimble, saying, 'Right, Senator, five o'clock.' That meant he was ready to return to the plenary. Ervine and everyone else were on tenterhooks awaiting the outcome.

A final plenary meeting, seen on television, took place where all parties present accepted the Agreement. They did not sign a document. That could be done only by the two heads of government afterwards. Many viewers in Northern Ireland, and farther afield, watched with incredulity and relief. It seemed that the impossible had, at last, been achieved. The nightmare of successive lifetimes seemed to be over for good.

A few black doubts fluttered in the bright, sunshiny Good Friday air. Was Blair's letter the last bandage that would cure the Ulster body politic's infection or a useless sticking-plaster to cover it over while poison festered away in the wound? A raft of issues integral to the Agreement still had to be deliberated upon and given substance, like decommissioning and policing. Most puzzling of all, why had Sinn Féin attached itself to a settlement which institutionalised partition? But these specks of doubt paled into insignificance on a glorious day of belief in a better future for all in Northern Ireland.

On Tuesday of the following week, 14 April, a case of champagne was delivered to the offices of the Progressive Unionist Party, courtesy of 'the senator'. It was preserved until the announcement of the result of the referendum, held on 22 May, which endorsed the Good Friday Agreement with 71.5 per cent in favour, when it was swiftly drunk.

It is likely that a few glasses were raised in Dublin, too.

AFTER AGREEMENT

ONY BLAIR, CAMPAIGNING for the referendum on the Good Friday Agreement, in a speech at Coleraine on 20 May 1998, unveiled a handwritten set of five pledges to the people of Northern Ireland, one of which was that 'Those who use or threaten violence [would be] excluded from the Government of Northern Ireland'. Unionists accepted the personal pledges of their trusted British prime minister. The IRA, at that time, had not decommissioned any of its arsenal.

After the referendum had been won there was some relief and a great deal of hope that implementation of the Agreement through the political process would lead to stability and a better way of life for all. It was unrealistic to expect the process to unfold smoothly. The prolonged period before an Executive could be established proved to be merely an overture to a symphony of discordant notes.

An unwieldy Ulster Unionist Party was always as likely to revert to its most traditional and conservative character as to move forward into a new and fruitful relationship with nationalism. A party nostalgic about its past as sole exercising power, and addicted to infighting to the detriment of cohesion and influence, now had to cope with even greater division caused by the prospect of sharing government. Much depended upon David Trimble's astuteness, powers of persuasion and determination to fashion the party into an organisation regarding political issues as opportunities to do successful business, to have influence and to preserve the Union.

Sinn Féin, having signed up to an accord which legitimised all they had fought against with physical force for nearly thirty years, could be as obstructive as the most intransigent of Ulster Unionists. They could endanger further progress by simply procrastinating, while all the time protesting their peaceful and fraternal intentions. As optimism receded and the implications of full implementation of the Agreement were realised, it was recalcitrant, and sadly predictable, unionists who gathered in reaction to pull down the Agreement with the hook of insistence on IRA decommissioning.

On 15 July 1999 at Stormont, as government ministers were due to be appointed in proportion to party voting strength, the unionists failed to attend. They accused republicans of reneging on their part of the Agreement, to decommission their arms. Thus devolved government was postponed for five months.

On the stroke of midnight, Thursday 2 December 1999, 601 days after the signing of the Agreement, and after twenty-five years of Direct Rule, political power in Northern Ireland was devolved to a local administration. And, on the same day, the IRA issued a statement of intent to appoint a representative to liaise with the Independent International Commission on Decommissioning (IICD) chaired by General John de Chastelain.

The tone of discord continued in 2000. On 27 January David Trimble threatened to resign as first minister if the IRA had not begun disarming before the end of the month. Unionist perception was that republicans were strategising to take all they could from the Good Friday Agreement without conceding anything of substance, so that unionists in frustration would collapse the Assembly, leaving joint authority between London and Dublin as the only means of governing Northern Ireland. On 12 February the power-sharing Executive was suspended because de Chastelain's report of the previous day, that the IRA might be ready to consider putting its arms beyond use, was not considered definite enough by the UUP. Three days later the IRA withdrew its offer. However, on 6 May, it announced that it would allow 'a number of' its arms dumps to be inspected on a regular basis by independent agreed inspectors, and reentered discussions with the IICD. Former Finnish president, Martti Ahtisaari, and former

ANC general secretary, Cyril Ramaphosa, were agreed as the two inspectors. Secretary of State Peter Mandelson signed an order, on 28 May, lifting the suspension of Northern Ireland institutions, and from midnight 30 May devolution was restored. The Executive met on 1 June and the Assembly on 5 June. On 26 June, the two inspectors reported, after their inspection of IRA weapons, that they 'cannot be used without detection'.

The troubled nature of the Assembly's birth continued in its infancy in 2001, dogged by unionist mistrust over decommissioning. On 1 July, Trimble resigned as first minister, though Seamus Mallon of the SDLP stayed as deputy first minister. On 10 August the Assembly was suspended for one day and restored the next day, for technical reasons, to allow a space of six weeks in which the position of first minister could be resolved. However, nothing was resolved. On 21 September the Assembly was again suspended for one day and restored on 22 September, for the same purpose. The DUP angrily threatened to take Secretary of State Dr John Reid to court because it felt he should have called fresh elections. There were no developments on decommissioning, and on 18 October the UUP ministers resigned. Then, on 23 October, it was announced that the IRA had put some of its weapons beyond use.

In a scenario that bordered on farce, on 6 November, the incumbent first minister and new deputy first minister Mark Durkan of the SDLP were elected. The first vote had failed, but then three of the non-aligned Alliance members and one Women's Coalition member had redesignated themselves as unionists to massage the required number of unionist votes for the motion to be carried. The DUP called the whole thing a fix. Many unionists argued that their Agreement, the people's Agreement, had been expropriated by politicians for cynical reasons. Further, they had lost faith in the integrity of the prime minister and his pledges so publicly given at Coleraine.

The Good Friday Agreement marked a transition in society, but not from one clearly demarcated era to another. There were, as yet, too many unfulfilled hopes and sensitive matters still to be negotiated. But within loyalism the desire for change had now achieved real expression. The thoughts of the UVF commander, who set loyalism on the political path in the 1980s, enunciate a hope that those decades which engulfed the community in so much misery and wrecked so many lives could now be left behind. On the flyleaf of a book he gave to an indispensable contact in Dublin the UVF man wrote: 'When this war is over and I see your face again, I'll tell you of some volunteers who put peace before revenge.'

Peace can only be nurtured and safeguarded through politics, advanced by brave, committed people. As Senator Mitchell has said: 'What takes courage is to compete in the arena of democracy where the tools are not bombs and bullets, but reason, logic, advocacy and where the risk of failure is high . . . and very public.'

Decommissioning has been used by other unionists to criticise Ervine, as the UVF has refused to decommission and thereby deflected moral pressure from the IRA. The UVF has declared that it will not put away its weapons before it is certain the 'War of the Troubles' is over. Spence extracted from them a 'no first strike' policy, but only implementation of the Good Friday Agreement, cessation of republicans' attrition against the Northern state, and acceptance by them that future developments lie in democratic politics, will persuade the UVF that decommissioning is an option for them.

Ervine is in no doubt that the IRA has indeed put weapons beyond use and estimates the amount to be at least one bunker that Cyril Ramaphosa and Marrti Ahtisaari had previously inspected. Equally, he is certain that the effect on American political and public opinion of the terrorist attacks upon New York and Washington on 11 September 2001 has hugely influenced republican action to decommission further – to assuage Irish-American opinion, that is, rather than unionists.

Ervine is on public record as stating that in the context of a political resolution the issue of demanding decommissioning is a nonsense. Although it is logical to remove illegal weapons from a normal society, the unionist demand conforms to a maxim of Northern Ireland politics: ask for that which you know you cannot have, and get upset when you cannot have it. Real decommissioning, in Ervine's view, is achieved by political stability making paramilitaries irrelevant. An important gesture in that direction would be a public utterance from the IRA saying that they, the soldiers, had passed the mantle of the delivery of the republican ideal to the politicians. Unionists, he says, need to hear republicans declare that the war is over. Such a declaration would indicate that republicans were serious about making the Good Friday Agreement work. It would signal that a United Ireland could only be achieved through persuasion and consent, which Gerry Adams stated in New York on 3 February 2002, at the World Economic Forum: 'I don't think we can force on unionism an all-Ireland state that doesn't have their assent or consent, and doesn't reflect their sense of being comfortable.'

Ervine recognised the significance of Adams' statement but asked for whom was Adams speaking. Did his comments signal that the republican movement realised that a collective strategy, covering each community's needs, was the way forward after all? And did they signal that the war was over?

In an atmosphere of uncertainty, disaffection about the Good Friday Agreement's capacity to deliver peace and provide opportunities to create a decent society has spread among a sizeable percentage of unionists who voted for it. Ervine identifies a multiplicity of causes.

The political leaders who were the architects of the Agreement have, he says, failed to implement it in a spirit of collective responsibility and mutual support, in which there is a sharing and spreading of pain. Instead, some have seen the Agreement as unfinished business and have continued to work to their own agendas, lobbying the British and Irish governments.

For him, the historic inter-communal battle is over, and problems are now intra-communal. However, politicians have interpreted the Agreement in ways that are tailored to appeal to their constituents' fears.

Ervine argues that the British and Irish governments have indulged unionists and nationalists respectively, that the supplicants who travelled to London and Dublin should have been turned back and told to negotiate with the other parties to the Agreement.

The capacity of moderate unionists to stay inside the process and continue to support it has been diminished by confrontational street politics and deals done outside the Agreement, which have given opportunities to opponents within unionism to strive even harder against compromise and encourage doubters into their camp. David Trimble finds himself in difficulty and makes harsher demands of Sinn Féin. Gerry Adams offers to deliver, but the British government has to pay a price and is criticised by unionists who consider the price too high. If unionists had not made demands in the first place – for decommissioning, for example – republicans would not have received more concessions.

Both nationalists and republicans have used sectarian arguments to justify policy to their own constituents, and this has had the effect of destroying unionists' faith in the Good Friday Agreement. Unionists feel that the argument on the nationalist side goes that if the unionists are doing badly then nationalists are doing well, and that unionist suffering is just retribution for past misrule and misdeeds in government. From a unionist perspective it seems that decades of bombing and murder from the republican side are forgotten. This perceived hypocrisy from their political opponents, whom unionists had hoped would move forward as partners in bringing the Good Friday Agreement to fruition, has eroded much middle-ground unionist support.

Ervine characterises Sinn Féin's strategy as two-faced. Republicans massage their constituents' difficulties in coming to terms with the new political dispensation in Northern Ireland through negative practical outcomes – for example, not joining the new policing board – whilst, at the same time, embracing the new Stormont establishment but not telling their foot-soldiers that their dream of a unitary thirty-two county socialist republic is no longer a priority on the republican agenda.

Initial enthusiasm and strong support for the Agreement has been dissipated, he argues, by its political architects failing to follow through collectively to implementation based upon each others' needs, not wants.

Developments in loyalism since the signing of the Good Friday Agreement have seen both internecine conflict within paramilitarism and sectarian confrontation with nationalists. When a feud broke out between the UDA and the UVF on the Shankill Road in the summer of 2001 it was portrayed in the media as two sprawling gangster mobs fighting a turf war over drugs, and control over other money-spinning criminal activities. Ervine knows the reality was more complex and sinister.

A metamorphosis has taken place within loyalist paramilitarism. There are those who have decided the war is over and have gone off to get on with the things of a normal life, like jobs and families. Some have chosen to work for their country rather than fight for it, and have moved into community development or politics. Another dangerous element, people who cannot cope with change which denies them their sense of importance, have decided upon a lifestyle of criminality.

On the ground Ervine analyses three causes for the internecine out-break of violence. First, the confrontational street politics of Sinn Féin and private deals between them and the British government gave cred-ibility to the anti-compromise elements within loyalist paramilitarism which could self-righteously respond with what they are good at, vio-lence. Secondly, a degree of gangsterism had always existed within loyalism, and some wanted to demolish restraints against drug-deal-ing, extortion and lawlessness. Thirdly, someone wanted to destroy the Combined Loyalist Military Command (CLMC) so that measured political analysis would not take place through cross-fertilisation across loyalist paramilitary groupings.

The PUP suffered because of the feud. Bertie Rice, who manned Billy Hutchinson's constituency office, was shot dead. The mafia-type causes of the feud propagated in the media damaged the party's image. The UDA/UVF feud was one part of shifts taking place in unionism for control of hearts and minds. Specific elements of the UDA wanted to expand their sphere of influence and dominate loy-alist paramilitarism. The feud was about power, position, influence and lucrative sources of income.

Ervine is convinced that the British establishment – not the British government, he stresses – had reason to be not unhappy at the dis-mantling of the CLMC and the perpetuation of violence. Its strategy, advanced by MI5 and Whitehall civil servants, is to solve the North-ern Ireland problem through joint administration with the govern-ment of the Republic of Ireland. Why, Ervine wonders, do the security forces in the South have, proportionately, a greater success rate in combating terrorism than those in the North with all their experience and professionalism?

The flux in loyalist paramilitarism has contributed to the flare-up of inter-communal strife in north Belfast, but the roots of this violent confrontation lie in sectarianism. In a sectarian society external threats turn a community in upon itself for security. Consequently, barriers, whether psychological or physical, prevent negotiation. Yet in north Belfast that stereotype is being broken down. Local politi-cians have combined to resolve immediate tensions and work towards a means for hostile communities to co-exist. The message is getting across that the only effective guarantees are those which come from opposing camps.

The enthusiasm with which local unionist politicians of the PUP and UUP have negotiated across a divide of hatred indicates that, a few years into multi-party power-sharing, some unionists at least have gained a real understanding of the work required of politicians. To their credit, they provide a sharp contrast to the distant middle-class figures who would deign in earlier years to visit working-class areas at election times; they differ, too, from those other unionists, perhaps the most gifted of their generation, who loudly withdrew from the talks which prepared the way for agreement.

In the years since the signing of the Good Friday Agreement the PUP has stayed the pace. The party's work has continued on several fronts: high-profile politics; local council matters; exploitation of the media to get its message of compromise over; development of party policies over a wide range of issues. The party has proven its stamina in these areas. Yet the development and expansion of the party have been below expectations. The unionist community is nervous about its future. A rash of sectarianism has disfigured the face of urban, working-class districts. In such times people run for succour to the loudest and largest bulwark against external threat. Consequently, support in the polling booth has been disappointing in the light of the amount of work done on behalf of individuals who pass through con-stituency offices. In local council elections one candidate in North Down and another in Newtownabbey failed to be re-elected.

Nevertheless, Ervine remains positive, especially when the PUP still garners cross-community votes. Perhaps, just as in the past the loyal-ist politicians needed a paramilitary ceasefire before launching them-selves into the electoral arena, a period of calm when normal politics fills the headlines is a pre-requisite for PUP consolidation and growth. Members of the party are determined to maintain a long-term view. Ervine observes: 'As Van Morrison wrote, "Open up the windows and let me breathe", and if we can get over the hurdles, get the breath of freedom from our brutal past, then I think the politics of the Pro-gressive Unionist Party will become more and more relevant.'

Today, before you cross the river Lagan and take one of the fan of roads which lead into east Belfast, a marvel of the contemporary cityscape confronts you along the riverbanks. New, tall buildings stand proud against the city skyline in a regenerated area which is a symbol of a different Belfast from that of previous decades.

On the east bank, the once mighty fly-over that used to carry the traffic from the humming shipyards to the lone Queen's Bridge is dwarfed beneath two yellow cranes, Samson and Goliath, like sentries at the gate of east Belfast. A sedate, fusty atmosphere awaits as you walk up the the Lower Newtownards Road, past the iron railings of a darkened church, and a solitary signpost indicating a 'Goodwill Centre'. A gable is covered by a mural in praise of loyalist paramilitaries. A fringe of union flags tops an archway before a redbrick square where the kerbs are painted red, white and blue, and pretty rows of modern houses sit snug under spreading green branches. The end of a low hedge gives way to brown-bricked maisonettes, and a gable shows a portrait of 'King Billy'.

Neat shops and trim streets of well-kept houses lead to another church, stern Westbourne Presbyterian just next to Tower Street, where the Further Education College stands across a playground, all glass windows and peeling paint. Tidy streets of terraced houses continue the line of the road and a public shrine to loyalism sprawls along walls regaled in tableaux, painted in vivid colours and drawn with care:

Their Only Crime Is Loyalty
UVF East Belfast Brigade
Release the Prisoners
Safeguarding our Nationhood – One Island Two Nations
UDR B-Specials
Our Message to the Irish is Simple – Hands Off Ulster – Irish Out
The Ulster Conflict is About Nationality
CUCHULAIN Ancient Defender of Ulster from Irish Attacks
UDA Ulster Freedom Corner

A church tower soars above the street: Church of Ireland, Parish of Ballymacarrett, St Patrick's, separated physically by a few yards from an Elim Pentecostal Church. Past the confluence of competing claims on Protestants, commerce gets on with its life on the Lower Newtownards Road. Here, as on any British high street, businesses stand ready to trade, seeking to attract households whose multifarious needs and aspirations are replicated throughout the land. Over on the right-hand side can be seen Westbourne Glentoran Supporters Club, and Megain Memorial Presbyterian Church. Off both sides of the road run streets of redbrick terraced houses, of which Chamberlain Street is one, where lives and breathes a working-class, staunch Protestantism whose predominant political outlook expresses itself in uncompromising unionism. A daunting environment for those who would reform unionism; a task taken on by Ervine, who was born in its bosom.

And yet it was from these streets, and others like them in inner-Belfast Protestant working-class districts, before the 'Troubles' started in 1969, that the Northern Ireland Labour Party, supported by people like Ervine's father and John Malone, headmaster of Orangefield school, sent MPs to the old Stormont Parliament. Is the PUP destined to be a passing phenomenon too? A factor in the PUP's make-up, and liable to make it endure, is the common origin, unique in unionism, of political activists of working-class origins taking their own leadership, never again to be exchanged for the big house, big job or big church leader. Gusty Spence and David Ervine refer to themselves with pride as 'back street boys'. They also share political intelligence. Having experienced manipulation by a crude unionist establishment, they set out to learn and have proved themselves to be effective and astute. They took responsibility upon themselves to work out a resolution of their political difficulties, and did not turn to London to settle things for them. Moreover, they no longer expect London to look after their interests, nor do they insult or offend Dublin with gratuitous incivility. They are in the business of politics, displaying a confidence forged upon self-reliance in negotiations from grass roots to heads of government, and have breathed a fresh dynamic into a unionism whose roots run deep in the old Labour tradition of the 1930s in urban working-class areas of Belfast, and were found postwar in the left-wing attitudes expressed by the poet John Hewitt and in Sam Thompson's plays.

The influence of Ervine, Spence, Hutchinson and Smyth may, in time, allow space to be cleared encouraging a richer regional identity to flower within the United Kingdom, at the same time finding a sense of Irishness which defines itself outside the travesty of an exclusively Roman Catholic, nationalist and Gaelic-speaking image.

Ervine talks politics with verve and passion. He speaks well, knows how to turn an original phrase and is diplomatic over points of disagreement, though within Loyalism there are some who denigrate him for his use of 'big words'. He crafts his arguments with coherence and a flair for words, but the pervading sense that abides is honesty. Ervine does not dissemble when challenged about his past involvement with the UVF. That is in the public domain but, equally, he challenges the public to accept that what he does now is politics. He speaks with the UVF, but is not a spokesman for them. With them he has had forceful arguments. He argues that it is beneficial to have influence to curb extremist 'super-Prod' behaviour, rather than cut himself off completely and have none at all. And he is a free agent to develop policies that will promote the well-being of his whole community.

Ervine enjoys a certain credibility and regard in the nationalist community, where the assumption is that he is a positive influence on the move from division to accommodation. There is a sense that Ervine's reaching across is genuine, that he treats nationalist political views and aspirations as valid and equal.

Ervine, working-class to his toes and proud of it, moves naturally between classes, and is well received across communities because that was his way when, as a young man, he first started seeking employment. He received encouragement from his father's example, consolidated later under Gusty Spence's influence. Ervine's enterprise to promote an inclusive unionism has been looked upon favourably by establishment figures who have been offended by Paisleyite politics and impatient with the UUP's dearth of initiative and lack of engagement with nationalism. The Rt Rev Robin Eames, Archbishop of Armagh, wrote in 1998:

> Ervine has brought a new element to loyalist thinking and has challenged traditional unionist thinking. His approach to historic divisions has been like a breath of fresh air and his grasp of political theory has been amazing. He is an excellent communicator and has won much more support for his views than the ballot box would suggest. His personal influence on the peace process has been immense.

APPENDIX ONE

PROPOSITIONS ON HEADS OF AGREEMENT
issued by the British and Irish governments, 12 January 1998

Balanced constitutional change, based on commitment to the principle of consent in all its aspects by both British and Irish governments, to include both changes to the Irish Constitution and to British constitutional legislation.

Democratically elected institutions in Northern Ireland, to include a Northern Ireland assembly, elected by a system of proportional representation, exercising devolved executive and legislative responsibility over at least the responsibilities of the six Northern Ireland departments and with provisions to ensure that all sections of the community can participate and work together successfully in the operation of these institutions and that all sections of the community are protected.

A new British-Irish agreement to replace the existing Anglo-Irish Agreement and help establish close co-operation and enhance relationships, embracing:

- An intergovernmental council to deal with the totality of relationships, to include representatives of the British and Irish governments, the Northern Ireland administration and the devolved institutions in Scotland and Wales, with meetings twice a year at summit level.

- A North/South ministerial council to bring together those with executive responsibilities in Northern Ireland and the Irish government in particular areas. Each side will consult, co-operate and take decisions on matters of mutual interest within the mandate of, and accountable to, the Northern Ireland assembly and the Oireachtas respectively. All decisions will be by agreement between the two sides, North and South.

- Suitable implementation bodies and mechanisms for policies agreed by the North/South council in meaningful areas and at an all-island level.

- Standing intergovernmental machinery between the Irish and British governments, covering issues of mutual interest, including non-devolved issues for Northern Ireland, when representatives of the Northern Ireland administration would be involved.

Provision to safeguard the rights of both communities in Northern Ireland, through arrangements for the comprehensive protection of fundamental human, civil, political, social, economic and cultural rights, including a Bill of Rights for Northern Ireland supplementing the provisions of the European Convention and to achieve full respect for the principles of equity of treatment and freedom from discrimination, and the cultural identity and ethos of both communities. Appropriate steps to ensure an equivalent level of protection in the Republic.

Effective and practical measures to establish and consolidate an acceptable peaceful society, dealing with issues such as prisoners, security in all its aspects, policing and decommissioning of weapons.

APPENDIX TWO

Selected extracts from Senator Mitchell's 'Draft Paper for Discussion'

TABLE OF CONTENTS

Annex C: List of Implementation Bodies in specified areas in which the Council is to take decisions on action at an all-Island and cross-border level.

5. Strand Three:
British-Irish Council

British-Irish Intergovernmental Conference

6. Rights, Safeguards and Equality of Opportunity
Human Rights

United Kingdom Legislation

New Institutions in Northern Ireland

Comparable Steps by the Irish Government

A Joint Committee

Victims of Violence and Reconciliation

Economic, Social and Cultural Issues

7. Decommissioning

8. Security

9. Policing and Justice
Annex A: Commission on Policing for Northern Ireland
Annex B: Review of the Criminal Justice System

10. Prisoners

11. Validation, Implementation and Review
Validation and Implementation
Review Procedures Following Implementation.

Following the Table of Contents, there followed a Declaration of Support, an outline of Constitutional Issues, and the description of a series of measures that were expected to be put in place, including the Assembly, under Strand One, and the North/South Ministerial Council under Strand Two.

North/South Ministerial Council

1. Under a new British/Irish Agreement dealing with the totality of relationships, and related legislation at Westminster and in the Oireachtas, a North/South Council to be established to bring together those with executive responsibilities in Northern Ireland and the Irish Government, to develop consultation, cooperation and action within the island of Ireland – including through implementation on an all-island basis – on matters of mutual interest within the competence of the administrations, North and South. . .

4. Agendas for all meetings to be settled by prior agreement between the two sides, but open to either to propose any matter for consideration or action.

5. The Council:

(i) to exchange information, discuss and consult with a view to co-operating on matters of mutual interest within the competence of both administrations;

(ii) to use best endeavours to reach agreement on the adoption of common policies in the areas listed in Annex A, making determined efforts to overcome any disagreements.

(iii) in specified areas set out in Annex B to take decisions on action for implementation separately in each jurisdiction;

(iv) in other specified meaningful areas set out in Annex C to take decisions on action at an all-island and cross-border level through implementation bodies to be established as set out in paragraphs 7 and 8 below.

Annex A
List of specified areas where the Council to use the best endeavours to reach agreement on the adoption of common policies [para 5 (ii)]

Agriculture
- research, training and advisory services
- development of the bloodstock and greyhound industries
- rural development

Education and Training

- tourism training
- education for students with special needs
- education for mutual understanding
- teacher qualifications and exchanges
- higher and further education
- combating educational disadvantage

Health

- general hospital services and accident/emergency planning
- food safety

Industrial and Trade Matters

- management development services to industry
- trading standards
- public purchasing
- supervision of credit unions
- occupational health and safety

Marine and Waterways

- inland fisheries
- approaches to the Common Fisheries Policy
- fish health
- fisheries education, research and training

Energy and Transport

- geological survey
- energy projects
- road and rail issues

Environment

- physical planning and development strategy
- road safety

Annex B

List of specified areas in which Council is to take decisions on action
for implementation separately in each jurisdiction [para 5 (ii)] [*Items
in brackets are not agreed*]

Agriculture

- Animal and plant health
- [Approaches to Common Agricultural Policy].

Education and Youth

Education and Training programmes

Social Welfare/Community Activity

- entitlements of cross-border workers and fraud control
- support for voluntary community activity

The Environment

- environmental protection, waste management and pollution control
- mapping
- wildlife conservation

Culture, Heritage and the Arts

- heritage protection and restoration
- cultural promotion abroad

Health

- disease registries, clinical trials and high cost, high technology areas
- post-graduate medical teaching and training
- health promotion strategies

Marine and Waterways

- aquaculture and marine matters [including research?] and drainage.

Sport

- promotion and support of joint activities and strategic planning of facilities.

Science and Technology

- promotion of scientific and technological research and its application.

Annex C
List of Implementation Bodies in specified areas in which the Council is to take decisions on action at an all-island and cross-border level (paras 5 (iv) and 7.) [*Items through Inland Waterways Body are agreed; all items thereafter are not agreed.*]

- a **Tourism Body** . . .
- an **Environmental Protection Body** . . .
- an **EU Programmes Implementation Body** . . .
- a **Transport Planning Body** . . .
- an **Inland Waterways Body** . . .
- an **Irish Language Promotion Body** . . .
- a **Trade Promotion and Indigenous Company Development Body** . . .
- an **Arts Body** . . .

7. For the areas listed in Annex C, where it is agreed that new implementation bodies are to be established, the two Governments to make all necessary legislative and other preparations to ensure the establishment of these bodies at the inception of the British/Irish Agreement or as soon as feasible thereafter, such that these bodies function effectively as rapidly as possible. The bodies to have a clear operational remit. To implement, on an all-island and cross-border basis, policies agreed in the Council. To report to the Council while remaining subject to normal accountability to the Northern Ireland Assembly and the Oireachtas, through the Council.

GLOSSARY

Alliance Party	A small moderate political party which wishes to maintain the Union with Britain.
Árd Fheis	Annual convention, usually of a political party.
Baton round	Rubber or plastic bullet.
CLMC	Combined Loyalist Military Command.
CLPA	Combined Loyalist Political Alliance.
CO	Commanding Officer.
Compound	In Long Kesh prison, area enclosed by wire fencing, in open air, where prisoners were housed in H-Blocks.
Crown	A term used to denote the British government and all the forces, such as the British army, and institutions that compose the British state, whose constitutional head is the Queen.
Dáil Éireann	Seat of Irish parliament.
DUP	Democratic Unionist Party – right-wing unionist party, led by Rev Ian Paisley.
Fenian	A term, usually pejorative, for a Catholic that implies that he or she is a republican. The original Fenians were an Irish-American revolutionary group in the 1860s.
Fianna Fáil	The Republic of Ireland's largest political party, founded by Éamon de Valera in 1926.
Fine Gael	The Republic of Ireland's second largest political party, founded in 1933.

H-Blocks	Single-storey buildings in Long Kesh/the Maze Prison.
IRA	Irish Republican Army, the major republican paramilitary organisation.
IRSP	Irish Republican Socialist Party, political wing of the Irish National Liberation Army (INLA).
Loyalist	A term, often with working-class and paramilitary connotations, used to describe those opposed to a united Ireland and in favour of maintaining the Union with Great Britain.
LVF	Loyalist Volunteer Force, loyalist paramilitary group whose first leader, Billy Wright, was murdered by the INLA in the Maze Prison in 1997.
MI5	The British domestic intelligence service that has overall control of the British government's battle against the IRA.
Nationalist	Someone who aspires to a reunited Ireland.
NIO	Northern Ireland Office – the administrative headquarters during Direct Rule.
OC	Officer Commanding.
Official IRA	Republican paramilitary faction. The IRA split in 1969 left two organisations, the Provisional IRA and the Official IRA. The Official IRA declared a ceasefire in 1972.
Oireachtas	Name to cover both houses of the Irish Parliament (i.e. The Dáil and the Seanad) and the President.
Orange Order	Organisation of Protestant men, opposed to Catholicism, defenders of Protestantism, who demonstrate by marching in regalia.
PIRA	Provisional Irish Republican Army, the major republican paramilitary organisation.
Provos, Provies	Provisional IRA
PSNI	Police Service of Northern Ireland, succeeded the Royal Ulster Constabulary (RUC) in November 2001.
PUP	Progressive Unionist Party, associated with the Ulster Volunteer Force (UVF).
Republican	A supporter of a united Ireland by any means.
RTÉ	Radio Telefís Éireann, the state-run broadcasting authority in the Republic of Ireland.
RUC	Royal Ulster Constabulary – the overwhelmingly Protestant police force of Northern Ireland, which was succeeded in November 2001 by the Police Service of Northern Ireland (PSNI).

SAS	Special Air Services, an undercover wing of the British Army.
SDLP	Social Democratic and Labour Party – the main nationalist political party which aspires to a united Ireland through democratic and peaceful means.
Sinn Féin	The main republican political party, often labelled the political wing of the (Provisional) IRA.
Stormont	The seat of government in Northern Ireland; the location of the Assembly and the multi-party talks.
Taoiseach	Prime Minister of the Republic of Ireland.
Tánaiste	Deputy Prime Minister of the Republic of Ireland.
TD	Teachta Dála (Member of the Dáil).
UDA	Ulster Defence Association, the largest Protestant paramilitary organisation.
UDP	Ulster Democratic Party, small unionist party linked to the UDA/UFF, which dissolved itself in November 2001.
UDR	Ulster Defence Regiment. Branch of the British army, set up in 1970 to replace the B-Specials. After disbandment in 1992, the UDR was replaced by the Royal Irish Regiment (RIR).
UFF	Ulster Freedom Fighters, loyalist paramilitary group synonymous with the UDA.
Unionist	Umbrella term for those in favour of remaining within the United Kingdom; specifically a supporter of one of the unionist parties.
UTV	Ulster Television – the independent commercial television channel serving Northern Ireland.
UUP	Ulster Unionist Party, the largest political party in Northern Ireland, led by David Trimble.
UVF	Ulster Volunteer Force, the smaller of the Protestant paramilitary organisations; some ex-members gravitated towards the Progressive Unionist Party (PUP).

INDEX